Symbolic Dynamics and Geometry

Symbolic Dynamics and Geometry

Using D* in Graphics and Game Programming

Brian Guenter * Sung-Hee Lee

CRC Press
Taylor & Francis Group
Boca Raton London New York

CRC Press is an imprint of the
Taylor & Francis Group, an **informa** business

CRC Press
Taylor & Francis Group
6000 Broken Sound Parkway NW, Suite 300
Boca Raton, FL 33487-2742

First issued in paperback 2020

© 2010 by Taylor & Francis Group, LLC
CRC Press is an imprint of Taylor & Francis Group, an Informa business

No claim to original U.S. Government works

ISBN-13: 978-1-56881-280-9 (hbk)
ISBN-13: 978-0-367-65930-1 (pbk)

**Visit the Taylor & Francis Web site at
http://www.taylorandfrancis.com**

**and the CRC Press Web site at
http://www.crcpress.com**

To Evelyn and Grant
—B. G.

To Mina
—S.-H. L.

Contents

I Tutorial   I

I Symbolic Geometric Modeling   3

2 Interactive Mechanism Modeling   7
   2.1 Introduction   7
   2.2 Building a Rigid-Body System   8

II Procedural Applications   15

3 D* Tutorial   17
   3.1 Introduction   17
   3.2 D* Functions   17
   3.3 Differentiation   19
   3.4 More Complex Functions   21
   3.5 Recursive Functions   22
   3.6 Piecewise Functions   24
   3.7 Evaluating D* Functions   27
   3.8 Expression Optimization   32
   3.9 Related Work   34
   3.10 Advantages of the D* Algorithm   35
   3.11 Limitations of the Current Implementation   35

4 Geometry Functions   37
   4.1 Surface Properties   37
   4.2 Geometry Operators   40
   4.3 Surface Curvature   43

5   Mechanism Functions   **51**
   5.1   Lagrangian Mechanics   51
   5.2   Modeling a Mechanism   56
   5.3   Example Mechanisms   58
   5.4   Complex Constraints   67
   5.5   Enforcing Additional Constraints   76
   5.6   Inverse Kinematics   80
   5.7   Inverse Dynamics   82

6   Miscellaneous Problems   **85**
   6.1   Synthetic Examples   85
   6.2   Spherical Harmonics   86
   6.3   Structure from Motion   89

III   Theory   **91**

7   The D* Algorithm   **93**
   7.1   Graph Structure of the Chain Rule   94
   7.2   Factoring the Derivative Graph   97
   7.3   Other Symbolic Forms   108
   7.4   Analysis of Forward and Reverse   111

8   Lagrangian Mechanics   **115**
   8.1   Kinematics of Mechanical Systems   118
   8.2   Derivatives   120
   8.3   Lagrangian Equations of Motion   126
   8.4   Tree Structures   136
   8.5   Dynamics Applications   136
   8.6   Conclusion   143

9   CSG on Procedural Geometry   **145**
   9.1   Previous Work   146
   9.2   Overview of the Algorithm   147
   9.3   Finding Exact Curves of Intersection   149
   9.4   Orienting the Curve of Intersection   156
   9.5   Triangulation   157
   9.6   Results   162
   9.7   Conclusion   166

A   List of Symbols   **167**

B   Properties of a Unitary Mapping   **169**

C   Kantorovich's Theorem   171

D   Implicit Differentiation   173

E   Code Listings   175
    E.1   Geometry Programs 175
    E.2   Dynamics Programs 176
    E.3   Miscellaneous 178

Bibliography   181

Index   185

Preface

Who Is This Book Intended For?

This book explains how to use the new symbolic differentiation system D*
for applications in computer games and engineering simulation. You will
want to read this book if

- you want to create a 3D mechanical system and simulate its physical
  behavior,

- you want to learn how to create compact functional representations of
  3D geometry that can be efficiently evaluated in real time on modern
  GPUs,

- you work in an engineering or scientific discipline that requires the
  computation of complex derivatives.

Several applications of D* are covered but two, real-time Lagrangian physics
simulation and procedural 3D geometric modeling, are developed in great
detail.

As you read the book, we are confident you will be pleased and sur-
prised by how much the symbolic differentiation capabilities of D* simplify
previously difficult tasks. For example, computing the Jacobian of a robot
manipulator to do inverse kinematics (Section 5.6) is just one line of code,
a call to the D* differentiation function. All the details of the differentiation process are handled by D*. By contrast, a typical robotics text such
as [28] takes 18 pages to describe algorithms for computing the Jacobian.
Computing surface curvature (Section 4.3) is another example. The derivatives are complicated and tedious to evaluate manually, but in D* all the
differentiation is handled by the system, greatly simplifying the process.

What Will You Need?

A solid understanding of C# programming is assumed. To use the software associated with this book, you will have to download the D* dll, the C# sources for SymMech and SymGeom (the interactive symbolic geometric modeling and mechanism construction programs), and XNA Game Studio. You can download XNA Game Studio from http://creators.xna.com; SymMech, SymGeom, and other example codes can be downloaded from http://research.microsoft.com/en-us/um/people/bguenter/, or by searching for the download "Dynamics Simulation and Geometric Modeling Using D* Symbolic Differentiation" on the main Microsoft Research website (http://research.microsoft.com/). No executables are included in our download, so you will have to compile the projects using Visual Studio 2008 or Visual Studio Express. You will also need a DX10-compatible graphics card that supports Shader Model 1.1 or higher and DirectX 9.0c or higher. Finally, to get the maximum benefit from this book, you will want to write programs of your own that use D*.

We have tried to make the presentation of geometric modeling and Lagrangian dynamics as self-contained and simple as possible. No knowledge of calculus is required to *use* the procedural geometric modeling or Lagrangian dynamics simulation software associated with this book. However, basic first-year calculus and linear algebra are essential for understanding the theory behind these software packages.

What Will You Learn from This Book?

When you are finished reading this book, you will be able to create procedural three-dimensional geometric models, link them together to form multibody physical systems, and simulate and display their physical behavior in real time. You will also be able to use the symbolic differentiation capabilities of D* in a wide variety of technical applications, including computer graphics, engineering, and mechanical simulation.

Organization of the Book

The book is split into three parts: Part I—Tutorial, Part II—Procedural Applications, and Part III—Theory.

Part I—Tutorial describes

- how to use the interactive geometric modeling tool SymGeom,

- how to use the the interactive mechanism and dynamic simulation tool SymMech.

If you do not intend to write your own custom software using D*, this is the only section you will need to read.

Part II—Procedural Applications describes

- how to use the D* language to write your own simple programs,

- how to create a toolkit of custom D* geometric operators for building your own geometric modeling system,

- how to create mechanical systems with joint constraints that are more sophisticated than those provided by SymMech,

- miscellaneous graphics applications of D*.

If SymGeom and SymMech cannot do what you want, and you are not intimidated by programming and a little math, then you should read this part.

Part III—Theory explains

- how the D* symbolic differentiation algorithm works,

- how Lagrangian mechanics must be formulated to give efficient solutions using D*,

- how the simple geometric modeling primitives of Chapter 4 can be extended to do constructive solid geometry (CSG), a much more powerful set of modeling operations.

You will want to read this part if you are the sort of person who just has to know why things work, or if you want to extend and improve D* or the geometric modeling and dynamics simulation algorithms.

Acknowledgments

It is our hope that this book, and the associated software, will be a living, growing thing with many future contributions from new users of D*. Two who have already contributed are Leonid Velikovich, who wrote the geometric modeling program, and Benjamin Hernandez Arreguin, who wrote the interactive mechanism construction program. Leonid is a former Microsoft employee who wanted to do something fun, completely unrelated to his job responsibilities. He wrote the geometric modeling program in a few months while also working full-time. Benjamin was an intern at Microsoft

Research. Both programs are in an early stage of development; if you see improvements that need to be made, then make them, and share them with the D* community.

If you find a bug or an error in the book, if you add functionality to the existing software, or if you develop entirely new software built on top of D*, send us the improvements. We will do our best to include fixes and new functionality in the next release of the software.

Brian Guenter

Sung-Hee Lee

Tutorial

This first part of the book contains tutorials on the interactive modeling programs made possible by the symbolic differentiation capabilities of D*.

Chapter 1 describes how to use the symbolic geometric modeling tool SymGeom to create three-dimensional geometry.

Chapter 2 describes how to use the interactive mechanism simulation program SymMech to create complex mechanisms and to simulate their dynamic properties. Models created in SymGeom can be imported into SymMech and used to construct mechanisms.

All of the source code for these interactive systems is available for free at http://research.microsoft.com (search for "Dynamics Simulation and Geometric Modeling Using D* and Symbolic Differentiation").

Symbolic Geometric Modeling

The interactive modeling tool SymGeom will allow you to model two-dimensional parametric surfaces. Surfaces can be made from three types of spline curves: profile, wire, and cross-section. Using these curve types you can create a surface of revolution, a profile product surface, or a wire product surface.

Surfaces of revolution are the most basic surfaces you can model; you only need to specify the profile curve and the tool will generate the surface. This kind of surface is useful for modeling rotationally symmetrical shapes such as balls, glasses, or cups.

The profile product surfaces allow you to model more complex surfaces such as trees, chess pieces, etc. This type of surface is generated from a profile curve, which defines the profile of the body, and a cross-section curve, which defines the orthographic projection of your body from the position of a plane through the object, i.e., one slice of your body.

The wire product surfaces are generated from a wire curve and a cross-section curve; the wire curve specifies the path the cross-section curve will follow. Wire product surfaces are useful for modeling tube-like bodies.

When you first start SymGeom, it will display a window like the one shown in Figure 1.1. The window is divided into two main parts. On the left, you will see four grids where you can draw spline curves, with a set of controls at the bottom that allow you to load/save a surface, specify the type of surface you are modeling, and specify the color and material of your surface. On the right, you will see the three-dimensional view of your surface; the sliders at the bottom are used to rotate and translate your body.

If you take a closer look at the grid section, you will notice that each grid allows you to draw four different curves: profile/wire curve, cross-section curve, and two auxiliary curves. You can create a profile curve by adding control points on the grid. Control points are added by right-clicking on the grid for profile curves.

Let us try to draw the curve shown in Figure 1.2. You might notice that the curve does not complete a closed circle. You can close the curve by right-clicking on the control points at the end of the curve to add more

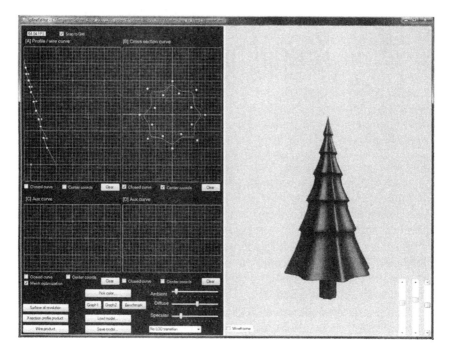

Figure 1.1. SplineEditor interface (see Plate I).

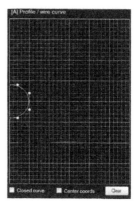

Figure 1.2. Profile curve.

Figure 1.3. Changing the weight of control points (see Plate II).

"weight" to them (Figure 1.3). Notice that each time you right-click on a point, the color of the point changes: one right-click gives a yellow point, two right-clicks give an orange point, and three right-clicks, the maximum,

Figure 1.4. Cross-section curve.

Figure 1.5. Left, an egg-like body. Right, a ball.

give a red point. If you want to reduce the weight of your control point, left-click on it. If you left-click enough times, the control point will be erased.

Now let us make a circular cross-section spline similar to the one shown in Figure 1.4. When you finish the cross-section curve, click on "X-section profile product" to create a profile product surface. The mesh you have just created has an egg-like shape. Now click on "Surface of revolution" and this will generate a ball (Figure 1.5).

2 Interactive Mechanism Modeling

2.1 Introduction

The mechanism construction tool SymMech will allow you to interactively create mechanical systems made up of linked rigid bodies. You can change the size, inertial properties, and types of joints that connect the rigid bodies, as well as the external forces, such as gravity, and torques that are applied to the system. After you have set the properties of your system you can run a real-time dynamic simulation. This system does not expose the full power of the `MultiBodySystem` class,[1] which allows you to define arbitrary parametric joint types. However, you can create systems that have revolute, translational, surface-surface, or surface-point joint types.

When you first start SymMech, you will see a window like the one in Figure 2.1. The window is divided into four parts: at the top you will see the file menu and the toolbar, on the left a tree view of the rigid-body system, on the right the properties of each body, and in the center a 3D view of the rigid-body system.

In the file menu and toolbar section, you can create, open, and save rigid-body systems; you will also be able to generate, play, and pause your animation. In the tree-view section, you can specify the hierarchy of your bodies by dragging and dropping the bodies you have added. You will also see two buttons at the top of the tree view; they will allow you to add and delete bodies from the system. The properties section will allow you to specify characteristics of your body, such as name, position, and orientation; physical properties, such as forces, mass, and torque; and shape type, such as sphere, cylinder, torus, surface of revolution, or a custom shape made in SymGeom. You can also specify the transformation constraints for each body.

---

[1]Described in Chapter 5.

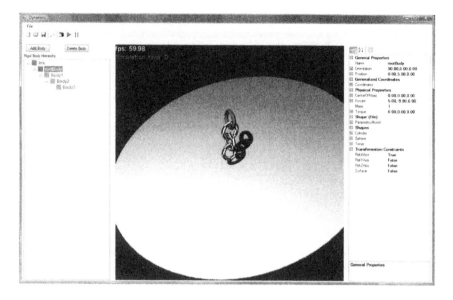

Figure 2.1. Interface.

2.2   Building a Rigid-Body System

2.2.1   Creating a New System

The first task is to create a new rigid-body system. In the toolbar menu, click on the "New" button; a dialog box will pop up asking you to introduce the name of your new rigid-body system (Figure 2.2) Type "Test" and press "OK." You should see a sphere displayed in the 3D view (Figure 2.3).

You can modify the properties of the body using its property grid, located on the left-hand side of the interface (Figure 2.4). The first step is to select the "rootBody" label, located in the tree view; notice that the body is colored in red, indicating that it has been selected. Create a name for the body by locating the "Name" property in the body properties

Figure 2.2. New rigid-body system dialog; notice that the name you have specified is the name of the root in the tree-view section.

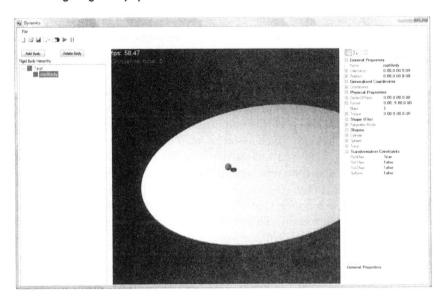

Figure 2.3. Body added to the system. The sphere shape is the geometrical representation of your body by default; if you select the body in the tree view, it will appear in red (see Plate III).

Figure 2.4. Body properties.

and changing it to "FirstBody." Notice that the name is changed in the tree-view label too.

To change the position of the body, click on the "Position" label and change its y value to 5 units; you will notice that your body moves upward. Change the x and z values to observe which way the body moves.

To change the orientation of your body, first click on the "Show XYZ Axis" button. A display of the coordinate frame will appear at the center of your body, making it much easier to keep track of the orientation as you rotate the body. The red axis is the positive x-axis, the blue axis is the positive z-axis, and the green axis is the positive y-axis.

To add a new body, click on the "Add Body" button at the top of your tree view; you will notice that the coordinate frame disappears and your root body has a new child. This child appears in the coordinate frame of its parent, since its local coordinate system depends on the parent coordinate system.

Select the child body by clicking on its label in the tree view. Now the child is marked in red because it has been selected. You can display its coordinate frame by clicking on "Show XYZ Axis." Now you can move and rotate the body; try several values and notice that all transformations are local transformations, not global. If you would like to apply a transformation to the whole system, you must change the position/orientation of the root body.

2.2.2   Building a Chain

Let us build the rigid body shown in Figure 2.1. This system will have the physical behavior of a chain.

1. In the toolbar menu, click on "New." A dialog box will pop up asking you to enter the name of your new rigid-body system. Type "link" and press "OK."

2. Click on "Add Body" to create the first body of your system. You will see a new body in the 3D view and its name in the tree-view hierarchy.

3. Replace the sphere shape by a torus shape. Select the body in the tree view by clicking on it to see its properties in the right-hand area of your interface. Locate the "Shapes" group and click on "Torus"; click on "Use_Torus" and select "True" (Figure 2.5).

4. Change the position and orientation of the body. In the "General Properties" section, change the x-axis orientation to 45 degrees and the y-axis position to 7 units.

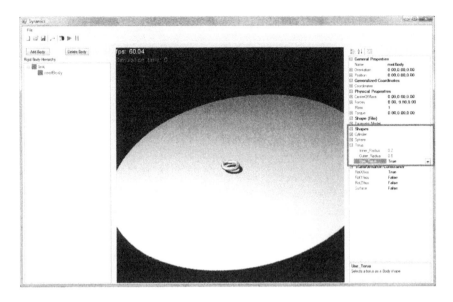

Figure 2.5. Torus options. The "Shapes" group is selected.

5. Insert a new body by clicking on "Add Body." Select the body by clicking on the "Body1" in the tree view and follow Step 3 to change the shape of the body. Follow Step 4 to change the z-axis orientation to 90 degrees and the z-axis position to 0.2 units. Figure 2.6 shows the new body. The translation and rotation transformations of your body are given in local coordinates. Locate the "Transformation Constraints" section in the properties area and change the "Surface" constraint to "True."

6. Click on "Add Body" to add another body to the system. Click on "Body2" in the tree-view section and drag it inside the "Body1" label. Click again on "Body2" to change its shape to torus, the z-axis orientation to 90 degrees, and the z-axis position to 0.2 units. Change the "Surface" constraint to "True." Finally, click on "Add Body" to insert the last body of your system. Click on "Body3" in the tree-view section and drag it inside the "Body2" label. Click again on "Body3" to change its shape to torus, the z-axis orientation to 90 degrees, and the z-axis position to 0.2. Change the "Surface" constraint to "True." Figure 2.7 shows the chain made of four links.

7. Finally, by clicking on the "Calculate Dynamic Equations" button in the toolbar section, you will see your chain moving. You can

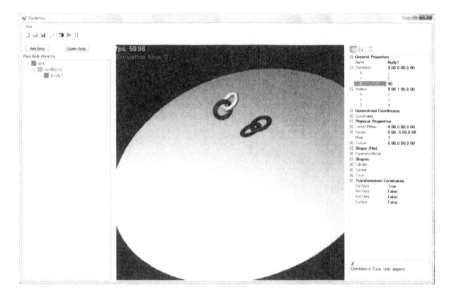

Figure 2.6. Building the chain.

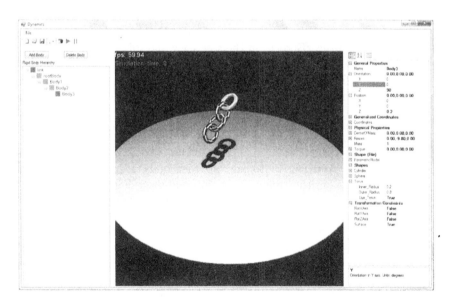

Figure 2.7. Four-links chain.

play/pause your animation by clicking on the "Play" and "Pause" buttons in the toolbar section.

Play around in the "Physical Properties" section of each body to see what can happen. Every time you change the properties of the body in your system, you need to click on "Play" to see it in motion.

2.2.3   Loading/Saving Your System

You can save your rigid-body system by clicking on the "Save" icon in the toolbar or the "Save" option in the file menu. In the same way, you can load a rigid-body file by clicking on "Open" in the toolbar or file menu.

Procedural Applications

In previous chapters, you learned how to use the interactive tools Sym-Geom and SymMech to create symbolic geometric objects and mechanical systems. These are useful tools but they have limitations. If the tools cannot do what you want, then you will need to write your own programs in D*.

Chapter 3 explains how to write programs in D* and describes some of the high-level optimizations used by the D* code generator.

Chapter 4 explains how to create a small set of geometric operators that can be composed with each other and with simple basic shapes to generate a wide variety of surfaces.

Chapter 5 explains

- how to create mechanisms containing arbitrary joint constraints,

- how to compute inverse kinematics,

- how to compute inverse dynamics,

- how to model closed-loop kinematic constraints.

Chapter 6 shows how to apply D* to a range of other problems in computer graphics.

3 ⟐ D* Tutorial

3.1 Introduction

D* is a language for conveniently expressing and computing efficient symbolic derivatives. There are many applications that require computing derivatives, and future chapters will describe several in great detail. This chapter will teach you how to write D* programs.

The D* language is implemented using a technique called language embedding. When you write a D* program you are actually programming in C#. Each type in the D* language has a corresponding C# class. D* mathematical operations are implemented by overloading the standard C# arithmetic operators and by providing special definitions for all the standard mathematical functions, such as sine and cosine.

The D* and C# code can be freely intermingled, with a few caveats. The most important is that the function `Function.NewContext` must be called before beginning the definition of any D* program. This sets up global data structures to keep track of all D* variable and function definitions.

3.2 D* Functions

Every D* program is a function from $\mathbb{R}^n \to \mathbb{R}^m$. For example, this program creates the $\mathbb{R}^2 \to \mathbb{R}^1$ function $f = ab$:

```
Function.NewContext(); //must be called before defining any D*
     variables or functions

Variable a = new Variable(), b = new Variable();
Function f = a*b;
f.print();
```

The print function displays the symbolic form of the D* program. The console output looks like this:

```
v0*v1
```

Expressions are automatically named by the system if you do not provide a name. Variable names can be assigned in the variable constructor, and functions can be named using the lhsName property:

```
Function.NewContext(); //must be called before defining any D*
    variables or functions

Variable a = new Variable("a"), b = new Variable("b");
Function f = a*b;
f.lhsName = "f";
f.print();
```

This gives the more readable printout

```
a*b
```

In general, $\mathbb{R}^n \to \mathbb{R}^1$ functions are defined by a statement of the following form:

```
f = expression
```

where the expression can contain any combination of arithmetic operators and function composition. The $\mathbb{R}^n \to \mathbb{R}^m$ functions are defined differently, by using the Function constructor. The following code creates the $\mathbb{R}^2 \to \mathbb{R}^2$ function $\mathbf{g} = (ab, \sin(b))$:

```
Variable a = new Variable("a"), b = new Variable("b");
Function g = new Function(a*b,Function.sin(b));
g.lhsName = "g"
g.print();
```

which prints out like this:

```
g[0]
a*b
g[1]
SINb
```

Individual range elements of a function are accessed with an indexer:

```
Function h = g[0]*g[1]; //(a*b)*sin(b)
```

3.3   Differentiation

The most powerful feature of D* is the ability to easily specify and compute symbolic derivatives that can be evaluated very efficiently. You specify derivatives of arbitrary order with the Function.D function:

```
Variable a = new Variable(), b = new Variable();
Function f = a*b;
Function dfa = Function.D(f,a); // Df/Da

//equality of mixed partials wrt variables
Function dfab = Function.D(f,a,b); // D(Df/Da)/Db
Function dfba = Function.D(f,b,a); // D(Df/Db)/Da

// does D(Df/Db)/Da = D(Df/Da)/Db?
Console.WriteLine((dfab == dfba));
```

which prints out

```
true
```

Notice that D* automatically detects that the two mixed partials are equal and computes only one of them. This will work regardless of the order or number of terms in the mixed partials.

For $\mathbb{R}^n \to \mathbb{R}^m$ functions, you must specify the index of the range element you are taking the derivative of, except if computing a parametric partial:

```
Variable a = new Variable("a"), b = new Variable("b");
Function g = new Function(a*b,Function.sin(b));

Function dg0 = Function.D(g[0],a); // D(a*b)/Da
Function dg1 = Function.D(g[1],b); // D(sin(b))/Db

//take derivative of all range elements
Function dgda = Function.D(g,a);
//dgda[0] = dg[0]/da
//dgda[1] = dg[1]/da
```

Derivatives can be used as arguments to other functions:

```
Function df = Function.D(f,a);
Function sindf = Function.sin(df));
Function ddf = Function.D(df,a);
Function derivExpression = ddf*sindf/df;
```

You can create functions of a variable without specifying what the function is, and you can compute derivatives of the unspecified function:

```
Variable a = new Variable("a");
UnspecifiedFunction q = UnspecifiedFunction.functionOf("q",a);


Function h = Function.D(Function.sin(q),a);
```

You can also take derivatives with respect to functions. Given a function $f(q(t), \dot{q}(t))$, you can specify the derivatives $\frac{\partial f}{\partial q}$ and $\frac{\partial f}{\partial \dot{q}}$:

```
Variable a = new Variable("t");
UnspecifiedFunction q = UnspecifiedFunction.functionOf("q",t);


Function dq = Function.D(Function.sin(q),q); // D(sin(q))/Dq


Function qdot = Function.D(q,t); // Dq/Dt
Function L = Function.sin(qdot);
Function dL_dqdot = Function.D(L,qdot); // DL/Dqdot
Function dL_dqdot_dt = Function.D(L,qdot,t); // D(DL/Dqdot)/Dt


Function et = Function.exp(t);
Function dsin_det = Function.D(Function.sin(et),et);
// D(sin(e^t))/D(e^t)
```

This type of derivative pops up occasionally, perhaps most importantly in the Euler-Lagrange equations of the calculus of variations. These equations are central to classical mechanics, covered in Chapter 8.

Equality of mixed partials taken in different order no longer holds when you take derivatives with respect to functions. This is because the things you are differentiating with respect to are not independent. For a function $f(p(t))$,

$$\frac{\partial f}{\partial p \partial t} = \frac{\partial}{\partial p}\left(\frac{\partial f}{\partial p}\frac{\partial p}{\partial t}\right) = \frac{\partial^2 f}{\partial^2 p}\frac{\partial p}{\partial t} + \frac{\partial f}{\partial p}\left\{\frac{\partial}{\partial p}\left(\frac{\partial p}{\partial t}\right)\right\},$$

but

$$\frac{\partial f}{\partial t \partial p} = \frac{\partial}{\partial t}\left(\frac{\partial f}{\partial p}\right) = \frac{\partial}{\partial p}\left(\frac{\partial f}{\partial p}\right)\frac{\partial p}{\partial t} = \frac{\partial^2 f}{\partial^2 p}\frac{\partial p}{\partial t}.$$

The derivatives will be the same if the term $\frac{\partial}{\partial p}\left(\frac{\partial p}{\partial t}\right)$ is zero. An example where this is not true is the function $\cos(e^t)$ with $f = \cos()$ and $p = e^t$:

$$\frac{\partial(\cos(e^t))}{\partial t \partial p} = \frac{\partial}{\partial t}\left(-\sin(e^t)\right) = -\cos(e^t)e^t,$$

but

$$\frac{\partial(\cos(e^t))}{\partial p \partial t} = \frac{\partial}{\partial p}\left(-\sin(e^t)e^t\right) = -\cos(e^t)e^t - \sin(e^t).$$

3.4   More Complex Functions

So far all of the D* functions we have written have been simple expressions. What if your function is too complicated to fit on a single line or if there are complex conditional expressions that have to be evaluated during its creation?

Because D* is embedded in C#, it is easy to write C# functions that return D* functions. Let us write a program, revSurf, that will take as input a two-dimensional profile curve, represented as an $\mathbb{R}^1 \to \mathbb{R}^2$ D* function,

$$f(t) := [x(t), y(t)]^{\mathrm{T}},$$

and return a new $\mathbb{R}^2 \to \mathbb{R}^3$ D* function,

$$g(\theta, t) = [x(\theta, t), y(\theta, t), z(\theta, t)]^{\mathrm{T}},$$

which represents a surface of revolution along the y-axis:

```
Function revSurf(Variable theta, Variable t, Function f){
    const int x = 0, y = 1;
    Function cosTheta = Function.cos(theta),
            sinTheta = Function.sin(theta);
    Function df = Function.D(f, t);
    Function denominator = Function.sqrt(df[x]*df[x] + df[y]*df[y]);
    Function d = 1 / denominator;
    return new Function(cosTheta * f[x], f[y], sinTheta * f[x]);
}
```

If we are given some D* function xyfunction as our profile curve input, then we can create the D* function representing the surface of revolution like this:

```
//returns a D* function from R1->R2
Function xyfunction(Variable var){...}

//make the surface of revolution
Variable theta, t;
Function surface = revSurf(theta,t,xyFunction(t));
```

3.5   Recursive Functions

It is easy to define recursive C# functions that return D* functions. We will
do a simple example here, Chebyshev polynomials, and a more complicated
example later, in Section 6.2. The recursion equation for the Chebyshev
polynomial, T_n, of order n is

$$T_0(x) = 1,$$
$$T_1(x) = x,$$
$$T_{n+1}(x) = 2xT_n(x) - T_{n-1}(x) \quad n \geq 1.$$

The C# function implementing this recursion looks almost exactly like the
mathematical equations:

```
//returns n degree Chebyshev polynomial
Function T(Function x, int n){
    if(n == 0){return 1;}
    if(n == 1){return x;}
    return 2*x*T(x,n-1) - T(x,n-2);
}
```

Let us print out the symbolic form of the Chebyshev polynomial of
degree 4 and compare that to the number of operations in the D* expression graph. The printOperatorCounts method will print out the total
number of operations of each kind that are present in the graph:

```
Variable x = new Variable("x");
Function res = T(x,4);

res.printOperatorCounts();
res.print();
```

which prints out

```
-:4  *:8

(x*(x*(x*(x*x*2 - 1)*2 - x)*2 - (x*x*2 - 1))*2 - (x*(x*x*2 - 1)*2
    - x))
```

There are 4 subtractions and 8 multiplications in the D* graph, but there
are 14 multiplications and 7 subtractions in the symbolic printout. This
is because there are many common subexpressions in the graph; the print
function recursively expands the graph into a tree, and this, in the worst

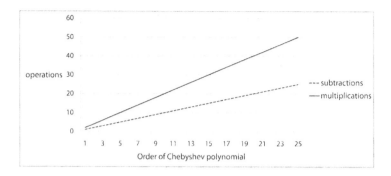

Figure 3.1. Arithmetic operations in D* Chebyshev polynomial function.

case, will lead to a symbolic printout that will be exponentially larger than the expression graph.

In Figure 3.1 you can see that the number of arithmetic operations in the D* function increases linearly as the order of the Chebyshev polynomial increases; D* has automatic common subexpression elimination, which detects and eliminates the many common terms that result from the recursion.

The *time* it takes to compute these polynomials is a different matter, however. Looking at the curve labeled "non-memoized" in Figure 3.2, you can see that computation time increases exponentially as a function of polynomial order; D* eliminates the common subexpressions as it finds them, but they are still created, which takes exponential time.

Because recursive definitions of mathematical functions are common, and we do not want to waste time computing them, D* has a feature called

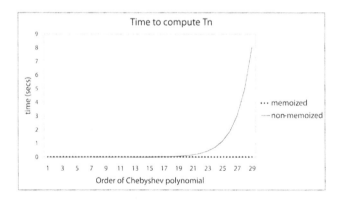

Figure 3.2. Memoized versus non-memoized recursive function execution time.

memoization. Memoization caches the values of recursive function calls so that they do not have to be recomputed. We can redefine our Chebyshev function as a lambda expression and then apply the Memoize method extension to memoize the function:

```
Func<Function, int, Function> T = null;
T = (Function x, int n) => {
   if (n == 0) { return 1; }
   if (n == 1) { return x; }
   return 2 * x * T(x, n - 1) - T(x, n - 2);
};


//memoize the function
T = T.Memoize();

//create Chebyshev polynomial of order 10
Variable y = new Variable("y");
Function cheb10 = T(y,10);
```

There is a big difference in the execution time of the memoized function vs. non-memoized function, as shown in Figure 3.2. The memoized function has essentially constant execution time as a function of polynomial order;[1] for $n = 29$ the memoized function takes approximately .02 seconds, while the non-memoized function takes 8 seconds, roughly 400 times longer.

3.6   Piecewise Functions

Some functions are most easily represented in piecewise fashion; piecewise polynomial splines are a widely used example we will see much more of in Chapter 4. In a piecewise function the symbolic function definition itself is a function of some other function or variable.

The FArray class, along with the operators Function.floor, Function.ceiling, Function.max, and Function.min, applies this functionality. To create an FArray you use Function.array. Each element in an FArray is an independent function:

```
Variable r = new Variable("r");
Variable s = new Variable("s");
FArray arr = Function.array(1.0, s, r * s);
```

---

[1] For $n < 17$ the overhead of setting up the memoization is greater than the cost of evaluating the Chebyshev recursion. This is why you should not blindly use memoization all the time; for small functions it is faster not to memoize.

```
arr.lhsName = "a";
arr.get(0).print();
arr.get(1).print();
arr.get(2).print();
```

which prints out

```
a[0] // references 1.0
a[1] // references s
a[2] // references r*s
```

Note that the get function does not return the contents of the array element being indexed. Instead it returns an instance of type Reference, which is a function referencing the array element.[2]

We can use arrays to create a C# class that will make D* functions representing cubic B-splines (see Listing 3.1).

There are several new features in this code: the IntegerValue class, the Function.floor function, and the exponentiation operator ^. The argument to the get function for FArray must be of type IntegerValue. Function.floor returns a function of type IntegerValue, which computes the floor of its argument. The ^ operator performs exponentiation by integer powers. Because the ^ operator has the lowest precedence of the C# operators, you must enclose your exponentiation expression in parentheses to avoid unexpected results.

Using the BSpline class, you can make a B-spline with constant coefficients:

```
BSpline c = new BSpline(1, 2, 3, 4, 5);
Variable t = new Variable("t");
Function ct = c.curveValue(t);
```

or with variable coefficients:

```
Variable a0 = new Variable("a0"),
         a1 = new Variable("a1"),
         a2 = new Variable("a2"),
         a3 = new Variable("a3"),
         a4 = new Variable("a4");

BSpline c = new BSpline(a0,a1,a2,a3,a4);
Variable t = new Variable("t");
Function ct = c.curveValue(t);
```

---

[2]Why? This is one of those technical details to be explained in Section 3.3.

```
public class BSpline{
  FArray P; //controlPoints
  public BSpline(params Function[] controlPoints){
    P = Function.array(controlPoints);
  }

  public Function curveValue(Function t){
    IntegerValue index = Function.floor(t + 3);
    t = t - Function.floor(t);
    Function B3 = ((1 - t)^3);
    Function B2 = 3 * (t^3) - 6 * (t^2) + 4;
    Function B1 = 3 * (-(t^3) + (t^2) + t) + 1;
    Function B0 = (t^3);
    return (1.0 / 6.0) * (B0 * P.get(index) +
                     B1 * P.get(index - 1) +
                     B2 * P.get(index - 2) +
                     B3 * P.get(index - 3));
  }

  public Function tangent(Function t){
    fTangent = Function.D(fCurveValue, t);
    fTangent = Function.derivative(fTangent);
    return fTangent;
  }

  public Function acceleration(Function t){
    if (fTangent == null){
      fTangent = tangent(t);
    }
    fAcceleration = Function.D(fTangent, t);
    fAcceleration = Function.derivative(fAcceleration);
    return fAcceleration;
  }
}
```

Listing 3.1. Cubic B-spline function.

You can also have coefficients that are mixtures of functions, variables, and constants:

```
Variable r = new Variable("t"),
       s = new Variable("s");

BSpline c = new BSpline(Function.sin(r),(r^2),s*r,3,r);
```

```
Variable t = new Variable("t");
Function ct = c.curveValue(t);
```

You can compute derivatives of piecewise functions, but not with respect to a variable or function that is in one of the FArray elements that make up the piecewise function:

```
Variable r = new Variable("r"), t = new Variable "t";
FArray arr = Function.array(1.0, r, (r^2));
Function ct = t*arr.get(Function.floor(t));
```

```
ct1 = Function.D(ct, t); // okay: t is not an element of the array
```

```
ct2 = Function.D(ct, r); // not okay: r is an element of the array
```

3.7   Evaluating D* Functions

You may have noticed that none of the previous examples had a printout of a D* function which contained a derivative. Let us make an example that does this right now:

```
Variable a = new Variable("a"), b = new Variable("b");
Function f = new Function(a * b);
Function g = Function.D(f, b); // D(a*b)/Db = a
g.lhsName = "g";
g.print();
```

This prints out

```
(a*b derivative b)
```

This is surprising; instead of what you would expect, $\frac{d(a*b)}{db} = a$, you get this funny (a*b derivative b) thing. What is going on here? When Function.D executes, it does not immediately compute a derivative; it creates a specification of a derivative, a placeholder in the expression graph for the actual derivative. This is because the D* derivative analysis algorithm[3] needs definitions of *all* the derivatives in your function so that it can globally analyze the entire graph to determine the most efficient way to compute all the derivatives at once. To actually compute the symbolic derivative you use Function.derivative. This function invokes the

---

[3]Explained in Chapter 7.

global derivative analysis algorithm and computes a new symbolic expression graph which has actual symbolic derivatives rather than placeholders. If we apply this to our example function we get

```
g = Function.derivative(g);
g.print();
```

which prints out

```
a
```

3.7.1   Compiling D* Functions

Interpretive evaluation of the function graph would be very slow, so evaluation of D* functions is done by transforming the D* expression graph to an intermediate high-level language and then compiling to an executable. The D* code generator has two back-ends: C# and C++. C# code can be dynamically compiled and immediately executed in the calling function. C++ code must be written to a file, compiled offline, and then manually combined with the user code that calls the D* function.

For functions with fewer than 64 local variables, the C# and C++ code have eqivalent performance. However, for code with more than 64 local variables, the C# .NET jit compiler does not provide register allocation,[4] which results in code that can be five to ten times slower than offline-compiled C++ code.[5] If you have large functions and need maximum performance, you should use the C++ back-end, invoked by the function

```
compileCCodeToFile(string filename)
```

To see how this compilation process works, let us define a simple $\mathbb{R}^2 \to \mathbb{R}^2$ function, $\mathbf{g} = (ab, \sin(b))$:

```
Function.newContext();
Variable a = new Variable("a"), b = new Variable("b");
Function f = new Function(a * b, Function.sin(b));
Function g = Function.D(f, b);
Function e = Function.derivative(g);

e.lhsName = "e";
e.print();
```

---

[4] As of the middle of 2009.
[5] The more local variables, the slower the code.

This prints

```
e[0]
a
e[1]
cosb
```

Now you can compile this function into an executable using the `compile` method, which by default dynamically compiles C# intermediate code. You can see the intermediate C# code that the system creates by setting the `Function.printCompilerSource` to true:

```
Function.printCompilerSource = true;
RuntimeFunction erun = e.compile();
```

This prints the following automatically generated source code:

```
using System;
using System.Collections;
using System.IO;
namespace DifferentiableFunction {
    public class newClass0:DifferentiableFunction.RuntimeFunction{
        public int rangeDimension{get{return 2;}}
        public int domainDimension{get{return 2;}}
        protected double Square(double a){return a*a;}

        public void eval(double[] result, params double[] vars){

// DOMAIN variables
// a = index:0
// b = index:1

// RANGE variables
// a = index:0
// Dv3_Db = index:1

        double a,b;
        double Dv3_Db;

        a= vars[0];
        b= vars[1];
//**** a

//**** Dv3_Db
```

```
        Dv3_Db = Math.Cos(b);
        result[0] = a;
        result[1] = Dv3_Db;
    }
  }
}
```

To compute the value of the derivative at a particular point, use the `eval` method:

```
double[] result = new double[2], vars = {1,Math.PI};
erun.eval(result,vars);
Console.WriteLine("e[0]:" + result[0] + "e[1]:" + result[1]);
```

This prints out

```
e[0]:
1
e[1]:
-1
```

In this case we know that `vars[0]` corresponds to variable a and `vars[1]` corresponds to variable b because we printed out the automatically generated source code. It is possible, though, that if the e function was defined in a different context, the correspondence might be different; `vars[1]` might correspond to variable a and `vars[0]` to b. There is no way to know exactly what order D* will put variables in, since the algebraic simplification rewrite rules can change the order in which they occur in an expression. Things become even more complicated if the expression has `UnspecifiedFunction` elements. For example, to compute

$$\frac{d[ab, \sin(q_0(t)]^{\mathrm{T}}}{db} = [a, \cos(q(t))\dot{q}_0(t)]^{\mathrm{T}},$$

the code is as follows:

```
Variable a = new Variable("a"), t = new Variable("t");
UnspecifiedFunction q0 = UnspecifiedFunction.functionOf("q0", t);

Function f = new Function(a * t, Function.sin(q0));
Function g = Function.D(f, t);
Function e = Function.derivative(g);
e.lhsName = "e";
e.print();
```

This prints

```
e[0]
a
e[1]
cosq0*q0_d_t
```

The printout for the function e[1] has a new UnspecifiedFunction, q0_d_t, corresponding to $\dot{q}_0(t)$, which was not explicitly declared in the code. The system has created this new UnspecifiedFunction term automatically.

You use the Function.orderVariablesInDomain function to specify the correspondence between variables and indices in the vars argument of the eval function. Once you order the variables in a function, they are guaranteed to stay in that order. Variables are always ordered first followed by unspecified function terms:

```
Function dq0db = Function.D(q0,b);

e.order(new[]{a, b}, new[]{q0,dq0db});

Function.printCompilerSource = true;
RuntimeFunction grun = e.compile();
```

If we look at just the portion of the automatically generated C# source code that relates to the mapping between variables and indices, you see that the mapping is the way we specified it:

```
public void eval(double[] result, params double[] vars){// DOMAIN
    variables
// a = index:0
// b = index:1
;
// UNSPECIFIED function variables
// q0 = index:2
// q0_d_b = index:3

// RANGE variables
// a = index:0
// Dv6_Db = index:1

double a,b;
double Dv6_Db,v13,v5,q0,v15,v14,q0_d_b;
```

```
a= vars[0];
b= vars[1];

q0= vars[2];
q0_d_b= vars[3];
```

Function expressions with many operations[6] can take a long time to differentiate. If the symbolic derivative is not changing between invocations, then it can be much faster to save the evaluation function to disk and then read it in again when you need it. To save the code for the evaluation function to disk use the compileToFile function. Use the Function.compileFromFile function to compile the evaluation function stored in a file. Here is a code snippet showing the use of these functions:

```
Variable a = new Variable("a"), b = new Variable("b"),
    c = new Variable("c"), d = new Variable("d");

Function f = (a + b) $*$ (c + d);

f.compileToFile(filename);
RuntimeFunction r = Function.compileFromFile(filename);
double[] result = new double[1], vars = { 1, 1, 1, 1 };
r.eval(result, vars);
```

3.8 Expression Optimization

Two kinds of expression optimization can be performed by D*: common subexpression elimination, and algebraic simplification. Before an expression is created, its hash code is used to see if it already exists. If it does, the existing value is used; otherwise, a new expression is created. Commutative operators, such as + and * test both orderings of their arguments. Similarly, the variable arguments to Function.D are sorted by their unique identifier before computing the hash code. This ensures that $\frac{\partial^2 g}{\partial^2 ab}$ and $\frac{\partial^2 g}{\partial^2 ba}$ will hash to the same value.

Algebraic simplification is performed by creating special constructors for each operator. For example, here is a constructor for the * operator:

```
public static Function operator *(Function a,Function b)
    Function alreadyExists = commutativeOperators(typeof(Times),a,b);
```

---

[6]Thousands of operations or more.

```
if (alreadyExists != null) return alreadyExists;
//do various simple constant optimizations
Constant ca = a as Constant,cb = b as Constant;
if (ca != null && cb != null) return ca * cb;
//will use Constant * operator overloading
if (ca != null){
    if (ca.leafValue == 0) return 0;
    if (ca.leafValue == 1) return b;
    if (ca.leafValue == -1) return -b;
    if (ca.leafValue < 0) return -(b * (-ca.leafValue));
    return (new Times()).compose(b,a);
}
if (cb != null){
    if (cb.leafValue == 0) return 0;
    if (cb.leafValue == 1) return a;
    if (cb.leafValue == -1) return -a;
    if (cb.leafValue < 0) return -(a * (-cb.leafValue));
    return (new Times()).compose(a,b);
}
return (new Times()).compose(a,b);
```

It performs the following symbolic algebraic simplifications:

$$a*1 \;\to\; a \qquad a*-1 \;\to\; -a$$
$$a*0 \;\to\; 0 \qquad c_0*c_1 \;\to\; \text{Constant}(c_0*c_1),$$

where a is a variable argument to the $*$ operator, c_0, c_1 are constant arguments to the $*$ operator, and Constant() is the constructor for the Constant class, which creates a new node that has a constant value.

Similar algebraic simplification rules can be incorporated in the constructors for other arithmetic and functional operations. This is much less powerful then the algebraic simplification performed by a program like Mathematica, but powerful enough for these important common cases:

$$
\begin{aligned}
a*1 &\to a & a*-1 &\to -a \\
a*0 &\to 0 & a \pm 0 &\to a \\
a/a &\to 1 & a/-1 &\to -a \\
a-a &\to 0 & f(c_0) &\to \text{Constant}(f(c_0)) \\
c_0*c_1 &\to \text{Constant}(c_0*c_1) & c_0 \pm c_1 &\to \text{Constant}(c_0 \pm c_1) \\
c_0/c_1 &\to \text{Constant}(c_0/c_1)
\end{aligned}
$$

3.9   Related Work

There are several methods of computing derivatives that are commonly used: first-order finite differencing, Richardson's extrapolation to the limit (a high-order form of finite differencing), automatic differentiation, and symbolic differentiation.

The first-order finite difference method is both inaccurate and much less efficient, in general, than other techniques, so it will not be discussed further. Richardson's extrapolation to the limit [22] can yield very accurate derivatives, but it requires many evaluations of the function to be differentiated, making it extremely inefficient. For $f : \mathbb{R}^n \to \mathbb{R}^m$, nk function evaluations and $O(mk^2)$ arithmetic operations are required, where k is typically 5 t0 10. In addition, the user must specify h, the initial step size. A principled selection of h requires knowledge of the second derivative, which is normally unavailable.

Forward and reverse automatic differentiation are nonsymbolic techniques independently developed by several groups in the 1960s and 1970s, respectively[7] [16, 31]. In the forward method, derivatives and function values are computed together in a forward sweep through the expression graph. In the reverse method, function values and partial derivatives at each node are computed in a forward sweep and then the final derivative is computed in a reverse sweep. Users generally must choose which of the two techniques to use on the entire expression graph, or whether to apply the forward form to some subgraphs and the reverse form to others. Some tools such as ADIFOR [7] and ADIC [8] automatically apply one method at the statement level and a different one at the global level. Forward and reverse are the most widely used of all automatic differentiation algorithms.

The forward method is efficient for $\mathbb{R}^1 \to \mathbb{R}^n$ functions but may do n times as much work as necessary for $\mathbb{R}^n \to \mathbb{R}^1$ functions. Conversely, the reverse method is efficient for $f : \mathbb{R}^n \to \mathbb{R}^1$ but may do n times as much work as necessary for $f : \mathbb{R}^1 \to \mathbb{R}^n$. For $f : \mathbb{R}^n \to \mathbb{R}^m$, both methods may do more work than necessary.

Efficient differentiation can also be cast as the problem of computing an efficient elimination order for a sparse matrix using heuristics which minimize fill-in [16, 17]. However, as of the time of [17], good elimination heuristics that worked well on a wide range of problems remained to be developed. An extensive list of downloadable automatic differentiation software packages can be found at http://www.autodiff.org.

Symbolic differentiation has traditionally been the domain of expensive, proprietary symbolic math systems such as Mathematica. These systems work well for simple expressions, but computation time and space grow

---

[7]See Section 7.3 for symbolic versions of these algorithms.

rapidly, often exponentially, as a function of expression size, in practice frequently exceeding available memory or acceptable computation time.

3.10 Advantages of the D* Algorithm

The D* algorithm combines some of the best features of current automatic and symbolic differentiation methods. Like automatic differentiation, D* can be applied to relatively large, complex problems, but instead of generating a numerical derivative, as automatic differentiation does, D* generates a true symbolic derivative expression; consequently any order of derivative can be easily computed by applying D* successively. Unlike with forward and reverse techniques, the user does not have to make any choices about which algorithm to apply—the symbolic derivative expression is generated completely automatically with no user intervention.

D* exploits the special nature of the sum-of-products graph that represents the derivative of a function using two new greedy algorithms. The first computes a factorization of the derivative graph and the second computes a grouping of common product terms into subexpressions. While not guaranteed to be optimal, in practice these two algorithms together produce extremely efficient derivatives. D* also symbolically executes the expression graph at compile time to eliminate common subexpressions and perform simple algebraic simplification. Because D* is embedded in a conventional programming language,[8] D* programs can be seamlessly interleaved with other code, which is very beneficial from a software engineering perspective.

3.11 Limitations of the Current Implementation

The current implementation of D* inlines all functions and unrolls all loops at expression-analysis time. Inlining is not required for the factorization algorithm to work; it is a software engineering choice analogous to the inlining trade-offs made in conventional compilers. This approach exposes maximum opportunities for optimization, and it simplifies the embedding of D* in C#. A side effect of this design choice is that the compiled derivative functions may be larger than desired for some applications. It also requires loop-iteration bounds to be known at compile time. For our initial set of applications this design trade-off worked quite well but future implementations may perform less inlining to allow for a broader range of application of the algorithm.

---

[8]D* is currently embedded in C# but can easily be embedded in other languages, such as C++, which support operator overloading.

The time to compute the symbolic derivative is guaranteed to be polynomial in the size of the expression graph. For an expression graph $f : \mathbb{R}^n \to \mathbb{R}^m$ with v nodes, the worst-case time to compute the symbolic derivative is $O(nmv^3)$. More details are provided in Sections 7.2.1 and 8.5.3. In practice, the current algorithm is fast enough to compute the symbolic derivative of expression graphs with hundreds to thousands of nodes in a few seconds, and tens of thousands of nodes in an hour or less.

Geometry Functions

In Chapter 1 you learned how to use the interactive procedural modeling program to generate objects. This chapter will explain how to use D* to define three-dimensional surfaces as functional objects, and how to triangulate and render surfaces.

The three-dimensional surfaces we will be dealing with are general parametric functions[1] of two variables,

$$\mathbf{f}(u, v) = \begin{bmatrix} x(u, v) \\ y(u, v) \\ z(u, v) \end{bmatrix} : \mathbb{R}^2 \to \mathbb{R}^3.$$

Rather than writing each surface function from scratch, we will create a small set of geometric operators that can be composed with each other and with simple basic shapes to generate a wide variety of surfaces. The set of operators we describe here is by no means complete, but once you have seen the basic structure it will be easy for you to develop your own.

The surface function code is split into several classes: DDiff, DGeom, DMat, DOp. The DDiff class defines functions for computing differential properties of surfaces such as parametric partials, surface normals, and surface curvature. The DGeom class has predefined curve and surface definitions. The DOp class defines geometric operators. Some of the geometric operators can be formulated as matrices; the composition of these operators becomes matrix multiplication. The DMat class provides this functionality.

4.1   Surface Properties

Given a surface

$$\mathbf{f}(u, v) = \begin{bmatrix} x(u, v) \\ y(u, v) \\ z(u, v) \end{bmatrix} : \mathbb{R}^2 \to \mathbb{R}^3,$$

---

[1]Not to be confused with parametric polynomial surfaces. Our system allows you to use any differentiable function, not just polynomials.

the parametric partials, $\mathbf{f}_u$, $\mathbf{f}_v$, are

$$
\mathbf{f}_u = \begin{bmatrix} \frac{\partial x(u,v)}{\partial u} \\ \frac{\partial y(u,v)}{\partial u} \\ \frac{\partial z(u,v)}{\partial u} \end{bmatrix}, \quad
\mathbf{f}_v = \begin{bmatrix} \frac{\partial x(u,v)}{\partial v} \\ \frac{\partial y(u,v)}{\partial v} \\ \frac{\partial z(u,v)}{\partial v} \end{bmatrix}.
$$

We can compute the parametric partial with the following function:

```
public static Function parametricPartial(Function surface, Variable
    parameter){
  List<Function> derivs = new List<Function>();
  //take partials with respect to parameter
  for (int i = 0; i < surface.rangeDimension; i++){
    derivs.Add(Function.D(surface, i, parameter));
  }
  return new Function(derivs);
}
```

In order to compute the shading on the surface, we need to know not just the points on the surface but also the normal. The normal, $\mathbf{n}$, of a parametrically defined surface $\mathbf{f}$ is the cross product of the two parametric partials:

$$
\mathbf{n} = \frac{\partial \mathbf{f}}{\partial u} \times \frac{\partial \mathbf{f}}{\partial v}
$$

$$
= \begin{bmatrix} \frac{\partial x(u,v)}{\partial u} \\ \frac{\partial y(u,v)}{\partial u} \\ \frac{\partial z(u,v)}{\partial u} \end{bmatrix} \times \begin{bmatrix} \frac{\partial x(u,v)}{\partial v} \\ \frac{\partial y(u,v)}{\partial v} \\ \frac{\partial z(u,v)}{\partial v} \end{bmatrix},
$$

where the cross product is computed by this function:

```
public static Function cross(Function a,Function b) {
  return new Function(a[1]*b[2] - a[2]*b[1],
              a[2]*b[0] - a[0]*b[2],
              a[0]*b[1] - a[1]*b[0]);
}
```

If we put these two together we end up with a completely generic function for computing the surface normal of an arbitrary parametric surface:

```
public static Function normal(Function surface, Variable u,
    Variable v){
  //compute the normal to the surface
```

```
Function dsdu = parametricPartial(surface,u);
Function dsdv = parametricPartial(surface,v);
return cross(dsdu,dsdv);
}
```

You may have noticed that the magnitude of this normal vector may not be 1; i.e., it is not necessarily a normalized vector. Because the graphics hardware can normalize vectors very quickly, it is generally faster to leave surface normals unnormalized and to let the hardware do it at runtime.[2] However, sometimes we need a normalized normal in the definition of a surface—this happens for example when creating an offset surface; then we can use this function to normalize any vector:

```
public static Function normalize(Function a) {
    int len = a.rangeDimension, i;
    List<Function> res = new List<Function>();
    Function sum = 0.0d;

    foreach(Function subfunc in a){sum += subfunc * subfunc;}
    sum = 1.0d / Function.sqrt(sum);
    foreach (Function subfunc in a) { res.Add(a * sum); }
    return new Function(res);
}
```

Now let us create a function that gives us all the geometric properties we need to render the surface on the GPU. There is not much to do—we just need to make a new function that combines the surface and normal functions. By convention, we will assume that the parameterizing variables of the surface are the first two domain variables:

```
public static Function surfaceAndNormal(Function surface){
    Variable u = surface.domain[0];
    Variable v = surface.domain[1];

    Function normal = normal(surface, u, v);
    //combine surface and normal functions
    Function result =
        new Function(surface[0], surface[1], surface[2],
                normal[0], normal[1], normal[2]);

    //give range variables human readable names
```

---

[2]The standard HLSL code wrapper that goes around every D* functional object includes code that uses the vector normalization instruction to normalize the surface normal.

```
result.allRangeNames =
   new string[] { "x","y","z","Nx","Ny","Nz" };
return result;
}
```

4.2   Geometry Operators

Let us begin with operators that transform two-dimensional curves into three-dimensional surfaces. We will assume that all two-dimensional curves are defined in the xy-plane.

Let us see what kinds of surfaces we can make using just the circle, shown in Figure 4.1, and our geometric operators. The circle function is already defined for us in the DGeom class:

```
public static Function circle(Variable theta){
   return new Function(Function.cos(theta), Function.sin(theta));
}
```

The extrude function is defined in the DOp class:

```
public static DMat extrude(Function d){
   return new DMat(
     new Function[,]{{1,0,0,0},
                     {0,1,0,0},
                     {0,0,0,d[0]},
                     {0,0,0,1}});
}
```

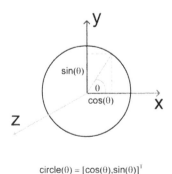

$$circle(\theta) = [\cos(\theta), \sin(\theta)]^\top$$

Figure 4.1. Circular curve defined in the xy-plane.

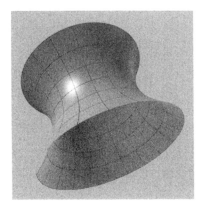 

Figure 4.2. 3D scoop cylinder.   **Figure 4.3.** Sphere surface.

It can be used to make a cylinder by composing it with the circle function (in this case using matrix multiplication):

```
protected Function cylinder(){
    Variable theta = new Variable("theta"), d = new Variable("d");
    Function cylinder = DOp.extrude(d) * DGeom.circle(theta);
    cylinder.order(theta, d);
    return cylinder;
}
```

By defining the radius of a circle as a function of the extrusion, you can create a 3D scoop cylinder as shown in Figure 4.2. The ordering of the domain variables determines the direction of the surface normal. The surface normal is $\frac{\partial \mathbf{f}}{\partial v_1} \times \frac{\partial \mathbf{f}}{\partial v_2}$, where v_1 is the first variable and v_2 is the second; by convention the surface normal points outward from the surface. For the cylinder the outward-pointing normal is $\frac{\partial \mathbf{f}}{\partial \theta} \times \frac{\partial \mathbf{f}}{\partial d}$. If we reverse the order of the variables, the normal will point inward and the surface will not render properly. The following code defines a sphere (see Figure 4.3):

```
public static Function sphere(Variable theta, Variable phi,
                    double radius,
                    double ox, double oy, double oz){

    //compute the surface function
    Function sinphi = Function.sin(phi);
    Function cosphi = Function.cos(phi);
    Function sintheta = Function.sin(theta);
```

Figure 4.4. Parametric offset surface.

```
Function costheta = Function.cos(theta);
Function sphere =
  new Function(radius * sinphi * costheta + ox,
               radius * cosphi + oy,
               radius * sinphi * sintheta + oz);
  return sphere;
}
```

We can create bumpy surfaces like the one shown in Figure 4.4 by defining a normal offset function that perturbs a smooth surface in and out along the surface normal:

```
public static Function wigglyTube(Function theta1,Function theta2,
    double tubeRadius,double slope,double wiggleHeight) {
  const double numWiggles = 12;
  const double twist = 15;
  const double r = 1;

  Function sinTheta1 = Function.sin(theta1)
  Function cosTheta1 = Function.cos(theta1);
  Function sinTheta2 = Function.sin(theta2)
  Function cosTheta2 = Function.cos(theta2);
  Function cosNumWiggles =
    Function.cos(thetaV1*numWiggles + theta2*twist)*wiggleHeight;
  Function helix =
    new Function((r+cosTheta1*tubeRadius)*cosTheta2,
                 slope*theta2+sinTheta1*tubeRadius,
                 -(r+cosTheta1*tubeRadius)*sinTheta2);
```

```
Function normal = normalize(normal(helix,theta2,theta1));
Function temp = cosNumWiggles*wiggleHeight;
Function scaledNormal = normal*temp;
Function wiggleSurf = helix + scaledNormal;
Function surf =
    new Function(wiggleSurf[0], wiggleSurf[1], wiggleSurf[2]);
return surf;
}
```

4.3 Surface Curvature

Computing the curvature of a surface can be useful for many applications: adaptive tessellation, ray sampling, etc.

The curvature is computed as follows. Assume we have a surface, $\mathbf{f}(u,v) : \mathbb{R}^2 \Rightarrow \mathbb{R}^3$, a curve in the plane, $\mathbf{c}(s) = (u(s), v(s)) : \mathbb{R}^1 \Rightarrow \mathbb{R}^2$, and a curve on the surface, $\mathbf{f}(\mathbf{c}(s))$, parameterized by arc length so that the tangent to the curve, $\|\mathbf{f}(\mathbf{c}(s))_s\|$, equals 1. The surface normal, $\hat{\mathbf{n}}(u,v)$, at any point on the curve is

$$\hat{\mathbf{n}}(u,v) = \frac{\mathbf{f}_u \times \mathbf{f}_v}{\|\mathbf{f}_u \times \mathbf{f}_v\|},$$

where $\mathbf{f}_u = \frac{\partial \mathbf{f}}{\partial u}$ and $\mathbf{f}_v = \frac{\partial \mathbf{f}}{\partial v}$.

The surface normal and curve tangent, $\mathbf{f}(\mathbf{c}(s))_s$, are orthogonal, so

$$\mathbf{f}(\mathbf{c}(s))_s \cdot \hat{\mathbf{n}}(\mathbf{c}(s)) = 0. \tag{4.1}$$

If we differentiate Equation (4.1), we get an expression for the projection of the second parametric derivative onto the normal,

$$\{\mathbf{f}(\mathbf{c}(s))_s \cdot \hat{\mathbf{n}}(\mathbf{c}(s))\}_s = 0,$$
$$\mathbf{f}(\mathbf{c}(s))_{ss} \cdot \hat{\mathbf{n}}(\mathbf{c}(s)) + \mathbf{f}(\mathbf{c}(s))_s \cdot \hat{\mathbf{n}}(\mathbf{c}(s))_s = 0, \tag{4.2}$$
$$\mathbf{f}(\mathbf{c}(s))_{ss} \cdot \hat{\mathbf{n}}(\mathbf{c}(s)) = -\mathbf{f}(\mathbf{c}(s))_s \cdot \hat{\mathbf{n}}(\mathbf{c}(s))_s.$$

Rearranging the terms in Equation (4.2), we get the following equation relating the curvature, $k = \mathbf{f}(\mathbf{c}(s))_{ss} \cdot \hat{\mathbf{n}}(\mathbf{c}(s))$, to the tangents and normal of the surface:

$$k = \left(\begin{bmatrix} \mathbf{f}_u \\ \mathbf{f}_v \end{bmatrix}^{\mathrm{T}} \begin{bmatrix} u_s \\ v_s \end{bmatrix} \right)^{\mathrm{T}} \begin{bmatrix} n_u \\ n_v \end{bmatrix}^{\mathrm{T}} \begin{bmatrix} u_s \\ v_s \end{bmatrix}$$

$$= \begin{bmatrix} u_s \\ v_s \end{bmatrix}^{\mathrm{T}} \begin{bmatrix} \mathbf{f}_u \\ \mathbf{f}_v \end{bmatrix} \begin{bmatrix} n_u \\ n_v \end{bmatrix}^{\mathrm{T}} \begin{bmatrix} u_s \\ v_s \end{bmatrix}. \tag{4.3}$$

If we want to compute the geometric curvature of the surface rather than the parametric curvature, we need to locally reparameterize the derivative using the linear transformation

$$\begin{bmatrix} u_s & v_s \end{bmatrix} = \begin{bmatrix} \acute{u}_s & \acute{v}_s \end{bmatrix} \mathbf{A}, \tag{4.4}$$

with the constraint that

$$\left\| \begin{bmatrix} \acute{u}_s & \acute{v}_s \end{bmatrix} \right\| = 1,$$
$$\|\acute{\mathbf{u}}\| = 1.$$

The reparameterized curvature equation is

$$k = \begin{bmatrix} \acute{u}_s & \acute{v}_s \end{bmatrix} \mathbf{A} \begin{bmatrix} \mathbf{f}_u \\ \mathbf{f}_v \end{bmatrix} \begin{bmatrix} \mathbf{n}_u \\ \mathbf{n}_v \end{bmatrix}^{\mathrm{T}} \mathbf{A}^{\mathrm{T}} \begin{bmatrix} \acute{u}_s \\ \acute{v}_s \end{bmatrix}.$$

Because $\mathbf{f}(\mathbf{c}(s))$ is parameterized by arc length, we know that

$$\|\mathbf{f}(\mathbf{c}(s))_s\| = 1,$$
$$\left\| \begin{bmatrix} u_s & v_s \end{bmatrix} \begin{bmatrix} \mathbf{f}_u \\ \mathbf{f}_v \end{bmatrix} \right\| = 1,$$
$$\left\| \begin{bmatrix} \acute{u}_s & \acute{v}_s \end{bmatrix} \mathbf{A} \begin{bmatrix} \mathbf{f}_{u}{}' \\ \mathbf{f}_v \end{bmatrix} \right\| = 1,$$
$$\|\acute{\mathbf{u}}^{\mathrm{T}} \mathbf{P}\| = 1. \tag{4.5}$$

Because $\|\acute{\mathbf{u}}\|=1$, Equation (4.5) can hold for arbitrary $\acute{\mathbf{u}}$ only if $\mathbf{P}$ is unitary:[3] the columns of $\mathbf{P}$ must have unit magnitude and be orthogonal to each other. Solving for the rows of $\mathbf{P}$,

$$\mathbf{P} = \mathbf{A} \begin{bmatrix} \mathbf{f}_u \\ \mathbf{f}_v \end{bmatrix}$$
$$= \begin{bmatrix} \mathbf{p}_1 \\ \mathbf{p}_2 \end{bmatrix},$$
$$\begin{bmatrix} \mathbf{p}_1 \\ \mathbf{p}_2 \end{bmatrix} = \begin{bmatrix} a_{11} & a_{12} \\ a_{21} & a_{22} \end{bmatrix} \begin{bmatrix} \mathbf{f}_u \\ \mathbf{f}_v \end{bmatrix}$$
$$= \begin{bmatrix} a_{11}\mathbf{f}_u + a_{12}\mathbf{f}_v \\ a_{21}\mathbf{f}_u + a_{22}\mathbf{f}_v \end{bmatrix}.$$

We can choose to have the first vector, $\mathbf{p}_1$, of our new coordinate system point in the same direction as $\mathbf{f}_u$ if we set $a_{12} = 0$. To make $\mathbf{p}_1$ unit length,

---

[3]$\mathbf{P}$ is unitary if $\|\mathbf{u}^{\mathrm{T}}\| = \|\mathbf{u}^{\mathrm{T}}\mathbf{P}\|$ for any $\mathbf{u}$: multiplication by $\mathbf{P}$ does not change the length of a vector (Appendix B).

we must have $\|a_{11}\mathbf{f}_u\| = 1$, which forces $a_{11} = \frac{1}{\|\mathbf{f}_u\|}$. The second vector, $\mathbf{p}_2$, of our new coordinate frame is

$$\mathbf{p}_2 = [a_{21}\mathbf{f}_u + a_{22}\mathbf{f}_v].$$

We need to choose the two remaining free parameters of $\mathbf{A}$ so that $\mathbf{p}_2$ is unit length and orthogonal to $\mathbf{p}_1$:

$$\mathbf{p}_2 = \frac{-\left(\hat{\mathbf{f}}_u^T \mathbf{f}_v\right)\hat{\mathbf{f}}_u + \mathbf{f}_v}{\left\|-\left(\hat{\mathbf{f}}_u^T \mathbf{f}_v\right)\hat{\mathbf{f}}_u + \mathbf{f}_v\right\|}$$

$$= \frac{-\left(\hat{\mathbf{f}}_u^T \mathbf{f}_v\right)}{\|\mathbf{f}_{v\text{perp}}\|\,\|\mathbf{f}_u\|}\mathbf{f}_u + \frac{1}{\|\mathbf{f}_{v\text{perp}}\|}\mathbf{f}_v$$

$$= a_{21}\mathbf{f}_u + a_{22}\mathbf{f}_v.$$

We now have all the elements of $\mathbf{A}$:

$$\mathbf{A} = \begin{bmatrix} \frac{1}{\|\mathbf{f}_u\|} & 0 \\ -\frac{\left(\hat{\mathbf{f}}_u^T \mathbf{f}_v\right)}{\|\mathbf{f}_{v\text{perp}}\|} & \frac{1}{\|\mathbf{f}_{v\text{perp}}\|} \end{bmatrix}.$$

Substituting Equation (4.4) into Equation (4.3), we get

$$k = \begin{bmatrix} \acute{u}_s & \acute{v}_s \end{bmatrix} \mathbf{A} \begin{bmatrix} \mathbf{f}_u \\ \mathbf{f}_v \end{bmatrix} \begin{bmatrix} \mathbf{n}_u & \mathbf{n}_v \end{bmatrix} \mathbf{A}^T \begin{bmatrix} \acute{u}_s \\ \acute{v}_s \end{bmatrix}$$

$$= \acute{\mathbf{u}}^T \mathbf{B} \acute{\mathbf{u}}.$$

The eigenvalues of $\mathbf{B}$ are the principal curvatures of the surface, and the eigenvectors are the principal curvature directions.[4] We can solve for the eigenvalues directly:

$$|\mathbf{B} - \lambda\mathbf{I}| = 0,$$

$$\begin{vmatrix} b_{11} - \lambda & b_{12}, \\ b_{21} & b_{22} - \lambda \end{vmatrix} = 0,$$

$$\lambda^2 - \lambda\left(b_{11} + b_{22}\right) - b_{21}b_{12} = 0,$$

which gives

$$\lambda_1 = \frac{-b - \text{sgn}(b)\sqrt{b^2 - 4c}}{2},$$

$$\lambda_2 = \frac{2c}{-b - \text{sgn}(b)\sqrt{b^2 - 4c}},$$

where $b = -\left(b_{11} + b_{22}\right)$, $c = -b_{21}b_{12}$.

---

[4] In differential geometry $\mathbf{B}$ is called the second fundamental form.

To find the eigenvectors, solve the following equation for $\mathbf{x}$:

$$(\mathbf{B} - \lambda_i \mathbf{I})\mathbf{x} = 0,$$

$$\left(\begin{bmatrix} b_{11} - \lambda_i & b_{12} \\ b_{21} & b_{22} - \lambda_i \end{bmatrix} \right) \mathbf{x} = 0.$$

The matrix $\mathbf{B} - \lambda_i \mathbf{I}$ is singular with rank 1, so we can arbitrarily set the value of one of the elements of $\mathbf{x}$. Two reasonable choices are $x_1 = b_{11} - \lambda_i$, which gives $x_0 = -b_{12}$, and $x_1 = b_{22} - \lambda_i$, which gives $x_0 = -b_{21}$. If $b_{jj} \approx \lambda_i$, then $b_{jj} - \lambda_i$ may lose many significant digits due to cancellation. We can choose the most accurate solution with the following rule:

$$\begin{cases} \dfrac{[-b_{12}, b_{11} - \lambda_i]^{\mathrm{T}}}{\|[-b_{12}, b_{11} - \lambda_i]\|} & \text{if } \left| \dfrac{b_{11} - \lambda_i}{b_{11}} \right| > \left| \dfrac{b_{22} - \lambda_i}{b_{22}} \right|, \\[4mm] \dfrac{[-b_{21}, b_{22} - \lambda_i]^{\mathrm{T}}}{\|[-b_{21}, b_{22} - \lambda_i]\|} & \text{otherwise.} \end{cases}$$

Once we have computed the principal curvature direction in the primed coordinate frame, we calculate the corresponding three-dimensional surface tangent vector using

$$\mathbf{c}_i = \begin{bmatrix} \mathbf{f}_u & \mathbf{f}_v \end{bmatrix} \mathbf{A}^{\mathrm{T}} \acute{\mathbf{u}}_i.$$

Here is a program[5] for computing the principal curvatures, and principal curvature directions, for an arbitrary two-parameter parametric surface:

```
public struct EigenData {
    public double lambda1;
    public double lambda2;
    public double[] firstEigenVector;
    public double[] secondEigenVector;

    public override string ToString() {
        StringWriter result = new StringWriter();
        result.WriteLine("lambda1:" + lambda1 + "lambda2:"
        + lambda2);
        result.Write("eigenVector1:");
        VM.print(result, firstEigenVector);
        result.Write("\neigenVector2:");
        VM.print(result, secondEigenVector);
        return result.ToString();
    }
}
```

---

[5]This is the library function `DifferentiableFunction.Utilities.curvature`.

```
/// <summary>
/// defined so that fu cross fv is the outward pointing
    normal of the surface
/// </summary>
/// <param name="surface"></param>
/// <param name="u"></param>
/// <param name="v"></param>
/// <returns></returns>
public static Func<double, double, EigenData> curvature(
    Function surface, Variable u, Variable v) {
  Function[] vecSurface = new[] { surface[0], surface[1],
      surface[2] };
  Function[] fu = Function.D(vecSurface, u), fv = Function.D
      (vecSurface, v);
  Function[] n = VM.normalize(Utilities.cross(fu, fv));
  Function[] nu = Function.D(n, u), nv = Function.D(n, v);
  Function[] fun = VM.normalize(fu), fvn = VM.normalize(fv);
  Function funDotfv = VM.dot(fun, fv);
  Function[] fvperp = VM.minus(fv, VM.mult(fun, funDotfv));
  Function[,] A = {{1.0/VM.length(fu), 0},
               {-funDotfv/(VM.length(fvperp)*VM.length(fu))
                  ,1.0/VM.length(fvperp)}};
  Function[,] fuv = {{fu[0],fu[1],fu[2]},
                  {fv[0],fv[1],fv[2]}};
  Function[,] nuv = {{nu[0],nv[0]},
                  {nu[1],nv[1]},
                  {nu[2],nv[2]}};
  Function[,] B = VM.mult(VM.mult(A, VM.mult(fuv, nuv)), VM.
      transpose(A));
  Function Bfunc = new Function(B[0, 0], B[0, 1], B[1, 0], B
      [1, 1]);
  RuntimeFunction Brun;
  Variable up = new Variable("up"), vp = new Variable("vp");
  Function[] uvp = { up, vp };
  Function transform = new Function(VM.mult(VM.transpose(fuv
      ), VM.mult(VM.transpose(A), uvp)));
  RuntimeFunction runTransform;


  Bfunc = Function.derivative(Bfunc[0], Bfunc[1], Bfunc[2],
      Bfunc[3]);
  Bfunc.orderVariablesInDomain(u, v);
  Brun = Bfunc.compile();
```

```
transform = Function.derivative(transform.range);
transform.orderVariablesInDomain(u, v, up, vp);
runTransform = transform.compile();


Func<double, double, EigenData> curve = (uval, vval) => {
    double[] res = new double[Bfunc.rangeDimension];
    EigenData result = new EigenData();
    Brun.eval(res, uval, vval);
    double b11 = res[0], b12 = res[1], b21 = res[2], b22 =
        res[3];


    double lambda1, lambda2;
    double b = -(b11 + b22), c = b11 * b22 - b21 * b12;
    double radical = Math.Sqrt(b * b - 4 * c);
    double q = -.5 * (b + VM.sign(b) * radical);

    lambda1 = q; //should be q/a but a is always 1
    lambda2 = c / q;


    result.lambda1 = lambda1;
    result.lambda2 = lambda2;

    double[] lambdas = { lambda1, lambda2 };
    double[][] eigenVectors = new double[2][];

    double[] vec;
    if ((b11 - lambdas[0]) / b11 > (b22 - lambdas[0]) / b22
        ) {
        vec = new[] { -b12, b11 - lambdas[0] };
        vec = VM.normalize(vec);
        eigenVectors[0] = vec;
    }
    else {
        vec = new[] { -b21, b22 - lambdas[0] };
        vec = VM.normalize(vec);
        eigenVectors[0] = vec;
    }

    eigenVectors[1] = new[] { -vec[1], vec[0] };

    runTransform.eval(res, new[] { uval, vval, eigenVectors
```

```
                    [0][0], eigenVectors[0][1] }); //res is length 4 so
                        can fit 3-vector in it
            result.firstEigenVector = new double[3];
            Array.Copy(res, result.firstEigenVector, 3);
            runTransform.eval(res, new[] { uval, vval, eigenVectors
                    [1][0], eigenVectors[1][1] }); //res is length 4 so
                        can fit 3-vector in it
            result.secondEigenVector = new double[3];
            Array.Copy(res, result.secondEigenVector, 3);


            return result;
        };

        return curve;
    }
```

5 Mechanism Functions

In this chapter, we will first show how to model a mechanical system and simulate its dynamics using the multibody dynamics software available in the download. While the detailed theory behind the software will be provided in Chapter 8, here we mention a few basic concepts of Lagrangian mechanics to the extent necessary for using the software.

Since the equations of motion of a mechanical system have the form of ordinary differential equations, and since and deriving them manually is very tedious and error-prone, D* can be used effectively to generate the symbolic form of the motion equations. Thus, you can not only simulate the dynamics of the mechanisms, but also perform advanced operations such as sensitivity analysis that require additional differentiation of the equations of motion. Additionally, unlike many dynamics simulation software packages, D* can help you model a broad scope of constraints (or joint types) to define a mechanism; you can use elementary joint types such as the revolute or prismatic joint, as well as more complex constraints such as curve or surface-type constraints, as we will demonstrate in this chapter.

5.1 Lagrangian Mechanics

The beauty of the Lagrangian dynamics formulation is that once you have specified the kinematics of your mechanical system using *generalized coordinates*, along with the inertia matrices for each of the rigid bodies, the equations of motion are generated completely automatically.

The generalized coordinates are a set of independent variables that completely specify the configuration (position and orientation) of every link in a mechanism.[1] The number of generalized coordinates is the same as the degrees of freedom of a system. For example, θ in Figure 5.1 can be used as the generalized coordinate of the hinged point-mass pendulum, since it

---

[1]How do you know if the generalized coordinates are independent? If the derivatives $\partial q_i / \partial q_j \equiv 0$ for all $i \neq j$, then the coordinates are independent. If you have a parameterization of the system, then this will be true by definition.

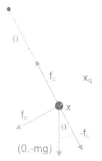

Figure 5.1. Point-mass pendulum with massless rigid rod.

completely specifies the configuration of the system. Using θ as the generalized coordinate, the equation of motion of the system is

$$\ddot{\theta}(t) = -g\sin(\theta(t)), \tag{5.1}$$

where g is the acceleration of gravity.[2] The dynamics equation is expressed in terms of the generalized coordinate θ, but not in terms of the (x,y) position of the mass. This is in contrast to Newtonian dynamics, in which the dynamics equation of the same system is

$$m\begin{bmatrix} \ddot{x} \\ \ddot{y} \end{bmatrix} = \mathbf{f}_c + \begin{bmatrix} 0 \\ -mg \end{bmatrix} \quad \text{subject to}\, \mathbf{x}^T\mathbf{x} = 1,$$

where $\mathbf{f}_c$ is the constraint force that enforces the constraint $\mathbf{x}^T\mathbf{x} = 1$, which specifies the distance from the point mass to the hinge point. As you can see, Lagrangian dynamics yields a simpler, more compact dynamics equation.

In general, it is possible to specify the kinematics of tree-structured systems using generalized coordinates. Figure 5.2 shows the topology of a tree-structured system. Each node of the tree is a rigid body, and the edge defines the relative transformation between a pair of connected bodies. Each transformation is defined as a function of the generalized coordinates.

Not every mechanism is tree structured; if a mechanism has closed loops it is frequently not possible to find independent generalized coordinates. In this case, it is necessary to augment the Lagrangian approach with Lagrange multipliers (Section 5.5.2). For now, we will consider only tree-structured mechanical systems.

The general form of the equations of motion is

$$\mathbf{Q} = \mathbf{M}(\mathbf{q})\ddot{\mathbf{q}} + \mathbf{c}(\mathbf{q}, \dot{\mathbf{q}}, \mathbf{f}_{\text{ext}}), \tag{5.2}$$

---

[2]The derivation of this equation is given in Chapter 8.

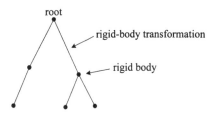

Figure 5.2. Tree-structured mechanism.

where $q \in \mathbb{R}^n$ is a vector of generalized coordinates with n as the number of degrees of freedom (DOFs) of the system, and $M \in \mathbb{R}^{n \times n}$ is the mass matrix expressing the inertial property of the system in the space of the generalized coordinates. The mass matrix has a special structure; it is a symmetric, positive definite matrix, and it is a function of the generalized coordinates (i.e., independent of the velocity of the generalized coordinate). The force $c \in \mathbb{R}^n$ accounts for all forces other than the generalized forces (i.e., it includes the Coriolis force, centrifugal force, and gravity, as well as other forces such as external forces f_{ext}); $Q \in \mathbb{R}^n$ denotes the generalized forces corresponding to the generalized coordinates. For instance, if you apply a torque τ to the hinge in Figure 5.1 (i.e., τ is the generalized force to θ), the equation of motion (5.1) becomes

$$\tau = m\ddot{\theta}(t) + mg\sin(\theta(t)).$$

Given a model of a multibody system, D* generates the equations of motion in the following form:

$$M(q)\ddot{q} = b, \tag{5.3}$$

where $b = Q - c(q, \dot{q}, f_{ext})$. By solving the matrix equation (5.3), you can compute the resulting acceleration given the current state and the input forces.

5.1.1 Simulation Procedure

Dynamics simulation is performed by determining the state (i.e., position and velocity) of a mechanical system at the next time step, given the state of the current time step and applied forces. In Lagrangian mechanics, the state of a system consists of the generalized coordinates q and their time derivatives $\dot{q}$. The following steps are executed repeatedly for dynamics simulation:

1. Determine the generalized forces Q and compute external forces f_{ext} such as gravity and contact forces.

2. Compute the acceleration of the system $\ddot{\mathbf{q}}$ by solving Equation (5.3).

3. Time integration: determine the state of the next time step $\mathbf{q}(t+\Delta t)$ and $\dot{\mathbf{q}}(t+\Delta t)$ by numerically integrating the position and velocity in time.

Note that additional steps are necessary if you want to detect and resolve collisions. Handling collision is usually done after the time-integration step or before computing the acceleration. It is essentially independent from solving forward dynamics, our main concern, so we do not deal with the topic further in this book.

There are various time-integration algorithms of differing accuracy and stability criteria. The most basic one among them is the forward Euler method, which determines the next state purely from the current state and the acceleration:

$$\mathbf{q}(t + \Delta t) = \mathbf{q}(t) + \dot{\mathbf{q}}(t)\Delta t,$$
$$\dot{\mathbf{q}}(t + \Delta t) = \dot{\mathbf{q}}(t) + \ddot{\mathbf{q}}(t)\Delta t.$$

5.1.2   The **MultiBodySystem** Class

MultiBodySystem is the class that you use to simulate the dynamics of your mechanism. Each of the three steps of the simulation procedure of Section 5.1.1 has corresponding functions in the MultiBodySystem class.

The functions in Listing 5.1 set or add the external forces, external torques, and generalized forces, respectively. The last function sets all the forces to zero.

Note that the external forces and torques must be expressed with respect to the world coordinate frame. Also, the external torques should be calculated about the center of mass of the link. For example, to apply gravity to a link i, you need to call

```
addExternalForce(i,mass*gravity);
```

but you do not need to apply a torque because gravity applies to the center of mass. However, if you apply a force to a point distant from its center of mass, a torque is induced by the force and you need to set it. The following function handles such a case:

```
public void addExternalForceAt(int idx, double[] localPos, double[]
    f)
```

where localPos is a 4-dim (homogeneous representation for a point with 1 at the last element) array representing the point to which a force f is

```
public void setExternalForce(int idx, double[] f) //idx: index of a
    link, f: force vector
public void setExternalTorque(int idx, double[] tau)
public void setGenForce(double[] Q)
public void addExternalForce(int idx, double[] f)
public void addExternalTorque(int idx, double[] tau)
public void addGenForce(double[] Q)
public void addGenForce(int i, double Qi) //add Qi to i'th entry in
    generalized force
public void setZeroAllForces()
```

Listing 5.1. Functions for Step 1 of simulation: setting generalized and external forces.

```
public void nextStepForwardEulerMethod(double h)
public void nextStepSymplecticEulerMethod(double h)
public void nextStepRK4(double h)
```

Listing 5.2. Functions for Steps 2 and 3 of simulation: computing acceleration, q̈, and doing time integration.

applied. For convenience, localPos is expressed with respect to the local frame of the link idx. The function addExternalForceAt adds external force as well as the torque induced by the force to the system.

The MultiBodySystem class has three numerical time-integration methods, shown in Listing 5.2, for proceeding to the next time step: forward Euler, symplectic Euler, and fourth-order Runge-Kutta. Each function performs Steps 2 and 3 in Section 5.1.1 together. The fourth-order Runge-Kutta method is more accurate than the other two methods, but it is slower.

You need to provide three parameters to the constructor:

```
public MultiBodySystem(Graph<Link> systemGraph, Variable t,
    Function[,] explicitConstraints)
```

Parameter t is the time variable. The explicitConstraints parameter specifies the constraints in the form of explicit functions. We will explain this parameter in detail later. For now, just note that you should set explicitConstraints to null for general mechanisms. Lastly, the systemGraph parameter is the target mechanism represented as a tree as in Figure 5.2. We will show how you can define this parameter for your mechanism next.

5.2   Modeling a Mechanism

In order to simulate dynamics of an articulated rigid-body system, you need to define the inertial properties of each link, as well as the kinematics of the system, in terms of the generalized coordinates.

5.2.1   Inertial Properties of a Rigid Body

The inertial properties of a rigid body consist of the mass, center of mass, and moment of inertia. The center of mass is the location of the mass center of a rigid body. The moment of inertia is a measure of the tendency to resist angular acceleration. It corresponds to the mass for the linear acceleration, but, unlike mass, the moment of inertia has different values depending on the reference frame. The formula for computing the moment of inertia is given in Equation (8.2).

An example of defining the inertial property of the rectangular object in Figure 5.3 is as follows:

```
//m: mass, x,y,z: lengths of a box
double Ix = 1/12.0*m*(y*y+z*z);
double Iy = 1/12.0*m*(x*x+z*z);
double Iz = 1/12.0*m*(x*x+y*y);
Function[,] centerOfMass = {{x/2},{y/2},{z/2},{1}};
Function[,] inertiaMatrix = Function[,]{{Ix,0,0,0},{0,Iy,0,0},
                {0,0,Iz,0},{0,0,0,0}};
```

Note that the center of mass is defined using the homogeneous representation of a vector and, likewise, the moment of inertia is defined as a 4×4 matrix where all the elements in the last row and column are zero. In our dynamics software, we assume that the moment of inertia is calculated

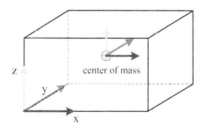

Figure 5.3. Center of mass of a rigid body. In our dynamics software, we assume without loss of generality that the moment of inertia is calculated with respect to the frame that is located at the center of mass and is parallel to the body-fixed frame.

with respect to the frame that is located at the center of mass and is parallel to the body-fixed frame (Figure 5.3). The `MultiBodySystem` class provides functions to calculate the moment of inertia of simple geometries such as the box, cylinder, and sphere.[3]

5.2.2 Defining Kinematics

Modeling the kinematics of a mechanical system is achieved by defining the relative configuration of a child link with respect to the parent link as a function of the generalized coordinates. We will be defining the kinematics of our tree-structured systems by connecting rigid bodies with joints, which can also be thought of as constraints on the motion of the link. Each joint, or constraint, has a corresponding transformation matrix, which can be a function of up to six generalized coordinates, although it is usually a function of just one or two. With a few basic kinds of connections you can model an incredible variety of systems. We will first introduce simple joint types.

Rotational joints. The simplest, and most commonly used, orientation constraints are rotations about either the x-, y-, or z-axes:

$$\mathbf{R}_x = \begin{bmatrix} 1 & 0 & 0 & 0 \\ 0 & \cos q & \sin q & 0 \\ 0 & -\sin q & \cos q & 0 \\ 0 & 0 & 0 & 1 \end{bmatrix},$$

$$\mathbf{R}_y = \begin{bmatrix} \cos q & 0 & \sin q & 0 \\ 0 & 1 & 0 & 0 \\ -\sin q & 0 & \cos q & 0 \\ 0 & 0 & 0 & 1 \end{bmatrix},$$

$$\mathbf{R}_z = \begin{bmatrix} \cos q & -\sin q & 0 & 0 \\ \sin q & \cos q & 0 & 0 \\ 0 & 0 & 1 & 0 \\ 0 & 0 & 0 & 1 \end{bmatrix}.$$

To simulate the effect of a joint with multiple rotational degrees of freedom, you can concatenate two or three rotation matrices, each a function of a different generalized coordinate. For instance, you can concatenate two rotation matrices to model a universal joint. If you use three rotational joints in order to model a ball joint, you are effectively parameterizing the orientation using Euler angles. This can lead to a phenomenon called *gimbal lock*, which happens when the coordinate frames align so that some

---

[3]Refer in the `MultiBodySystem` class to `public static Function[,] inertiaMatrix{Box|Cylinder|Torus|Sphere}()`.

of the rotations are redundant, causing the failure of the simulation. You should carefully choose the right Euler angle for your application so that gimbal lock does not occur for the range of motion of your mechanism.

Translational joints. In the most general case a translational joint is defined by the transformation

$$
\mathbf{T} = \begin{bmatrix} 1 & 0 & 0 & t_x(\mathbf{q}) \\ 0 & 1 & 0 & t_y(\mathbf{q}) \\ 0 & 0 & 1 & t_z(\mathbf{q}) \\ 0 & 0 & 0 & 1 \end{bmatrix},
$$

where the vector of generalized coordinates, $\mathbf{q}$, can have up to three elements, q_1, q_2, q_3. For example, a single degree-of-freedom joint that translates the child link in the x-direction is

$$
\mathbf{T} = \begin{bmatrix} 1 & 0 & 0 & q_x \\ 0 & 1 & 0 & 0 \\ 0 & 0 & 1 & 0 \\ 0 & 0 & 0 & 1 \end{bmatrix}.
$$

If the body is free to translate anywhere in space, then the transformation is

$$
\mathbf{T} = \begin{bmatrix} 1 & 0 & 0 & q_x \\ 0 & 1 & 0 & q_y \\ 0 & 0 & 1 & q_z \\ 0 & 0 & 0 & 1 \end{bmatrix}.
$$

5.3   Example Mechanisms

5.3.1   Visualization Using Microsoft XNA

The `MultiBodySystem` class provides only functions for computing the dynamics of a mechanical system but does not have visualization tools; you can incorporate the dynamics software into your preferred graphics environment to visualize the mechanism. Our download has software to simulate and visualize dynamics using Microsoft XNA. You should not need any additional XNA references to use the software if you have a basic knowledge of general three-dimensional graphics.

The MultiBodySystemXNA class. `MultiBodySystemXNA` is a derived class of `MultiBodySystem`; it additionally defines functions for visualization in the XNA environment. Likewise, `LinkXNA` is a derived class of `Link` for visualization in XNA. It defines the shape of a rigid body using XNA's `Model` class. The `MultiBodySystemXNA` and `LinkXNA` classes are the implementations of the simplest visualization; you can modify the classes if you want to write your own shaders for higher-quality rendering.

5.3.2 Two-Link Pendulum

Let us first create a simple two-link pendulum mechanism. The kinematics of a two-link pendulum in Figure 5.4 is specified by first defining the configuration of the first link, L_1, with respect to the world frame and then defining the configuration of the child link, L_2, with respect to L_1. The configuration of L_1 with respect to the world frame is the product of a translation $(p_x, p_y, 0)$ and a rotation by a generalized coordinate, q_1, around the z-axis:[4]

```
UnspecifiedFunction q1 = UnspecifiedFunction.functionOf("q1", t);
    //UnspecifiedFunction q1 of which domain variable is t
Function[,] A1 = VM.mult(VM.translate(px,py,0),VM.rotZ(q1,0,0,0));
```

VM is a class for basic matrix operations, translate(x,y,z) returns a transformation matrix for translation by (x,y,z), and rotZ(q,x,y,z) returns a transformation matrix for rotating by q about the z-axis. The last three parameters define the translation part of the transformation matrix.[5]

A link, L_1, is created by specifying its local transformation and inertial properties:

```
Link L1 = new Link(A1, new Function[] {q1}, centerOfMass, inertia,
    mass, name, t);
```

Parameter t is the time variable. Likewise, L_2 is defined as follows:

```
UnspecifiedFunction q2 = UnspecifiedFunction.functionOf("q2", t);
Function[,] A2 = VM.mult(VM.translate(1,0,0),VM.rotZ(q2,0,0,0));
Link L2 = new Link(A2, new Function[] {q2}, centerOfMass, inertia,
    mass, name, t);
```

After defining each link, you construct your mechanism by creating a graph representing its topology:

```
List<Link> allJoints = new List<Link>(); //list of all the links
allJoints.Add(L1); //add L1 to the list
allJoints.Add(L2); //add L2 to the list
```

---

[4]Section 3.3 explains unspecified functions. You may want to review this before continuing.

[5]Therefore, VM.mult(VM.translate(px,py,0),VM.rotZ(q1,0,0,0)) is actually equivalent to VM.rotZ(q1,px,py,0).

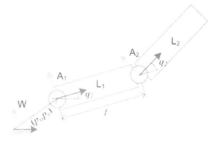

Figure 5.4. Kinematics of a two-link pendulum example.

```
L1.c(L2); // set L2 as a child of L1
Graph<Link> graph = new Graph<Link>(L1, allJoints.ToArray()); //
    create a graph whose root node is L1
MultiBodySystem TwoLinkPendulum = new MultiBodySystem(graph, t,
    null); //create a mechanism from the graph
```

Note that the order of the generalized coordinates is defined by the order of joints in the allJoints list. In this example, since the list contains L_1 and L_2, in that order, the vector of the generalized coordinates will be defined as (q_1, q_2).[6]

5.3.3   Simulating the Two-Link Pendulum

At each time step, you determine the input forces, and the dynamics routine determines the state of the mechanism at the next time step. Ideally the duration of the simulation time step should be the same as the display refresh frequency for a real-time simulation. The maximum simulation time step is determined by the properties of the mechanism, the dynamics algorithm, and the time-integration method. In many cases, the simulation step must be smaller than the display step to get stable results, so you will need to run the simulation step multiple times for each display refresh.

The code in Listing 5.3 shows how the input forces are defined for the two-link pendulum. Since there can be many sources of external forces, you need to set all the external forces and the generalized forces to zero by calling setZeroAllForces(), and then add forces appropriately. For the two-link pendulum, we apply gravity as well as the damping force. Note that damping forces are critical for stable simulation. If you use an explicit time integration method, such as the forward Euler method, the

---

[6]A link can have more than one generalized coordinate. For example, if link L_1 had two generalized coordinates (q_{11}, q_{12}) and L_2 had (q_{21}, q_{22}), the generalized coordinates would have been ordered $(q_{11}, q_{12}, q_{21}, q_{22})$.

```
protected void NextStep(GameTime gameTime){
  double simulationTimeStep = 0.016;
  int stepMult = (int)(displayTimeStep/simulationTimeStep);
  for (int i = 0; i < stepMult; i++){
    //clear all input forces
    rbs.setZeroAllForces();
    //add gravity
    double gravity = -9.8;
    for (int i = 0; i < rbs.numberOfNodes; ++i){
      double[] gforce = new double[] { 0, gravity * rbs.allNodes[i].
          mass(), 0 };
      rbs.addExternalForce(i, gforce);
    }
    //add damping forces
    double Kd = 1; //damping coefficient
    for (int i = 0; i < rbs.numberOfCoords; ++i){
      rbs.addGenForce(i, -Kd * rbs.dq[i]);
    }
    //proceed to the next time step
    rbs.nextStepForwardEulerMethod(timeStep);
  }
}
```

Listing 5.3. Two-link pendulum external and damping forces.

energy of the system will increase, due to numerical inaccuracies, even if no force is applied. Without damping forces to dissipate the energy, the simulation will soon become unstable.

Figure 5.5 is a screen capture of the simulation of the two-link pendulum example. The source code is provided with an XNA 3.0 Windows game project named "TwoLinkPendulum" in the downloaded software.

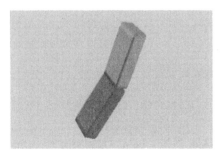

Figure 5.5. A two-link pendulum.

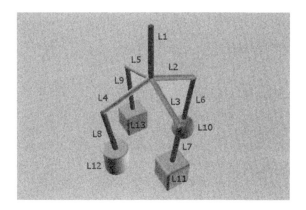

Figure 5.6. A tree-structured mechanism.

```
List<Link> all = new List<Link>();
all.Add(L1);
all.Add(L2), all.Add(L3), all.Add(L4), all.Add(L5);
all.Add(L6), all.Add(L7), all.Add(L8), all.Add(L9);
all.Add(L10), all.Add(L11), all.Add(L12), all.Add(L13);

//define topology
//L1 has 4 children
L1.c(L2);
L1.c(L3);
L1.c(L4);
L1.c(L5);
//Other links have only one child
L2.c(L6), L6.c(L10);
L3.c(L7), L7.c(L11);
L4.c(L8), L8.c(L12);
L5.c(L9), L9.c(L13);

//create a mechanism
Graph<Link> g = new Graph<Link>(L1, all.ToArray()); //create a
    graph of which root is L1
MultiBodySystemXNA tree = new MultiBodySystemXNA(g, t, null); //
    create a system
```

Listing 5.4. Definition of a tree-structured mechanism.

5.3.4   A Tree-Structured Mechanism

Since generalized coordinates always exist for a tree-structured mechanism, we can simulate such a mechanism under Lagrangian formulation. Figure 5.6 is an example of a tree-structured mechanism in which L1 has four children, from L2 to L5. Listing 5.4 shows the definition of the mechanism in D*. Source code is provided in the project "TreeExample."

5.3.5   A Serial Robot

The next example is the simple three-DOF serial robot in Figure 5.7. This system consists of three links connected by revolute joints. As we will repeatedly use this mechanism in the following sections, we first present its construction in the following code listing:

```
Function.newContext(); //always call this function first to use D*
List<LinkXNA> alljoints = new List<LinkXNA>(); //empty list of
    joints
Variable t = new Variable("t"); // time variable
Graph<Link> g = null; //mechanism graph

//link0 - rotation Y
UnspecifiedFunction q0 = UnspecifiedFunction.functionOf("q0", t);
    //gen. coordinate
Function[,] A0 = VM.rotY(q0, 0, 0, 0); //xform of link0
LinkXNA link0 = new LinkXNA(A0, new Function[] { q0 }, centerOfMass
    , inertia, mass, "link0", t);
alljoints.Add(link0); //add to joint list
```

Figure 5.7. A three-DOF serial robot.

```
//link1 - rotation Z
UnspecifiedFunction q1 = UnspecifiedFunction.functionOf("q1", t);
Function[,] A1 = VM.translate(lenY, 0, 0); //lenY is the height of
    link0
A1 = VM.mult(A1, VM.rotZ(-Math.PI / 4, 0, 0, 0)); //set default
    pose
A1 = VM.mult(A1, VM.rotZ(q1, 0, 0, 0)); //xform due to q1
LinkXNA link1 = new LinkXNA(A1, new Function[] { q1 }, centerOfMass
    , inertia, mass, "link1", t);
alljoints.Add(link1);
link0.c(link1); // declare link1 as a child of link0

//link2 - rotation Z
UnspecifiedFunction q2 = UnspecifiedFunction.functionOf("q2", t);
Function[,] A2 = VM.translate(lenX, 0, 0);
A2 = VM.mult(A2, VM.rotZ(-Math.PI / 2, 0, 0, 0)); //default pose
A2 = VM.mult(A2, VM.rotZ(q2, 0, 0, 0));
LinkXNA link2 = new LinkXNA(A2, new Function[] { q2 }, centerOfMass
    , inertia, mass, "link2", t);
alljoints.Add(link2);
link1.c(link2);

//create a mechanism
g = new Graph<Link>(link0, alljoints.ToArray()); //create a graph
    of which root is link0
MultiBodySystemXNA SerialRobot = new MultiBodySystemXNA(g, t, null)
    ; //create a system
```

5.3.6 Proportional-Derivative Control

By modeling a controller you can create a self-animating system such as a
robot. The simplest yet most popular control method is the proportional-
derivative (PD) control, in which the feedback force is determined from the
measurement of error,

$$\tau = k_s(q_d - q) + k_d(\dot{q}_d - \dot{q}),$$

where k_s and k_d are the proportional and derivative gain, respectively, and
q_d and $\dot{q}_d$ are the desired joint angle and velocity. Output torque τ is
linearly proportional to the positional error $(q_d - q)$ and the velocity error
$(\dot{q}_d - \dot{q})$. The PD controller is implemented as follows:

```
//PD control
double[] Ks = new double[] { 300, 200, 100 }; //proportional gains
```

```
double[] Kd = new double[] { 60, 40, 20 }; //derivative gains
for (int i = 0; i < rbs.numberOfCoords; ++i){ //for each joint
  rbs.addGenForce(i, Ks[i] * (qd[i] - rbs.q[i]) - Kd[i] * (dqd[i] -
      rbs.dq[i]))); //qd,dqd: desired joint angle, velocity
}
```

See the "RobotArm" project for the complete source code for this example.

5.3.7 Explicit Constraints

In general we cannot define generalized coordinates if a mechanism contains closed loops, because the coordinates depend on each other in highly nonlinear, noninvertible ways. However, for some simple closed-loop mechanisms, dependence of the generalized coordinates has a simple, explicit functional form.

Let us take the simple slider-crank mechanism in Figure 5.8 as an example. Its equations of motion can be expressed as those of the corresponding open-loop system (i.e., the closed-loop constraint is ignored and the terminal link can move freely) plus the constraint equations:

$$
\begin{bmatrix} Q_0 \\ Q_1 \\ Q_2 \end{bmatrix} = \mathbf{M}(\mathbf{q}) \begin{bmatrix} \ddot{q}_0 \\ \ddot{q}_1 \\ \ddot{q}_2 \end{bmatrix} + \mathbf{c}(\mathbf{q}, \dot{\mathbf{q}}, \mathbf{f}_{\text{ext}}), \tag{5.4}
$$

subject to

$$
q_0 + q_1 + q_2 = 2\pi,
$$
$$
l_1 \sin q_2 = l_0 \sin q_0.
$$

Since there are two constraint equations, the DOF of the system is $1 = 3$ (DOFs of the corresponding open-loop system) $- 2$ (number of additional

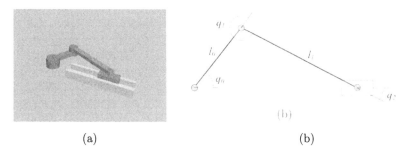

(a)   (b)

Figure 5.8. A slider-crank mechanism (a) and its corresponding open-loop system (b).

constraints). Let us arbitrarily choose q_0 as the generalized coordinate of the system. We can express the other two coordinates as explicit functions of generalized coordinate q_0:

$$q_1 = 2\pi - q_0 - q_2,$$

$$q_2 = \sin^{-1}\left(\frac{l_0}{l_1}\sin q_0\right). \tag{5.5}$$

We call generalized coordinate q_0 the independent coordinate of the closed-loop mechanism; q_1 and q_2 are the dependent coordinates. Dependent coordinates do not have their own DOF; their configurations are determined by the independent coordinates. By substituting Equation (5.5) into Equation (5.4), we can remove dependent coordinates q_1 and q_2 from the equations of motion and get a one-DOF equation of motion that is free from the additional constraint equations. The parameter explicitConstraint specifies the dependent coordinates as functions of the independent coordinates. The dynamics algorithm then eliminates the dependent coordinates from the equations of motion. Going back to the slider-crank mechanism example, the explicit constraints are defined as follows:

```
Function[,] explicitConstraints = new Function[,] { { q1, 2 * Math.
    PI - q0 - q2 }, { q2, Function.asin(lenX0 / lenX1 * Function.
    sin(q0)) } };
MultiBodySystem RBSTemp = new MultiBodySystem(g, t,
    explicitConstraints); //g defines the corresponding open-loop
    system with generalized coordinates q0, q1, q2.
```

The project name of this example is "ExplicitConstraints." The format of explicit constraints is

```
Function[,] explicitConstraints={{x1,g1(q)},{x2,g2(q)}...}
```

where x_i is a dependent coordinate and $g_i(\mathbf{q})$ is a function of the independent coordinates. Note that the explicit constraints are removed sequentially from $x_1, x_2, \ldots$. Therefore, g_i is actually allowed to be expressed as $g_i(\mathbf{q}, x_{i+1}, x_{i+2}, \cdots)$, because x_j $(j > i)$ will later be removed by g_j.

Figure 5.9 shows another example in which the generalized coordinates can be defined for a closed-loop mechanism. A total of 32 rigid bodies are constrained such that each joint angle of the link can be defined as a function of a single generalized coordinate; i.e., $q_i = q_i(q)$ for all i. A "fish" object is connected to a tong-like chain via a universal joint. In this case, our algorithm creates an ODE with only three independent variables. In contrast, nonsymbolic, conventional Lagrangian dynamics algorithms such as the Articulated-Body Algorithm [13] cannot achieve this level of reduction

Figure 5.9. A tong-like mechanism.

for the closed-loop system, because they endow independent coordinates to each mobile rigid body, followed by enforcing the loop constraints using Lagrange multipliers. For this example, they will obtain a 34-dimensional ODE coupled with 31 holonomic closed-loop constraints. Newtonian dynamics algorithms will generate a (33×6)–dimensional ODE for this type of mechanism.

5.4   Complex Constraints

The great strength of the dynamics algorithm using D* is that complex joints can be easily specified and robustly and rapidly simulated. In contrast, many physics engines support only a limited number of constraint types, such as the revolute or prismatic joint. In this section, we will show you some examples of the complex constraints that you can use.

5.4.1   General Translational Constraints

By parameterizing the position vector with one or more generalized coordinates, you can create various types of translational constraints. For a body constrained to move on a surface defined by two generalized coordinates,

q_u, q_v, the general form of the transformation is

$$
\mathbf{T}_{\text{surface}} = \begin{bmatrix} 1 & 0 & 0 & t_x(q_u, q_v) \\ 0 & 1 & 0 & t_y(q_u, q_v) \\ 0 & 0 & 1 & t_z(q_u, q_v) \\ 0 & 0 & 0 & 1 \end{bmatrix}.
$$

For example, to constrain a body to translate on the surface of a sphere, we could use the parameterization of the sphere

$$
f(q_\theta q_\phi) = [r \sin q_\phi \cos q_\theta + o_x, r \cos q_\phi + o_y, r \sin q_\phi \sin q_\theta + o_z]^{\mathrm{T}},
$$

where $[o_x, o_y, o_z]^{\mathrm{T}}$ is the fixed origin of the sphere, r is the radius, and q_ϕ, q_θ are the generalized coordinates. The transformation matrix for this translational joint is

$$
\mathbf{T}_{\text{sphere}} = \begin{bmatrix} 1 & 0 & 0 & r \sin q_\phi \cos q_\theta + o_x \\ 0 & 1 & 0 & r \cos q_\phi + o_y \\ 0 & 0 & 1 & r \sin q_\phi \sin q_\theta + o_z \\ 0 & 0 & 0 & 1 \end{bmatrix}.
$$

As another example of a surface translation constraint, we could constrain a body to translate on the surface of the plane passing through point $\mathbf{p}_o$, parameterized by generalized coordinates q_a, q_b and two noncolinear vectors $\mathbf{v}_a$, $\mathbf{v}_b$ in the plane. The corresponding transformation matrix is

$$
\mathbf{T}_{\text{plane}} = \begin{bmatrix} 1 & 0 & 0 & p_{o_x} + q_a v_{a_x} + q_b v_{b_x} \\ 0 & 1 & 0 & p_{o_y} + q_a v_{a_y} + q_b v_{b_y} \\ 0 & 0 & 1 & p_{o_z} + q_a v_{a_z} + q_b v_{b_z} \\ 0 & 0 & 0 & 1 \end{bmatrix}.
$$

The general form of the transformation that constrains a body to translate along a curve parameterized by the generalized coordinate q_t is

$$
\mathbf{T}_{\text{curve}} = \begin{bmatrix} 1 & 0 & 0 & t_x(q_t) \\ 0 & 1 & 0 & t_y(q_t) \\ 0 & 0 & 1 & t_z(q_t) \\ 0 & 0 & 0 & 1 \end{bmatrix}.
$$

To constrain translation to the line passing through the point $\mathbf{p}_o$, with direction $\mathbf{v}$, and parameterized by the generalized coordinate q_t, we could use the transformation matrix

$$
\mathbf{T}_{\text{line}} = \begin{bmatrix} 1 & 0 & 0 & p_{o_x} + q_t v_x \\ 0 & 1 & 0 & p_{o_y} + q_t v_y \\ 0 & 0 & 1 & p_{o_z} + q_t v_z \\ 0 & 0 & 0 & 1 \end{bmatrix}.
$$

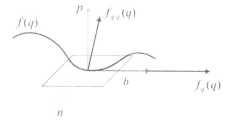

Figure 5.10. Traveling coordinate frame defined by the tangent, $f_q(q)$, and second derivative, $f_{qq}(q)$, of the curve $f(q)$.

5.4.2 General Orientation Constraints

A commonly used orientation constraint is a traveling coordinate frame along a curve. You could use this to constrain beads to slide along a wire, or to make a roller coaster or train roll along a track, or to make an airplane fly along a motion path.

If the curve, $f(q)$, has a continuous, nonzero second derivative everywhere in the region where you intend to evaluate it, then it is easy to define a coordinate frame that travels along the curve:

$$\mathbf{b} = \frac{f_q(t)}{\|f_q(t)\|},$$

$$\mathbf{n} = \frac{\mathbf{b} \times f_{qq}(t)}{\|\mathbf{b} \times f_{qq}(t)\|},$$

$$\mathbf{p} = \mathbf{n} \times \mathbf{b},$$

where $f_q = df/dq$ (see Figure 5.10).

There are three transformation matrices you can define with the column vectors $\mathbf{b}$, $\mathbf{n}$, $\mathbf{p}$ that do not change the handedness of your coordinate system.[7] One transformation rotates the x-axis into $\mathbf{b}$, the y-axis into $\mathbf{p}$, and the z-axis into $\mathbf{n}$:

$$\mathbf{R}_{\text{curve}} = \begin{bmatrix} \mathbf{b} & \mathbf{p} & \mathbf{n} & 0 \\ 0 & 0 & 0 & 1 \end{bmatrix}.$$

The other two transformations are

$$\mathbf{R}_{\text{curve}} = \begin{bmatrix} \mathbf{n} & \mathbf{b} & \mathbf{p} & 0 \\ 0 & 0 & 0 & 1 \end{bmatrix}$$

and

$$\mathbf{R}_{\text{curve}} = \begin{bmatrix} \mathbf{p} & \mathbf{b} & \mathbf{n} & 0 \\ 0 & 0 & 0 & 1 \end{bmatrix}.$$

---

[7] Assuming you do not change the sign of any of $\mathbf{b}$, $\mathbf{n}$, $\mathbf{p}$.

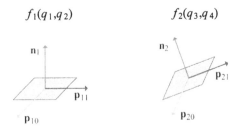

$$f_1(q_1, q_2) \qquad\qquad f_2(q_3, q_4)$$

Figure 5.11. Surface-surface coordinate frame constraints.

Moving up one dimension from curves, we can define an orientation constraint for surfaces. Given a function

$$\mathbf{f}(q_1, q_2) = [f_x(q_1, q_2), f_y(q_1, q_2), f_z(q_1, q_2)]^T$$

that describes the surface, we can use the two parametric tangent vectors of the surface,

$$\mathbf{p}_0 = \begin{bmatrix} \frac{\partial f_x}{\partial q_1} \\ \frac{\partial f_y}{\partial q_1} \\ \frac{\partial f_z}{\partial q_1} \end{bmatrix}, \qquad \mathbf{p}_1 = \begin{bmatrix} \frac{\partial f_x}{\partial q_2} \\ \frac{\partial f_y}{\partial q_2} \\ \frac{\partial f_z}{\partial q_2} \end{bmatrix},$$

and their cross product $\mathbf{n} = \mathbf{p}_0 \times \mathbf{p}_1$ to create the transformation matrix

$$\mathbf{R}_{\text{surface}} = \begin{bmatrix} \mathbf{p}_0 & \mathbf{p}_1 & \mathbf{n} & \mathbf{0} \\ 0 & 0 & 0 & 1 \end{bmatrix}.$$

We can force the surface coordinate frames of two surfaces, shown in Figure 5.11, to align by using the transformation

$$\mathbf{R}_{s_1 s_2} = \mathbf{R}_{s_1} \mathbf{R}_{s_2}^{-1}$$

$$= \begin{bmatrix} \mathbf{p}_{10} & \mathbf{p}_{11} & \mathbf{n}_1 & \mathbf{0} \\ 0 & 0 & 0 & 1 \end{bmatrix} \begin{bmatrix} \mathbf{p}_{20} & \mathbf{p}_{21} & \mathbf{n}_2 & \mathbf{0} \\ 0 & 0 & 0 & 1 \end{bmatrix}^{-1}$$

$$= \begin{bmatrix} \mathbf{p}_{10} & \mathbf{p}_{11} & \mathbf{n}_1 & \mathbf{0} \\ 0 & 0 & 0 & 1 \end{bmatrix} \begin{bmatrix} \mathbf{p}_{20}^T & 0 \\ \mathbf{p}_{21}^T & 0 \\ \mathbf{n}_2^T & 0 \\ \mathbf{0} & 1 \end{bmatrix}.$$

The matrix $\mathbf{R}_{s_1 s_2}$ is a function of four generalized coordinates: q_1, q_2, q_3, q_4.

By permuting and changing the sign of the column vectors of $\mathbf{R}_{s_1}$, you can control the mapping of the $f_2(q_3, q_4)$ coordinate frame to the $f_1(q_1, q_2)$

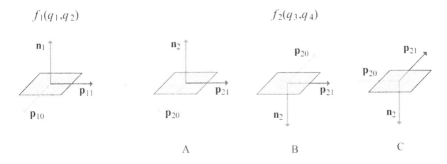

Figure 5.12. Different mappings from the $f_2(q_3, q_4)$ coordinate frame to the $f_1(q_1, q_2)$ coordinate frame.

coordinate frame. For example, suppose we wanted mapping B in Figure 5.12. We want the vectors of coordinate frame $f_2(q_3, q_4)$ to map like this:

$$\mathbf{p}_{20} \to -\mathbf{p}_{10}, \quad \mathbf{p}_{21} \to \mathbf{p}_{11}, \quad \mathbf{n}_2 \to -\mathbf{n}_1.$$

We can write this mapping in matrix form as

$$\mathbf{R}_B \begin{bmatrix} \mathbf{p}_{20} & \mathbf{p}_{21} & \mathbf{n}_2 & \mathbf{0} \\ 0 & 0 & 0 & 1 \end{bmatrix} = \begin{bmatrix} -\mathbf{p}_{10} & \mathbf{p}_{11} & -\mathbf{n}_1 & \mathbf{0} \\ 0 & 0 & 0 & 1 \end{bmatrix},$$

$$\mathbf{R}_B = \begin{bmatrix} -\mathbf{p}_{10} & \mathbf{p}_{11} & -\mathbf{n}_1 & \mathbf{0} \\ 0 & 0 & 0 & 1 \end{bmatrix} \begin{bmatrix} \mathbf{p}_{20} & \mathbf{p}_{21} & \mathbf{n}_2 & \mathbf{0} \\ 0 & 0 & 0 & 1 \end{bmatrix}^{-1}.$$

For mapping C we want

$$\mathbf{p}_{20} \to -\mathbf{p}_{11}, \quad \mathbf{p}_{21} \to -\mathbf{p}_{10}, \quad \mathbf{n}_2 \to -\mathbf{n}_1.$$

In matrix form this is

$$\mathbf{R}_C \begin{bmatrix} \mathbf{p}_{20} & \mathbf{p}_{21} & \mathbf{n}_2 & \mathbf{0} \\ 0 & 0 & 0 & 1 \end{bmatrix} = \begin{bmatrix} -\mathbf{p}_{11} & -\mathbf{p}_{10} & -\mathbf{n}_1 & \mathbf{0} \\ 0 & 0 & 0 & 1 \end{bmatrix},$$

$$\mathbf{R}_C = \begin{bmatrix} -\mathbf{p}_{11} & -\mathbf{p}_{10} & -\mathbf{n}_1 & \mathbf{0} \\ 0 & 0 & 0 & 1 \end{bmatrix} \begin{bmatrix} \mathbf{p}_{20} & \mathbf{p}_{21} & \mathbf{n}_2 & \mathbf{0} \\ 0 & 0 & 0 & 1 \end{bmatrix}^{-1}.$$

5.4.3 Combined Constraints

Most of the time you will have to use both translational and rotational constraints to specify the system kinematics. Let us look at a few examples to see how this is done.

Assume we want to constrain an object to move along a space curve, $\mathbf{f}(q_p) : \mathbb{R}^1 \to \mathbb{R}^3$, and that we want this object oriented so that the x-axis in object-model space always points in the direction of the tangent, $\partial \mathbf{f} / \partial q_p$,

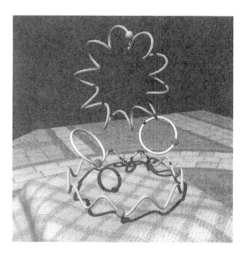

Figure 5.13. Path-following constraint: beads on a wire (see Plate IV).

to the curve. Let us assume also that we want to allow the object to rotate about the axis of the tangent vector. The system will be parameterized by two generalized coordinates, q_p, the parametric distance along the curve, and q_r, the rotation about the tangent vector. An example of several systems constrained this way is shown in Figure 5.13. The beads are forced to orient themselves along the tangent to the curve, but they are free to rotate about this tangent vector.

The combined constraint will use three transformation matrices: the curve orientation constraint matrix, the translational constraint matrix, and a rotation about the x-axis,

$$
\begin{aligned}
\mathbf{R}_{\text{path}} &= \mathbf{T}_{\text{curve}}\mathbf{R}_{\text{curve}}\mathbf{R}_x \\
&= \left[\begin{array}{cc} \mathbf{1} & \mathbf{f}(q_p) \\ \mathbf{0} & 1 \end{array}\right]\left[\begin{array}{cccc} \mathbf{b}(q_p) & \mathbf{p}(q_p) & \mathbf{n}(q_p) & \mathbf{0} \\ 0 & 0 & 0 & 1 \end{array}\right] \\
&\quad \times \left[\begin{array}{cccc} 1 & 0 & 0 & 0 \\ 0 & \cos q_r & \sin q_r & 0 \\ 0 & -\sin q_r & \cos q_r & 0 \\ 0 & 0 & 0 & 1 \end{array}\right] \\
&= \left[\begin{array}{cccc} \mathbf{b}(q_p) & \mathbf{p}(q_p) & \mathbf{n}(q_p) & \mathbf{f}(q_p) \\ 0 & 0 & 0 & 1 \end{array}\right]\left[\begin{array}{cccc} 1 & 0 & 0 & 0 \\ 0 & \cos q_r & \sin q_r & 0 \\ 0 & -\sin q_r & \cos q_r & 0 \\ 0 & 0 & 0 & 1 \end{array}\right].
\end{aligned}
$$

We can make a chain of torii, shown in Figure 5.14, by applying mapping C of Figure 5.12 to the sequence of torus objects. The torus surfaces are

Figure 5.14. Surface-surface constraint: torus chain (see Plate V).

Figure 5.15. Surface-surface constraint: wheels inside wheels (see Plate VI).

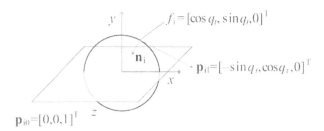

Figure 5.16. Wheel coordinate frame.

constrained by these mappings to translate across each other. The D* code to generate the torus chain is in Appendix E.2.

It is also possible to simulate certain types of rolling contact. In Figure 5.15 the wheels are constrained to roll rather than slide. The wheels, w_i, of radius r_i are arranged in a linear kinematic chain so that wheel w_{i+1} is inside wheel w_i. The transformation relating w_i and w_{i+1} is parameterized by a single generalized coordinate, q_{t_i}. Let us define all the wheel models so that they lie in the xy-plane and rotate about the z-axis, as shown in Figure 5.16.

For one pair of wheels, w_1, w_2, we have the translation functions

$$\mathbf{f}_1(q_t) = [\cos q_t, \sin q_t, 0]^{\mathrm{T}},$$

$$\mathbf{f}_2(q_t) = \left[\cos\left(\frac{r_1}{r_2}q_t\right), \sin\left(\frac{r_1}{r_2}q_t\right), 0\right]^{\mathrm{T}}.$$

The smaller wheel has to rotate in the ratio $\frac{r_2}{r_1}$ to maintain rolling contact. Looking at Figure 5.16, you can see that the coordinate frame for the larger wheel is

$$\mathbf{p}_{10} = [0, 0, 1]^{\mathrm{T}},$$

$$\mathbf{p}_{11} = \frac{\partial \mathbf{f}_1}{\partial q_t}$$

$$= [-\sin q_t, \cos q_t, 0]^{\mathrm{T}},$$

$$\mathbf{n}_1 = \mathbf{p}_{10} \times \mathbf{p}_{11}$$

$$= [-\cos q_t, -\sin q_t, 0]^{\mathrm{T}}.$$

The coordinate frame for the smaller wheel is similar except for the $\frac{r_1}{r_2}$ term:

$$\mathbf{p}_{20} = [0, 0, 1]^{\mathrm{T}},$$

$$\mathbf{p}_{21} = \frac{\partial \mathbf{f}_2}{\partial q_t}$$

$$= \left[-\frac{r_1}{r_2} \sin\left(\frac{r_1}{r_2} q_t\right), \frac{r_1}{r_2} \cos\left(\frac{r_1}{r_2} q_t\right), 0 \right]^{\mathrm{T}},$$

$$\mathbf{n}_2 = \frac{\mathbf{p}_{10} \times \mathbf{p}_{11}}{\|\mathbf{p}_{10} \times \mathbf{p}_{11}\|}$$

$$= \sqrt{2}\frac{r_1}{r_2} \left[-\cos\left(\frac{r_1}{r_2} q_t\right), \sin\left(\frac{r_1}{r_2} q_t\right), 0 \right]^{\mathrm{T}}.$$

The mapping we want is

$$\mathbf{p}_{20} \to \mathbf{p}_{10}, \quad \mathbf{p}_{21} \to \mathbf{p}_{11}, \quad \mathbf{n}_2 \to \mathbf{n}_1, \quad \mathbf{f}_2 \to \mathbf{f}_1.$$

If we define the matrices

$$\mathbf{A}_1 = \begin{bmatrix} \mathbf{p}_{10} & \mathbf{p}_{11} & \mathbf{n}_1 & \mathbf{f}_1 \\ 0 & 0 & 0 & 1 \end{bmatrix},$$

$$\mathbf{A}_2 = \begin{bmatrix} \mathbf{p}_{20} & \mathbf{p}_{21} & \mathbf{n}_2 & \mathbf{f}_2 \\ 0 & 0 & 0 & 1 \end{bmatrix},$$

then we can write the mapping as this matrix equation and solve for the constraint transformation:

$$\mathbf{R}_{\mathrm{roll}} \mathbf{A}_2 = \mathbf{A}_1,$$

$$\mathbf{R}_{\mathrm{roll}} = \mathbf{A}_1 \mathbf{A}_2^{-1}.$$

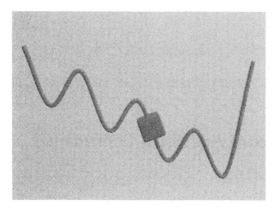

Figure 5.17. A box is constrained to move along a B-spline curve.

5.4.4 Constraint Modeling Using Piecewise Functions

You can also employ piecewise functions to model constraints of a mechanism.[8] Piecewise functions such as the B-splines can be effectively used for modeling constraints of complex shapes. As with the closed-form functions, in order to use piecewise function for modeling constraints, you need only to represent the transformation matrices of rigid bodies in terms of the piecewise functions. Figure 5.17 is such an example; in it, a cubic B-spline (Listing 3.1) constrains the position and orientation of a box object.

The procedure to model this mechanism is as follows. First, you need to define a cubic B-spline on which a box will be sliding. You also want to define the derivative of the spline function as it is used for defining the orientation of the box:

```
//spline
Function[] controlPoints = new Function[] { 5, 5, 5, 1, 5, 0, 4,
    -1, 3, -2, 5, 5, 5 };
BSpline spline = new BSpline(controlPoints);
Function f = spline.curveValue(q0);
Function df = spline.tangent(q0);
```

Having defined the spline function and its derivative, you represent a transformation matrix using the spline function as follows:

```
//link0
UnspecifiedFunction q0 = UnspecifiedFunction.functionOf("q0", t);
```

---

[8] As the functions will be differentiated twice by the dynamics algorithm, the piecewise functions must be twice differentiable.

```
Function[,] A0 = VM.rotZ(Function.atan(df), q0, f, 0);
LinkXNA rigidBody0 = new LinkXNA(A0, new Function[] { q0 },
    centerOfMass, inertia, mass, "link0", t);
```

Complete code is provided in the project "BSplineMechanism."

5.5   Enforcing Additional Constraints

5.5.1   Closed Loops

In Section 5.3.7, we have shown that we can create the equations of motion purely in terms of the generalized coordinates, without any additional constraint equations, if we can express the dependent coordinates as explicit functions of the independent coordinates. However, constraint equations generally have the form of implicit functions, and we cannot use the substitution technique in Section 5.3.7. In this case, the differential equations of motion are coupled by the algebraic constraint equations, and the Lagrange multiplier method is used for solving the differential-algebraic equations (DAEs).

Given the constraint, the equations of motion have the following form:

$$\mathbf{Q} = \mathbf{M}\ddot{\mathbf{q}} + \mathbf{c} + \mathbf{f_c}, \tag{5.6}$$

where $\mathbf{f_c}$ is the joint space constraint force created by the constraint. In this equation, the unknown is not only $\ddot{\mathbf{q}}$ but also $\mathbf{f_c}$, and we will compute both by solving (5.6) in conjuction with the constraint equations

$$\mathbf{g}(\mathbf{q}) = \mathbf{0}. \tag{5.7}$$

In order to relate Equation (5.7) to Equation (5.6), we differentiate Equation (5.7) to get

$$\frac{d\mathbf{g}}{d\mathbf{q}}\dot{\mathbf{q}} := \mathbf{J}\dot{\mathbf{q}} = \mathbf{0} \tag{5.8}$$

and differentiate once more to get

$$\mathbf{J}\ddot{\mathbf{q}} + \dot{\mathbf{J}}\dot{\mathbf{q}} = \mathbf{0}. \tag{5.9}$$

D'Alembert's principle is that constraint forces do no work; that is,

$$\mathbf{f_c}^{\mathrm{T}}\dot{\mathbf{q}} = \mathbf{0}. \tag{5.10}$$

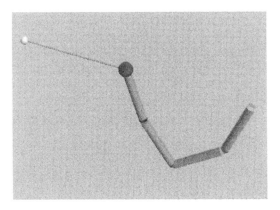

Figure 5.18. Closed-loop system example. The start and end points of the serial links are constrained to an imaginary plane, thus forming a closed loop.

Therefore, from Equations (5.8) and (5.10), we can see that the constraint forces must have the following form:[9]

$$\mathbf{f_c} = \mathbf{J}^{\mathrm{T}}\lambda, \qquad\qquad (5.11)$$

where the vector λ is unknown and is called the Lagrange multiplier. Plugging Equation (5.11) into Equation (5.6) yields

$$\mathbf{Q} = \mathbf{M}\ddot{\mathbf{q}} + \mathbf{c} + \mathbf{J}^{\mathrm{T}}\lambda.$$

Finally, the acceleration $\ddot{\mathbf{q}}$ and the Lagrange multiplier λ can be computed from the matrix equation

$$\begin{bmatrix} \mathbf{M} & \mathbf{J}^{\mathrm{T}} \\ \mathbf{J} & \mathbf{0} \end{bmatrix} \begin{bmatrix} \ddot{\mathbf{q}} \\ \lambda \end{bmatrix} = \begin{bmatrix} \mathbf{Q} - \mathbf{c} \\ -\dot{\mathbf{J}}\dot{\mathbf{q}} \end{bmatrix}. \qquad\qquad (5.12)$$

Figure 5.18 shows an example of a closed-loop mechanism. The two end points of a serial link are constrained on a plane (not shown), creating a closed loop. The loop constraint is enforced by Equation (5.12). Listing 5.5 shows how you can generate constraint Jacobian $\mathbf{J}$ and $\dot{\mathbf{J}}\dot{\mathbf{q}}$ using D*. First you differentiate $\mathbf{g}(\mathbf{q})$ twice to get $\ddot{\mathbf{g}} = \mathbf{J}\ddot{\mathbf{q}} + \dot{\mathbf{J}}\dot{\mathbf{q}}$. Then you construct $\mathbf{J}$ using the fact that J_{ij} is the coefficient of $\ddot{q}_j$ of g_i, where $\mathbf{g} = (g_1, \cdots, g_m)^{\mathrm{T}}$. D* provides the `coefficient` function for computing the coefficient; $\dot{\mathbf{J}}\dot{\mathbf{q}}$ is simply $\ddot{\mathbf{g}}|_{\ddot{\mathbf{q}}=\mathbf{0}}$.[10] We use a D* function, `substitute`, to substitute $\ddot{\mathbf{q}} = \mathbf{0}$ into $\ddot{\mathbf{g}}$. See the "ClosedLoop" project for the source code.

---

[9]You can verify that Equation (5.10) holds true if you substitute $\mathbf{f_c}$ with Equation (5.11).

[10]$\ddot{\mathbf{g}}|_{\ddot{\mathbf{q}}=\mathbf{0}}$ means $\ddot{\mathbf{g}}$ when $\ddot{q} = 0$.

```
RuntimeFunction createJacobianEval(){
  int n = rbs.numberOfCoords;
  Function qdt = Function.derivative(Function.D(rbs.genCoords1D,
      rbs.time));
  Function qddt = Function.derivative(Function.D(rbs.genCoords1D,
      rbs.time, rbs.time));

  //define constraint equation
  Function[] g = VM.mult(rbs.allNodes[rbs.numberOfNodes - 1].Wi,
      localPositionEndPoint); //position of the end point in world
      frame
  g = VM.minus(g, new Function[] { 2, 0, 0, 1 }); //(2,0,0) is the
      desired position of the end point

  //differentiate constraint twice
  Function gddt = Function.derivative(Function.D(VM.subArray(g, 0,
      3), rbs.time, rbs.time));
  //substituion map will be used to substitute qddt with 0
  Function[,] substitutionMap = new Function[n, 2];
  for (int i = 0; i < n; i++){
  substitutionMap[i, 0] = qddt[i];
  substitutionMap[i, 1] = 0;
  }
  Function[,] J = new Function[numConst, n];
  Function[] Jdtqdt = new Function[numConst];
  //J is the coefficient of qddt in gddt
  //Jdtqdt is qddt when qddt = 0
  for (int i = 0; i < J.GetLength(0); i++){
  Jdtqdt[i] = Function.substitute(gddt[i], substitutionMap);
  for (int j = 0; j < J.GetLength(1); j++){
    J[i, j] = gddt[i].coefficient(qddt[j]);
  }
  }
  //make 1d array
  Function J1d = new Function(VM.concatenate<Function>(VM.
      matrixToVector<Function>(J), Jdtqdt));
  //compile
  RuntimeFunction jacobianEval = J1d.compile();
  return jacobianEval;
}
```

Listing 5.5. Computing constraint Jacobian using D*.

As a matter of fact, solving Equation (5.12) does not exactly satisfy the constraint perfectly due to the numerical error. Note that we are enforcing $\ddot{\mathbf{g}} = \mathbf{0}$, but not $\mathbf{g} = \mathbf{0}$. Therefore, if there is a slight error in $\mathbf{g}$ (e.g., $\mathbf{g} = \epsilon$), the current method can only make sure that the acceleration of the constraint is zero, but it cannot reduce the error. This is why constraint-stabilization methods such as Baumgarte stabilization [5] should be employed to keep the constraint. Note that the constraint-resolution method that we have introduced here is the most basic one and there are other variations for solving this problem. Refer to books on multibody dynamics such as [14] for more details.

5.5.2 Nonholonomic Constraint

As you have seen in the previous section, a closed-loop constraint has the form

$$\mathbf{g}(\mathbf{q}) = \mathbf{0},$$

and a constraint of such a form is called a holonomic constraint.[11] By differentiating twice, the holonomic constraint can be enforced using Lagrange multipliers. In fact, not only can Lagrange multipliers be used for the holonomic constraint, but they can also be used for a certain type of nonholonomic constraint, called the Pfaffian constraint. The Pfaffian constraint has the following form:

$$\mathbf{P}(\mathbf{q})\dot{\mathbf{q}} = \mathbf{0}.$$

You can easily see that the differentiation of the Pfaffian constraint $\dot{\mathbf{P}}\dot{\mathbf{q}} + \mathbf{P}\ddot{\mathbf{q}} = \mathbf{0}$ has the same form as Equation (5.9), and thus we can use Lagrange multipliers in the same way we did to resolve the holonomic constraint.

A rolling constraint between surfaces is an example of the Pfaffian constraint. Figure 5.19 shows an ellipsoidal ball rolling over an ellipsoidal surface, with the rolling constraint enforced using Lagrange multipliers. To establish a rolling constraint between two surfaces, let $(\mathbf{R}_1, \mathbf{t}_1)$ and $(\mathbf{R}_2, \mathbf{t}_2)$ denote the orientation and position of the surface frames of the two surfaces. When the two surfaces do not slip, the velocities of the two surface frames must be the same; i.e., $\mathbf{R}_1^{\mathrm{T}}\dot{\mathbf{t}}_1 = \mathbf{R}_2^{\mathrm{T}}\dot{\mathbf{t}}_2$, which yields the constraint equation

$$\mathbf{P}\dot{\mathbf{q}} = \mathbf{0}, \tag{5.13}$$

where

$$\mathbf{P} = \left[\mathbf{R}_1^{\mathrm{T}}\frac{d\mathbf{t}_1}{d\mathbf{q}} \quad - \mathbf{R}_2^{\mathrm{T}}\frac{d\mathbf{t}_2}{d\mathbf{q}} \right].$$

---

[11]More precisely, a holonomic constraint has the form $\mathbf{g}(\mathbf{q},t) = \mathbf{0}$.

Figure 5.19. Rolling constraint: an ellipsoidal ball rolling over an ellipsoidal surface.

5.6   Inverse Kinematics

Inverse kinematics computes the generalized coordinates that will make the specified position and/or orientation of a part of interest (e.g., the gripper of a robot arm), called an end-effector. Inverse kinematics is an important process in computer animation and robotics. In this section, we will show how you can easily solve it using D^*.

The prerequisite of inverse kinematics is a forward kinematics function that represents the position (and/or orientation) of the end-effector in terms of the generalized coordinates. For simplicity, let us consider only the position of the end-effector:

$$\mathbf{p} = \mathbf{p}(\mathbf{q}).$$

Our goal is to compute $\mathbf{q}^*$ such that $\mathbf{p}^* = \mathbf{p}(\mathbf{q}^*)$, given a desired position $\mathbf{p}^*$ of the end-effector. Let $\mathbf{q}$ denote the current joint angle that is not far from $\mathbf{q}^*$. Then we can approximate the equation using the Taylor expansion:

$$\begin{aligned}
\mathbf{p}^* &= \mathbf{p}(\mathbf{q}^*) \\
&= \mathbf{p}(\mathbf{q} + \delta\mathbf{q}) \\
&\approx \mathbf{p}(\mathbf{q}) + \mathbf{J}(\mathbf{q})\delta\mathbf{q},
\end{aligned} \qquad (5.14)$$

with the kinematics Jacobian $\mathbf{J} = d\mathbf{p}/d\mathbf{q}$. The following example shows the creation of the runtime function that evaluates the Jacobian $\mathbf{J}$ in D*:

```
//el: index of the target link
//endEffectorLocalPos: local position of the end effector with
      respect to the target link
RuntimeFunction Jacobian(){
  Function[] P = VM.mult(rbs.allNodes[el].Wi, endEffectorLocalPos);
        //position of the end effector in world frame
  //Jacobian function. J = dP/dq
  Function[,] J = new Function[3,n];
  for (int i = 0; i < 3; ++i){
    for (int j = 0; j < n; ++j){
      J[i,j] = Function.D(P[i], rbs.genCoords1D[j]);
    }
  }
  J = Function.derivative(J);
  Function Jacobian1D = new Function(VM.matrixToVector<Function>(J)
        ); //make 1D array
  Jacobian1D.orderVariablesInDomain(rbs.genCoords1D);
  JacobianEval = Jacobian1D.compile();
}
```

Given the Jacobian function, you can compute $\mathbf{q}^*$ by iteratively updating $\mathbf{q}$ in solving Equation (5.14) until the distance between $\mathbf{p}(\mathbf{q})$ and $\mathbf{p}^*$ becomes less than a preset tolerance:

```
double[] inverseKinematics(double[] target, double[] q, double tol)
    {
  double[] qnew = new double[q.Length];
  q.CopyTo(qnew, 0); // qnew = q
  double[] pos = endEffectorPosition(qnew); // forward kinematics
      function
  double[] err = VM.minus(target, pos); // err = target - pos
  double dist = VM.length(err); // dist = || err ||
  while (dist > tol){
    double[,] J = computeJacobian(qnew);
    double[] delta = solve(J, err); // delta = J^{-1} * err
    qnew = VM.plus(qnew, delta); // qnew += delta
    pos = endEffectorPosition(qnew); // update pos
    err = VM.minus(target, pos); // update error
    dist = VM.length(delta);
  };
    return qnew;
}
```

Figure 5.20. Inverse kinematics computes the joint angles of the robot to place the end-effector at the target position indicated by a yellow sphere (see Plate VII).

Figure 5.20 shows an example of the inverse kinematics application. Given a target position of the end-effector (yellow sphere), the inverse kinematics algorithm computes the desired joint angles of the three-DOF serial robot. The project "InverseKinematics" provides the source code for this example.

5.7 Inverse Dynamics

Inverse dynamics computes the generalized forces that are necessary to generate a specified motion (more precisely, acceleration), while forward dynamics computes the motion that is generated by given force inputs. Inverse dynamics has wide application in areas such as motion analysis, planning, control, etc. Mathematically, inverse dynamics computes $\mathbf{Q}^*$ given $\ddot{\mathbf{q}}^*$ in Equation (5.2); that is,

$$\mathbf{Q}^* = \mathbf{M}(\mathbf{q})\ddot{\mathbf{q}}^* + \mathbf{c}(\mathbf{q}, \dot{\mathbf{q}}, \mathbf{f}_{\text{ext}}).$$

The MultiBodySystem class provides $O(n)$ inverse dynamics function for a tree-structured mechanical system:

```
public void inverseDynamics(double[] qddt, out double[] genForce)
```

This function outputs generalized force genForce to create given acceleration qddt. Also, the invDyn function of the MultiBodySystem class represents the symbolic expression of the inverse dynamics function. The project "InverseDynamics" performs the inverse dynamics for the three-DOF serial robot mechanism (Figure 5.21).

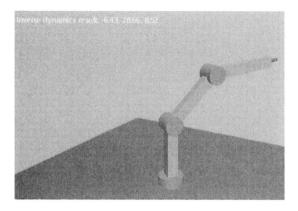

Figure 5.21. The numbers in the upper left corner are the joint torques computed by the inverse dynamics when a desired motion as well as the external forces are specified.

5.7.1 Computed Torque Control

Inverse dynamics can be used for the feedforward controller. If we know the accurate parameters of a mechanical system as well as the accurate sensor data of external forces, we can compute exact control input to create desired motions though inverse dynamics. In reality, since there are always errors in the system parameters and in the sensor data, the computed torque from the inverse dynamics is not accurate, making it necessary to add the feedback controller. Nonetheless, the computed torque control method yields more robust control performance and allows lower gain of the feedback controller, because the feedforward controller provides approximate control forces. The controller has the form

$$\mathbf{Q} = \mathbf{Q_{ff}} + \mathbf{K_s}(\mathbf{q_d} - \mathbf{q}) + \mathbf{K_d}(\dot{\mathbf{q}}_\mathbf{d} - \dot{\mathbf{q}}),$$
$$\mathbf{Q_{ff}} = \mathbf{M}(\mathbf{q})\ddot{\mathbf{q}}_\mathbf{d} + \mathbf{c}(\mathbf{q}, \dot{\mathbf{q}}, \mathbf{f}_{\text{ext}}),$$

where $\ddot{\mathbf{q}}_\mathbf{d}$ is the desired acceleration. $\mathbf{Q_{ff}}$ is computed from the inverse dynamics routine.

Miscellaneous Problems

There are two types of problems covered in this chapter. The first type is synthetic problems small enough so that we can compute the optimal derivative.

The second type is real-world problems that arise in many areas of graphics. The functions and their representation in D* are described in this section. All timings were performed on a single core of a 2.4-GHz Core2 Duo processor, with 2 GBytes of RAM.

6.1 Synthetic Examples

These problems are taken from Chapter 8 of [16], and are primarily useful for comparing D* to various automatic differentiation techniques. The computational graphs shown in Figures 6.1 and 6.2 represent difficult cases for automatic differentiation techniques and are used in [16] to highlight the trade-offs between different methods. The operations count given in the figures does not include the interpretive overhead of automatic differentiation, which can require far more computation than the arithmetic operations. It is strictly a count of the number of arithmetic operations required to compute the derivative. The operation counts for vertex elimination, greedy Markiewicz, and cross-country elimination are taken from [16]. In some cases the number of addition operations was not given, so we have not included these in the figures.

For each of these graphs D* computes an optimal derivative, one with the minimum number of multiplications and additions. No one automatic differentiation technique is optimal for all of the graphs. Quite the opposite is the case: only one technique, cross-country elimination, achieves optimal results, and only for one of the graphs. For three out of the four graphs none of the automatic differentiation techniques achieve optimal results.

While D* is not guaranteed to be optimal, it is encouraging to see that for small problems considered to be difficult cases, it does generates optimal results.

D*:22x 3+
vertex elimination: 34x
forward: 32x 6+
reverse: 36x 3+

D*:12x 1+
greedy Markiewicz: 16x
foreword: 19x 2+
reverse: 16x 1+

Figure 6.1. Synthetic examples.

D*: 8x 1+
cross-country elimination: 8x 1+
reverse: 14x 2+
forward: 14x 2+

D*:13x 1+
vertex elimination:
14x 3+ or
15x 1+
reverse: 21x 1+
forward: 16x 2+

Figure 6.2. Synthetic examples.

6.2 Spherical Harmonics

Spherical harmonics are used in many algorithms to approximate global illumination functions. For example, in the PRT algorithm [32], the smallest possible set of basis functions is sought that approximates a given illumination function. A gradient-based optimization routine is used to minimize the number of spherical harmonic coefficients. Computing the gradient is complicated by the fact that the spherical harmonics are most easily defined in a recursive fashion, and it is not obvious how to differentiate these recursive equations directly.

The spherical harmonic functions are defined by the following set of four recursive equations:

1. Legendre polynomials, P, divided by $\sqrt{(1-z^2)^m}, 0 \leq l < n, m \leq l$, functions of z,

$$
\begin{aligned}
P(0,0) &= 1, \\
P(m,m) &= (1-2m)P(m-1,m-1), \\
P(m+1,m) &= (2m+1)zP(m,m), \\
P(l,m) &= \frac{(2l-1)zP(l-1,m) - (l+m-1)P(l-2,m)}{(l-m)};
\end{aligned}
$$

2. sin/cos (written S, C) multiplied by $\sqrt{(1-z^2)^m}, 0 \le m < n$, functions of x, y,

$$
\begin{aligned}
S(0) &= 0, \\
C(0) &= 1, \\
S(m) &= xC(m-1) - yS(m-1), \\
C(m) &= xS(m-1) + yC(m-1);
\end{aligned}
$$

3. constants, $N, 0 \le l < n, m \le l$,

$$
\begin{aligned}
N(l, m) &= \sqrt{(2l+1)/(4\pi)}\, m = 0, \\
N(l, m) &= \sqrt{\frac{(2l+1)}{(2\pi)}\frac{(l-|m|)!}{(l+|m|)!}}\, m > 0;
\end{aligned}
$$

4. the spherical harmonic basis functions, $Y, 0 \le l < n, |m| \le l$,

$$
\begin{aligned}
Y(l, m) &= N(l, |m|)P(l, |m|)S(|m|)\, m < 0, \\
Y(l, m) &= N(l, |m|)P(l, |m|)C(|m|)\, m \ge 0.
\end{aligned}
$$

The order, L, of the spherical harmonic function is specified by the first argument, l, to the function $Y(l, m)$. At each order L there are $2L + 1$ basis functions. The total number of basis functions up to order L is

$$
\sum_{i=0}^{L} 2i + 1 = (L + 1)^2.
$$

There are three domain variables, x, y, z .and $(L + 1)^2$ basis functions up to order L. so $f : \mathbb{R}^3 \to \mathbb{R}^{(L+1)^2}$; there will be $3(L + 1)^2$ derivative terms in the gradient of f.

The D* functions are essentially identical to the recursive mathematical equations and require only 28 lines of code. including the code necessary to specify the derivatives to be computed:

```
F SHDerivatives(int maxL, double x, double y, double z){
    List harmonics = new List();
    for (int l = 0; l <= maxL; l++)
      for (int m = -l; m <= l; m++)
       harmonics.Add(Y(l,m,x,y,z));

    F[] dY = new F[harmonics.Count * 3];
    for (int i = 0; i < dY.GetLength(0) / 3; i++){
      dY[i * 3]     = D((F)harmonics[i],0,x);
      dY[i * 3 + 1] = D((F)harmonics[i],0,y);
```

```
    dY[i * 3 + 2] = D((F)harmonics[i],0,z);
    }

    return evalDeriv(dY);
}


F P(int l, int m, Var z){
    if(l==0 && m==0)return 1.0;
    if(l==m)return (1-2*m)*P(m-1,m-1,z);
    if(l==m+1)return (2*m + 1)*z*P(m,m,z);
    return(((2*l -1)/(l-m))*z*P(l-1,m,z) - ((l+m-1)/(l-m))*P(l-2,m,z)
        );
}


F S(int m, Var x, Var y){
    if(m==0)return 0;
    else return x*C(m-1,x,y) - y*S(m-1,x,y);
}


F C(int m, Var x, Var y){
    if(m==0)return 1;
    else return x*S(m-1,x,y) + y*C(m-1,x,y);
}


F N(int l, int m){
    int absM = Math.Abs(m);
    if(m==0)return Math.Sqrt((2*l+1)/(4*Math.PI));
    else return Math.Sqrt((2*l+1)/(2*Math.PI)*(factorial(l-absM)/
        factorial(l+absM)));
}


F Y(int l, int m, Var x, Var y, Var z){
    int absM = Math.Abs(m);
    if(m<0)return N(l,absM)*P(l,absM,z)*S(absM,x,y);
    else return N(l,absM)*P(l,absM,z)*C(absM,x,y);
}
```

Derivatives of spherical harmonics with values of L from 5 to 20 were computed. Table 6.1 shows the results.

Order, L	5	10	15	20
D* runtime evaluation	6,622,516	1,117,318	468,384	222,024
D* symbolic time (secs.)	.02	.55	4.9	53

Table 6.1. Spherical harmonics: number of derivative evaluations per second. The last line in the table shows the amount of time D* took to compute the symbolic derivative.

Order, L	5	15	19	20	5	15	19	20
Operation	±	±	±	±	×	×	×	×
Number of operations	57	412	642	707	139	1714	2820	3139

Table 6.2. Operation counts for various orders of spherical harmonics.

Table 6.2 shows the number of operations for various orders of spherical harmonics.

6.3   Structure from Motion

Structure from motion has been used for creating three-dimensional textured objects from photographs [10], for making multi-viewpoint panoramas [2], for placing photos in a virtual 3D space [33], for light field reconstruction [25], head tracking, and stereo reconstruction, and for many other graphics applications.

In the "Structure from Motion" problem, we are given a set of points in 3D space, observed by some number of cameras. The intrinsic and extrinsic camera parameters, as well as the 3D point positions, are unknown and must be estimated from the 2D projections of the 3D points onto each of the camera's image planes. In the following equations, $\mathbf{p}_t$ is a 3D point viewed by the camera; $\mathbf{r}$ is $\mathbf{p}_t$ rotated by the quaternion, $\mathbf{q}$; $\mathbf{k}$ is the matrix containing the intrinsic camera parameters; and $\mathbf{z}$ is the observed 2D projection, $\mathbf{p}_t$. The error vector, $\mathbf{e}$, is the difference between the measured position and the one predicted by the camera model.

$$\mathbf{r} = \mathbf{q}(\mathbf{p}_t),$$

$$\mathbf{k} = \begin{bmatrix} f & s & p_x \\ 0 & af & p_y \\ 0 & 0 & 1 \end{bmatrix} [\mathbf{r} + \mathbf{t}]^T,$$

$$\mathbf{e} = \begin{bmatrix} \dfrac{\mathbf{k}_x}{\mathbf{k}_z} - \mathbf{z}_x, & \dfrac{\mathbf{k}_y}{\mathbf{k}_z} - \mathbf{z}_y \end{bmatrix}.$$

A D* program implementing this computation is shown below:

```
F StructureFromMotionDerivs(Var f, a, s, px, py, ptx ,pty ,ptz , wx
    , wy, wz, tx, ty, tz){
  F[,] affine = f,s,px , 0,f * a,py , 0,0,1 ;
  F pt = new F(ptx,pty,ptz);
  F t = new F(tx,ty,tz);
  F q = quaternion(wx,wy,wz);
  F r = quaternionRotation(q,pt);
```

```
F[] T = VM.plus(r,t);
F K = new F(VM.mult(affine,new F[] T[0],T[1],T[2] )); F proj =
    new F(K[0] / K[2],K[1] / K[2]);
F error = new F(proj[0] - zx,proj[1] - zy);
F[,] derivs;derivs = D(new F[]error[0],error[1], new Var[] f,a,s,
    px,py,ptx,pty,ptz,wx,wy,wz,tx,ty,tz );
return evalDeriv(derivs);
}


F quaternion(Var wx,Var wy,Var wz){
  return new F(F.sqrt(1 - (wx * wx - wy * wy - wz * wz) / 4),wx /
    2,wy / 2,wz / 2);
}


F quaternionRotation(F q,F p){
  F x = q[0],y = q[1],z = q[2],w = q[3],px = p[0],py = p[1],pz = p
    [2];
  F[,] R = 1-2*(y*y) - 2*(z*z), 2*(x*y) - 2*(w*z), 2*(z*x) + 2*(w*y
    ), 2*(x*y) + 2*(w*z), 1- 2*(x*x) - 2*(z*z), 2*(y*z) - 2*(w*x)
    , 2*(z*x) - 2*(w*y), 2*(y*z) + 2*(w*x), 1 - 2*(x*x) - 2*(y*y)
    ;
  F[] temp = VM.mult(R,new F[] px,py,pz );
  F s = new F(temp);
  return s;
}
```

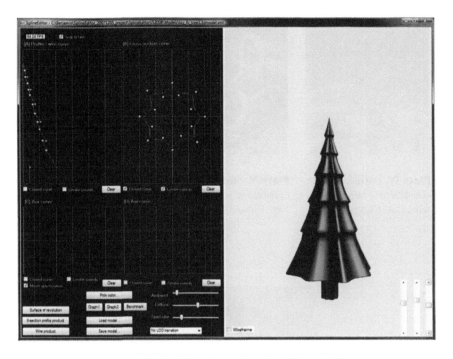

Plate I. SplineEditor interface (see Figure 1.1).

Plate II. Changing the weight of control points. The color of a point changes with each right-click. (see Figure 1.3).

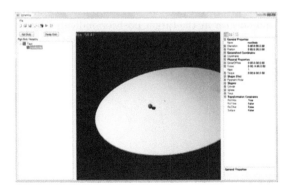

Plate III. Body added to the system. The sphere shape is the geometrical representation of your body by default; if you select the body in the tree view, it will appear in red (see Figure 2.3).

Plate IV. Path-following constraint: beads on a wire (see Figure 5.13).

Plate V. Surface-surface constraint: torus chain (see Figure 5.14).

Plate VI. Surface-surface constraint: wheels inside wheels (see Figure 5.15).

Plate VII. Inverse kinematics computes the joint angles of the robot to place the end-effector at the target position indicated by a yellow sphere (see Figure 5.20).

$$f_0^0 = \underbrace{\begin{matrix} \text{Path 1} \\ c \\ d_1 \quad d_4 \\ d_2 \quad d_3 \\ b \\ d_0 \end{matrix}}_{} + \underbrace{\begin{matrix} \text{Path 2} \\ c \\ d_1 \quad d_4 \\ d_2 \quad d_3 \\ b \\ d_0 \end{matrix}}_{}$$

$$f_0^0 = d_0 d_2 d_1 + d_0 d_3 d_4 = d_0(d_2 d_1 + d_3 d_4)$$

Plate VIII. Relationship between factoring and dominance: node b postdominates node c, so all paths from c to the leaf must include the common factor d_0 (see Figure 7.6).

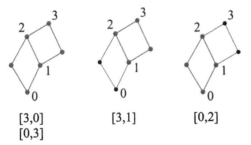

[3,0]
[0,3]   [3,1]   [0,2]

Plate IX. Factor subgraphs of the graph of Figure 7.7 (see Figure 7.8).

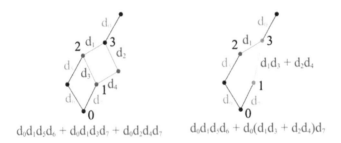

$d_0d_1d_5d_6 + d_0d_1d_3d_7 + d_0d_2d_4d_7$ $d_0d_1d_5d_6 + d_0(d_1d_3 + d_2d_4)d_7$

Plate X. The factorization rule does not change the value of the sum of products over all paths (see Figure 7.9).

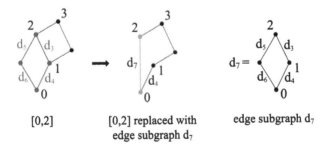

[0,2]   [0,2] replaced with   edge subgraph d_7
                 edge subgraph d_7

Plate XI. Factor subgraph $[0, 2]$, highlighted in blue and red in the leftmost graph, is factored out of the graph and replaced with an equivalent subgraph edge d_7 (see Figure 7.10).

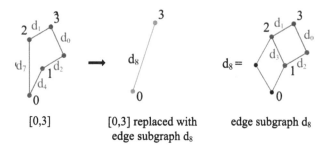

|[0,3]|[0,3] replaced with edge subgraph d_8|edge subgraph d_8|

Plate XII. Factor subgraph $[0, 3]$, highlighted in blue in the leftmost graph, is factored out of the graph and replaced with an equivalent subgraph edge d_8 (see Figure 7.11).

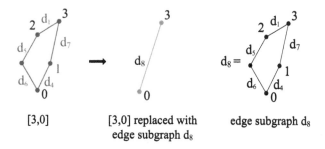

|[3,1]|[3,1] replaced with edge subgraph d_7|edge subgraph d_7|

Plate XIII. Factor subgraph $[3, 1]$ is factored out of the graph and replaced with an equivalent subgraph edge d_7 (see Figure 7.12).

|[3,0]|[3,0] replaced with edge subgraph d_8|edge subgraph d_8|

Plate XIV. Factor subgraph $[3, 0]$, highlighted in blue in the leftmost graph, is factored out of the graph and replaced with an equivalent subgraph edge d_8 (see Figure 7.13).

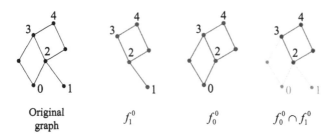

Plate XV. The derivatives f_0^0 and f_1^0 intersect only in the red highlighted subgraph (see Figure 7.14).

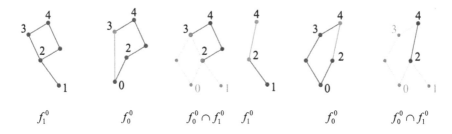

Plate XVI. Factor $[0,3]$ from f_0^0. $f_0^0 \cap f_1^0$, highlighted in red, does not contain a factor subgraph of either derivative (see Figure 7.15).

Plate XVII. Factor $[4,2]$ from both f_0^0 and f_1^0. $f_0^0 \cap f_1^0$ contains the common subgraph edge $4,2$ (see Figure 7.16).

Plate XVIII. The $\mathbb{R}^3 \rightarrow \mathbb{R}^2$ function on the left has six derivatives; all of the derivatives are completely factored. What is the best way to form the path products? The subproducts $d_1 d_2$ and $d_0 d_2$ can each be used in three path products. The subproducts $d_2 d_4$, $d_2 d_5$, and $d_2 d_3$ can each be used in only two path products (see Figure 7.17).

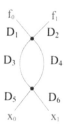

Plate XIX. Derivative graph for some arbitrary function (see Figure 7.18).

Forward: 4 multiplications, 3 additions.
Reverse: 6 multiplications, 2 additions.

Forward: 18 multiplications, 6 additions.
Reverse: 12 multiplications, 3 additions.

Plate XX. Failures of simple domain-range tests (see Figure 7.19).

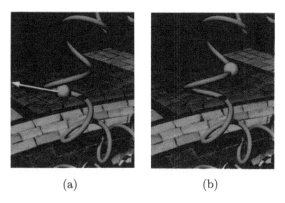

(a)   (b)

Plate XXI. (a) Yellow arrow shows differential equation step, ignoring constraints.
(b) Actual step with constraints (see Figure 8.7).

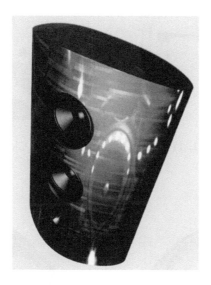

Plate XXII. Real-time screen capture of a generative model of a speaker (see Figure 9.1).

Plate XXIII. Wheel 0: 8.2KBytes (see Figure 9.10).

Plate XXIV. Wheel 1: 11.4 KBytes (see Figure 9.11).

Plate XXV. Closeup of Plate XXIV (see Figure 9.12).

Plate XXVI. Wheel 2: 7 KBytes (see Figure 9.13).

Plate XXVII. Rear view of the wheel in Plate XXVI (see Figure 9.14).

Plate XXVIII. Closeup of bolt cutouts in Plate XXVI (see Figure 9.15).

Plate XXIX. The tire treads are geometric detail resulting from CSG operations, not a bump or normal map. Tire by itself: 11.9 KBytes (see Figure 9.16).

Theory

In previous chapters you learned how to use D*, along with the interactive modeling tools SymGeom and SymMech, to solve problems in geometric modeling and dynamics simulation. This part of the book explains the theory behind what has come before.

Chapter 7 explains how the D* symbolic differentiation algorithm works. Chapter 8 contains a concise introduction to the mathematics of Lagrangian mechanics and derives the particular formulation of Lagrangian mechanics that makes efficient symbolic differentiation possible. Chapter 9 shows how to add constructive solid geometry (CSG) operations to the simple geometric operators described in Chapter 4.

7 The D* Algorithm

This chapter is concerned with the problem of efficiently computing the symbolic derivative of a function from $\mathbb{R}^m \to \mathbb{R}^n$. We will begin by defining the chain rule in a slightly unconventional way, which exposes the problem we have to solve in the clearest way. The conventional recursive form of the chain rule is

$$D(f(g_1(h_1, \ldots, h_m), \ldots, g_n(\ldots))) = \sum_{i=1}^{n} \frac{\partial f}{\partial g_i} D(g_i), \qquad (7.1)$$

where the $g_i(\ldots)$ are themselves functions of some h_j and so on. Expanding one level of this recursion for g_1, we get

$$\frac{\partial f}{\partial g_1} D(g_1) = \frac{\partial f}{\partial g_1} \sum_{j=1}^{m} \frac{\partial g_1}{\partial h_j} D(h_j)$$

$$= \frac{\partial f}{\partial g_1} \frac{\partial g_1}{\partial h_1} D(h_1) + \frac{\partial f}{\partial g_1} \frac{\partial g_1}{\partial h_2} D(h_2) + \ldots \frac{\partial f}{\partial g_1} \frac{\partial g_1}{\partial h_m} D(h_m).$$

If we expand all levels of the recursion this way, we see that the derivative, $D(f)$, is simply a sum of products. This form of the chain rule undoes the factorization implicit in Equation (7.1).[1]

We can write a simple recursive function to evaluate the derivative in this way. The function takes two arguments: the first argument is the product of the partials up to this level of recursion and the second argument is a list containing all of the partial products in the derivative sum:

```
expD (double product, List sum)
    if (this.isLeaf) sum.Append(product);
    else foreach(child ci) ci.D(product*partialWRTChild(ci), sum)
```

The expD function is initially called on the root node with product set to 1 and with sum set to the empty list. The partialWRTChild(ci) function returns the partial of the current node with respect to child ci.

---

[1] This has been noted many times; the earliest instance we are aware of is [4].

After execution is finished, each entry in sum corresponds to the product of all the partial derivatives on one path from the root to the leaf. Summing all the entries in sum gives the derivative.

This algorithm is not useful for computing derivatives, because its worst-case computation time is exponential, but it allows us to precisely state the problem we need to solve: to efficiently compute a symbolic derivative we need to minimize the number of operations required to compute a sum of products.

There are only two things we can do to reduce computation in a sum of products: factor, and reuse product subexpressions. For example, in the sum of products

$$d_1 d_3 d_4 d_6 + d_1 d_3 d_5 d_6 + d_2 d_3 d_4 d_6 + d_2 d_3 d_5 d_6, \tag{7.2}$$

the term d_6 is shared, so we can factor it out:

$$d_6 \left(d_1 d_3 d_4 + d_1 d_3 d_5 + d_2 d_3 d_4 + d_2 d_3 d_5 \right).$$

Similarly, the terms d_1 and d_2 are shared and can be factored out:

$$d_6 \left(d_1 \left(d_3 d_4 + d_3 d_5 \right) + d_2 \left(d_3 d_4 + d_3 d_5 \right) \right).$$

We can factor out the d_3 term,

$$d_6 \left\{ d_1 \left(d_3 \left(d_4 + d_5 \right) \right) + d_2 \left(d_3 \left(d_4 + d_5 \right) \right) \right\},$$

and reuse the product term $k_1 = d_3 \left(d_4 + d_5 \right)$:

$$d_6 \left\{ d_1 k_1 + d_2 k_1 \right\}. \tag{7.3}$$

The original expression, Equation (7.2), requires 15 arithmetic operations to evaluate. The final expression, Equation (7.3), requires only four arithmetic operations, more than a factor of four reduction.

Unfortunately, solving the problem of minimizing computation for a sum of products appears at first glance to be in the NP-hard category; it seems that we must examine a huge number of possible factorization and common product term possibilities. Fortunately, the sum of products produced by the chain rule has a special structure of which we can take advantage; this makes it possible to solve the problem in polynomial time.

7.1   Graph Structure of the Chain Rule

In the first stage of the new differentiation algorithm, the derivative expression is factored. To understand the factorization step, we must examine the

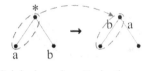

Original graph   Derivative graph

Figure 7.1. The derivative graph of multiplication. The derivative graph has the same structure as its corresponding expression graph, but the meaning of edges and nodes is different: edges represent partial derivatives and nodes have no operational function.

special structure of the graph resulting from differentiating a function, the *derivative graph*, and how this relates to the chain rule of differentiation. This will lead to a simple derivative algorithm that takes the worst-case time exponential in the number of edges, e, in the original graph. In Section 7.2 we will present a new algorithm that reduces this to polynomial time.

Before we can begin, we have to introduce some notation to minimize clutter in the illustrations. We will use the following notation for derivatives: for $f : \mathbb{R}^n \to \mathbb{R}^m$, f_j^i is the derivative of the ith range element with respect to the jth domain element. Range and domain indices start at 0. Higher-order derivatives are indicated by additional subscript indices. For example,

$$f_{jk}^i = \frac{\partial^2 f^i}{\partial f_j \partial f_k}.$$

The chain rule can be graphically expressed in a *derivative graph*. The derivative graph of an expression graph has the same structure as the expression graph, but the meaning of nodes and edges is different. In a conventional expression graph, nodes represent functions and edges represent function composition. In a derivative graph, an edge represents the partial derivative of the parent node function with respect to the child node argument. Nodes have no operational function; they serve only to connect edges.

As a simple first example, Figure 7.1 shows the graph representing the function $f = ab$ and its corresponding derivative graph. The edge connecting the $*$ and a symbols in the original function graph corresponds to the edge representing the partial $\frac{\partial ab}{\partial a} = b$ in the derivative graph. Similarly, the $*, b$ edge in the original graph corresponds to the edge $\frac{\partial ab}{\partial b} = a$ in the derivative graph.

The derivative graph for a more complicated function, $f = \sin(\cos(x)) * \cos(\cos(x))$, is shown in Figure 7.2. The nodes in the original function graph

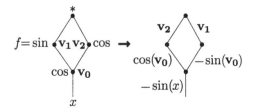

Figure 7.2. The derivative graph of an expression.

have been given labels $\mathbf{v}_i$ to minimize clutter in the derivative graph:

$$\mathbf{v_0} = \cos(x),$$
$$\mathbf{v_1} = \sin(\cos(x)) = \sin(\mathbf{v_0}),$$
$$\mathbf{v_2} = \cos(\cos(x)) = \cos(\mathbf{v_0}).$$

Given some $f : \mathbb{R}^n \to \mathbb{R}^m$, we can use the derivative graph of f to compute the derivative f_j^i as follows. Find all paths from node i to node j. For each path compute the product of all the partial derivatives that occur along that path; f_j^i is equal to the sum of these path products. In the worst case, the number of paths is exponential in the number of edges in the graph, so this algorithm takes exponential time and produces an expression whose size is exponential in the number of edges in the graph.

If we apply this differentiation algorithm to compute f_0^0, we get the result shown in Figure 7.3. For each path from the root we compute the product of all the edge terms along the path, then sum the path products:

$$f_0^0 = \mathbf{v_2}\cos(\mathbf{v_0})(-\sin(x)) + \mathbf{v_1}(-\sin(\mathbf{v_0}))(-\sin(x))$$
$$= \cos(\cos(x))\cos(\cos(x))(-\sin(x)) + \sin(\cos(x))(-\sin(\cos(x)))(-\sin(x)).$$

For $f : \mathbb{R}^n \to \mathbb{R}^m$ the path product sum may have redundant computations of two forms: common factors and common product subsequences.

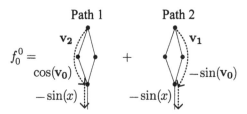

Figure 7.3. The sum of all path products equals the derivative.

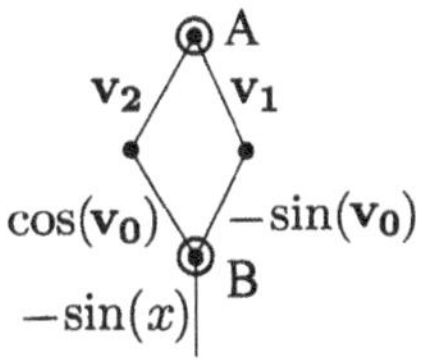

Figure 7.4. Each branching in the derivative graph corresponds to a factorization of the derivative. There is a branch at node A and at node B.

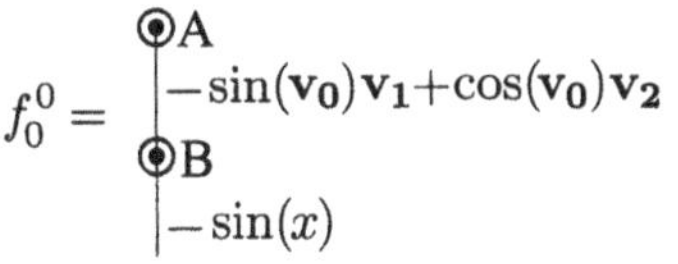

$$f_0^0 = \begin{array}{l} \text{A} \\ -\sin(\mathbf{v_0})\mathbf{v_1} + \cos(\mathbf{v_0})\mathbf{v_2} \\ \text{B} \\ -\sin(x) \end{array}$$

Figure 7.5. Factoring out the terms that share $-\sin(x)$ reduces the number of paths in the graph of Figure 7.3 from two to one.

Both will be discussed in more detail in Section 7.2, but we can get an intuitive grasp of common factor redundancy by looking at the simple example of Figure 7.4. Each branching of the graph, either upward or downward, corresponds to a factorization of the expression. All product paths that pass through the node marked B will include $-\sin(x)$ as a factor.

If we collapse the two product paths into a single edge that groups the terms sharing $-\sin(x)$ as a factor, we get the graph of Figure 7.5. This is mathematically the same as summing the product paths of the graph of Figure 7.3, but now there is a single product path where there used to be two.

7.2 Factoring the Derivative Graph

Since the derivative of $f : \mathbb{R}^n \to \mathbb{R}^m$ is just the derivative of each of its nm $\mathbb{R}^1 \to \mathbb{R}^1$ constituent functions, we will begin by developing an algorithm for factoring the derivative of $\mathbb{R}^1 \to \mathbb{R}^1$ functions, and then generalize to the more complicated case of $f : \mathbb{R}^n \to \mathbb{R}^m$ in Section 7.2.1.

The derivative graph, f_0^0, of an $\mathbb{R}^1 \to \mathbb{R}^1$ function has one root and one leaf; there is a potential factorization of f_0^0 when two or more paths must pass through the same node on the way to the root or to the leaf. As an example, in Figure 7.6 all paths from c to the leaf must pass through node b and therefore must include the common factor d_0.

Factoring is closely related to a graph property called *dominance*. If a node b is on every path from node c to the root, then b *dominates* c (b **dom** c). If b is on every path from c to the leaf, then b *postdominates* c (b **pdom** c). Looking again at Figure 7.6 we can see that node b postdominates node c, and so all paths from c to the leaf must include the common term d_0, which can be factored out.

A slightly more complicated example is shown in Figure 7.7. Here, node 0 postdominates nodes 1, 2, and 3 (0 **pdom** $\{1, 2, 3\}$), but node 2 does not dominate node 0. Node 3 dominates nodes 0,1, and 2 (3 **dom** $\{0, 1, 2\}$).

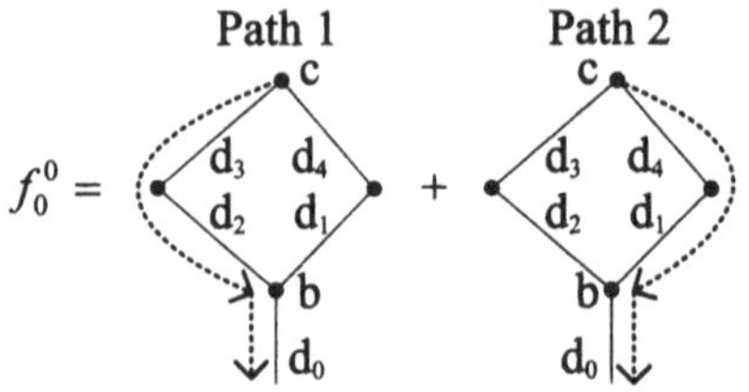

$$f_0^0 =$$ $$+$$

$$f_0^0 = d_0 d_2 d_3 + d_0 d_1 d_4 = d_0(d_2 d_3 + d_1 d_4)$$

Figure 7.6. Relationship between factoring and dominance: node b postdominates node c, so all paths from c to the leaf must include the common factor d_0 (see Plate VIII).

Figure 7.7. Dominance and postdominance relationships: node 0 postdominates nodes $1, 2,$ and 3 (0 **pdom** $\{1, 2, 3\}$), but node 2 does not dominate 0 or 1; node 3 dominates nodes $0, 1,$ and 2 (3 **dom** $\{0, 1, 2\}$), but node 1 does not postdominate 3 or 2.

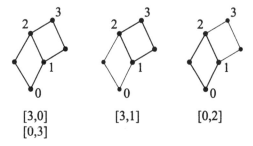

[3,0]
[0,3]   [3,1]   [0,2]

Figure 7.8. Factor subgraphs of the graph of Figure 7.7 (see Plate IX).

An efficient, simple algorithm (roughly 40 lines of code) for finding the dominators or postdominators of a graph is described in [9]. For a directed acyclic graph (DAG) this takes worst-case time $O(n^2)$, where n is the number of nodes in the graph. Much more complex linear time algorithms exist, but in practice these algorithms are slower until n becomes quite large.

Factorable subgraphs are defined by a dominator or postdominator node at a branch in the graph. If a dominator node b has more than one child, or if postdominator node b has more than one parent, then b is a *factor node*. If c is dominated by factor node b and has more than one parent, or c is postdominated by b and has more than one child, then c is a *factor base* of b. A factor subgraph $[b, c]$ consists of a factor node b, a factor base c of b, and those nodes on any path from b to c.

For example, the factor nodes in Figure 7.7 are 0 and 3. The factor subgraphs of node 3, highlighted in blue in Figure 7.8, are $[3, 1], [3, 0]$. Node 2 is not a factor node because the sole node dominated by 2 has only one parent and no node is postdominated by 2. Node 1 is not a factor node, because no nodes are dominated or postdominated by 1.

The factor subgraphs of node 0 are $[0, 2], [0, 3]$. Notice that $[3, 0]$ and $[0, 3]$ are the same graph. This is true in general; i.e., $[a, b] = [b, a]$ if both exist. However, you can see that $[1, 3]$ is not a factor subgraph even though $[3, 1]$ is. This is because 1 does not postdominate 3 in the graph of Figure 7.7. In general, the existence of $[a, b]$ does not imply the existence of $[b, a]$.

We can factor the graph by using the factor subgraphs and the dominance relations for the graph. We will assume that the graph has been depth-first-search numbered from the root, so the parents of node b will always have a higher number than b. Each edge, e, in the graph has nodes $e.1, e.2$ with the node number of $e.2$ greater than the node number of $e.1$; that is, $e.2$ will always be higher in the graph. The following algorithm computes which edges to delete from the original graph and which edges to add to a new factored edge:

```
given: a list L of factor subgraphs [X,Y] and a graph G

S = empty subgraph edge
foreach factor subgraph [A,B] in L{
    E = all edges which lie on a path from B to A

    foreach edge e in E{
        if(isDominator(A) //dominatorTest
            if(B pdom e.1){
                delete e from G
            }
        }
        else //postDominatorTest
            if(B dom e.2){
                delete e from G
            }
        }
        add e to S
```

```
    }
    add subgraph edge S to G, connecting node A to node B
    if any [X,Y] in L no longer exists delete [X,Y] from L
}
```

The *subgraph* edges that are added to the original graph are edges that themselves contain subgraphs. The subgraphs contained in subgraph edges are completely isolated from the rest of the original graph, and from the point of view of further edge processing behave as though they were a single edge.[2]

The correctness of this algorithm is easily verified for a **dom** b; the proof for b **pdom** a is similar. There are two classes of paths: those that pass through both a and b ($root \cdots a \cdots b \cdots leaf$) and those that pass through a but not b ($root \cdots a \cdots leaf$).[3] Starting with the first class: if we remove all edges $e \in [a,b]$ from the original graph and replace them by a single edge whose value is the sum of all path products from a to b, then the value of the sum of all path products over the paths $root \cdots a \cdots b \cdots leaf$ will be unchanged. Computation will be reduced because of the factorization, but algebraically the two sums will be identical. For example, in Figure 7.9 the factor subgraph $[3,1]$ has been replaced by a single edge from node 3 to node 1, and the paths that precede a and follow b in $root \cdots a \cdots b \cdots leaf$ have been factored out.

Edges $e \in [a,b]$, belonging to the second class of paths, $root \cdots a \cdots leaf$, cannot be deleted, because this would change the sum of products over all paths. In Figure 7.9, if edge d_1 is removed, then the product $d_0 d_1 d_5 d_6$ will be destroyed. All such e have the property that b **pdom** $e.1$ is not true; that is, there is a path through e to $leaf$ which does not pass through b. In Figure 7.9 b **pdom** $d_3.1$, so edge d_3 can be removed from the graph, but b **pdom** $d_1.1$ is not true, so edge d_1 cannot be removed from the graph.

Factorization does not change the value of the sum-of-products expression representing the derivative, so factor subgraphs can be factored in any order.[4]

In Figure 7.10 the factoring algorithm is applied to a postdominator case. Factor node 0 is a postdominator node; the red edge labeled d_4 does not satisfy the postDominatorTest, so it is not deleted from the original graph. The three blue edges labeled d_3, d_5, d_6 satisfy the test, so they are deleted. Since factor subgraph $[3,1]$ no longer exists in the graph, it is deleted from the list of factor subgraphs and not considered further.

---

[2]Except for the final evaluation step when the edge subgraphs are recursively visited to find the value of the factored derivative graph.

[3]Paths that pass through b but not a cannot occur, because a **dom** b.

[4]However, for $f : \mathbb{R}^n \to \mathbb{R}^m$ different orders may lead to solutions with very different computational efficiency.

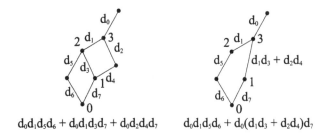

$$d_0d_1d_5d_6 + d_0d_1d_3d_7 + d_0d_2d_4d_7 \qquad d_0d_1d_5d_6 + d_0(d_1d_3 + d_2d_4)d_7$$

Figure 7.9. The factorization rule does not change the value of the sum of products over all paths (see Plate X).

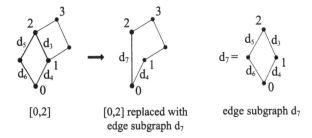

[0,2]   [0,2] replaced with   edge subgraph d_7
                         edge subgraph d_7

Figure 7.10. Factor subgraph $[0, 2]$, highlighted in blue and red in the leftmost graph, is factored out of the graph and replaced with an equivalent subgraph edge d_7 (see Plate XI).

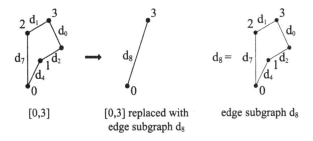

[0,3]   [0,3] replaced with   edge subgraph d_8
                         edge subgraph d_8

Figure 7.11. Factor subgraph $[0, 3]$, highlighted in blue in the leftmost graph, is factored out of the graph and replaced with an equivalent subgraph edge d_8 (see Plate XII).

The factor subgraphs for the new graph, shown in Figure 7.11 on the left-hand side, are $[3, 0], [0, 3]$. We choose $[0, 3]$ arbitrarily. All edges satisfy the `postDominatorTest`, so the final graph, in Figure 7.11 on the far right-hand side, has the single subgraph edge d_8.

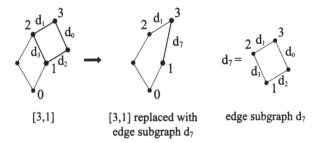

[3,1]   [3,1] replaced with   edge subgraph d_7
                         edge subgraph d_7

Figure 7.12. Factor subgraph $[3, 1]$ is factored out of the graph and replaced with an equivalent subgraph edge d_7 (see Plate XIII).

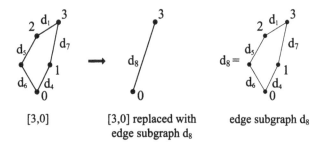

[3,0]   [3,0] replaced with   edge subgraph d_8
                         edge subgraph d_8

Figure 7.13. Factor subgraph $[3, 0]$, highlighted in blue in the leftmost graph, is factored out of the graph and replaced with an equivalent subgraph edge d_8 (see Plate XIV).

Alternatively we could have factored $[3, 1]$ first, as shown in Figure 7.12. Factor node 3 is a dominator node; the red edge labeled d_1 does not satisfy the dominatorTest, so it is not deleted from the original graph. The three blue edges labeled d_0, d_2, d_3 satisfy the test, so they are deleted. Since factor subgraph $[0, 2]$ no longer exists in the graph, it is deleted from the list of factor subgraphs and not considered further.

The factor subgraphs for this new graph are $[3, 0], [0, 3]$. We choose $[3, 0]$ arbitrarily. All edges satisfy the dominatorTest, so we get the result of Figure 7.13.

To evaluate the factored derivative, we compute the sum of products along all product paths, recursively substituting in subgraphs when necessary. For the factorization of Figures 7.10 and 7.11, we get

$$
\begin{aligned}
f_0^0 &= d_8 \\
&= d_1 d_7 + d_0 d_2 d_4 \\
&= d_1 (d_5 d_6 + d_3 d_4) + d_0 d_2 d_4,
\end{aligned} \tag{7.4}
$$

and for the factorization of Figures 7.12, 7.13 we get

$$
\begin{aligned}
f_0^0 &= d_8 \\
&= d_1 d_5 d_6 + d_7 d_4 \\
&= d_1 d_5 d_6 + (d_1 d_3 + d_0 d_2) d_4.
\end{aligned}
\tag{7.5}
$$

The two factorizations of (7.4) and (7.5) are trivially different; they have the same operations count.

For $f : \mathbb{R}^1 \to \mathbb{R}^1$, this algorithm is all we need. For $f : \mathbb{R}^n \to \mathbb{R}^m$, we will need the more sophisticated algorithm of Section 7.2.1.

7.2.1 Factoring $\mathbb{R}^n \to \mathbb{R}^m$ Functions

Two complications arise in factoring $f : \mathbb{R}^n \to \mathbb{R}^m$ that did not arise in the $f : \mathbb{R}^1 \to \mathbb{R}^1$ case. The first is that the order in which the factor subgraphs are factored can make an enormous difference in computational efficiency. The second is that after factorization, different derivatives may share partial product subsequences, so it is desirable to find product subsequences that are most widely shared. The order of factorization will be dealt with in this section, and the product subsequence issue will be dealt with in the next.

The derivative of f is just the derivative of each of its nm $\mathbb{R}^1 \to \mathbb{R}^1$ constituent functions. These nm $\mathbb{R}^1 \to \mathbb{R}^1$ derivative graphs will, in general, have a nonempty intersection, which represents redundant computation.

An example of this is shown in Figure 7.14. Here the derivatives f_0^0 and f_1^0 intersect in the red highlighted region, which is a common factor subgraph of f_0^0 and f_1^0. If we choose to factor $[0,3]$ from f_0^0, then we get Figure 7.15, where $f_0^0 \cap f_1^0$ does not contain a factor subgraph of either derivative.

If instead we factor $[4,2]$ from both f_0^0 and f_1^0, then we get Figure 7.16, where $f_0^0 \cap f_1^0$ contains the common subgraph edge 4,2.

The computation required for f_0^0 is independent of whether $[0,3]$ or $[4,2]$ is factored first. But the computation required to compute both f_0^0 and f_1^0 is significantly less if $[4,2]$ is factored first, because we can reuse the $[4,2]$ factor subgraph expression in the factorization of f_1^0.

The solution to the problem of common factor subgraphs is to count the number of times each factor subgraph $[i,j]$ appears in the nm derivative graphs. The factor subgraph that appears most often is factored first. If factor subgraph $[k,l]$ disappears in some derivative graph as a result of factorization, then the count of $[k,l]$ is decremented. To determine if factorization has eliminated $[k,l]$ from some derivative graph f_j^i it is necessary only to count the children of a dominator node or the parents of a post-dominator node. If either is one, the factor subgraph no longer exists. The

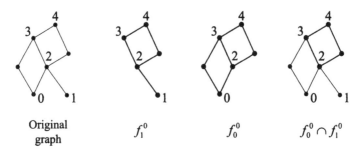

Figure 7.14. The derivatives f_0^0 and f_1^0 intersect only in the red highlighted subgraph (see Plate XV).

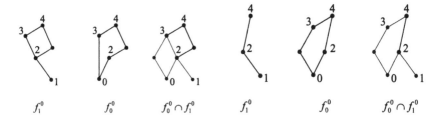

Figure 7.15. Factor $[0, 3]$ from f_0^0. $f_0^0 \cap f_1^0$, highlighted in red, does not contain a factor subgraph of either derivative (see Plate XVI).

Figure 7.16. Factor $[4, 2]$ from both f_0^0 and f_1^0. $f_0^0 \cap f_1^0$ contains the common subgraph edge $4, 2$ (see Plate XVII).

counts of the $[k, l]$ are efficiently updated during factorization by observing if either node of a deleted edge is either a factor or a factor base node. Ranking of the $[k, l]$ can be done efficiently with a priority queue. The complete factorization algorithm is:

```
factorSubgraphs(function F)
hash table Counts: counts of [k,l]
list Altered: [k,l] whose counts have changed due to factorization
priority queue Largest: sorted by factor subgraph count
   foreach(derivative graph Fij in F)
     compute factor subgraphs of Fij;
     foreach(factor subgraph [k,l] in Fij){
       if(Counts[[k,l]] == null){
         Counts[[k,l]] = [k,l];
       }
       else{
         Counts[[k,l]].count += 1;
```

```
    }
  foreach([k,l] in Counts){
    Largest.insert([k,l]);
    while(Largest not empty){
    maxSubgraph = Largest.max
  foreach(Fij in which maxSubgraph occurs){
    Altered.Add(Fij.factor(maxSubgraph))
  compute factor subgraphs of Fij;
    foreach([k,l] in Altered)Largest.delete([k,l])
    foreach([k,l] in Altered)Largest.insert([k,l])
```

For $f : \mathbb{R}^n \to \mathbb{R}^m$ with v nodes there are nm F_{ij}, each of which can have at most v factor subgraphs. At most v iterations will be required to factor all of these subgraphs. Recomputing the factor subgraphs takes worst-case time $O(v^2)$; this is done at each iteration. Multiplying these terms together gives a worst-case time of $O(nmv^3)$. We have never observed this worst-case running time for any of the examples we have tested, and in practice the algorithm is fast enough to differentiate expression graphs with tens of thousands of nodes.

In the current algorithm any time a factor subgraph is factored, all of the factor subgraphs of the F_{ij} are recomputed, which requires running the dominator algorithm on all the nodes in F_{ij}. We discuss the consequences of this inefficiency further in Section 8.5.3.

7.2.2   Computing Common Subproducts

After the graph has been completely factored, there is no branching; i.e., for each F_{ij} there is a single path from node i to node j. Figure 7.17 shows the derivative graph of an $\mathbb{R}^3 \to \mathbb{R}^2$ function. Each of the nm derivative functions is completely factored, giving six path products:

$$f_0^0 = d_1 d_2 d_4, \quad f_0^1 = d_0 d_2 d_4,$$

$$f_1^0 = d_1 d_2 d_5, \quad f_1^1 = d_0 d_2 d_5,$$

$$f_2^0 = d_1 d_2 d_3, \quad f_2^1 = d_0 d_2 d_3.$$

The subproducts $d_1 d_2$ and $d_0 d_2$ can each be used in three path products, whereas the subproducts $d_2 d_4$, $d_2 d_5$, and $d_2 d_3$ can each be used in only two path products. If we compute and reuse the subproducts $d_1 d_2$ and $d_0 d_2$ we can compute all six path products with only $2 + 2 * 3 = 8$ multiplications. If we compute and reuse the products $d_2 d_4$, $d_2 d_5$, and $d_2 d_3$ it will take $3 + 3 * 2 = 9$ multiplications. In this simple example it is easy to

$$d_1d_2d_3$$
$$d_1d_2d_4$$
$$d_1d_2d_5$$

$$d_0d_2d_3$$
$$d_0d_2d_4$$
$$d_0d_2d_5$$

$$d_1d_2d_4$$
$$d_0d_2d_4$$

$f^0 \qquad f^1$

$d_1 \qquad d_0$

d_2

$d_4 \qquad d_3$

d_5

$f_0 \qquad \qquad f_2$

f_1

$d_1 \qquad d_0$

d_2

$d_4 \qquad d_3$

d_5

$d_1 \qquad d_0$

d_2

$d_4 \qquad d_3$

d_5

$d_1 \qquad d_0$

d_2

$d_4 \qquad d_3$

d_5

$\cdots$

$$f : \mathbb{R}^3 \to \mathbb{R}^2$$

Figure 7.17. The $\mathbb{R}^3 \to \mathbb{R}^2$ function on the left has six derivatives; all of the derivatives are completely factored. What is the best way to form the path products? The subproducts d_1d_2 and d_0d_2 can each be used in three path products. The subproducts d_2d_4, d_2d_5, and d_2d_3 can each be used in only two path products (see Plate XVIII).

determine the best choice, but it becomes quite difficult for more complex graphs.

The solution to the problem of common subproducts is to compute the number of product paths that pass through each subproduct and then form the subproduct with the highest path count. This is performed in two stages. First the path counts of pairs of edges that occur in sequence along the path are computed. Then the highest-count pair is merged into an EdgePair that is inserted into all paths of all f_j^i derivative graphs containing the pair. The counts of existing edge pairs are updated. This takes time $O(1)$ per edge pair updated. This process is continued until all paths in all f_j^i are one edge long. Each edge pair may itself contain an edge pair, and edges may contain subgraphs, so the final evaluation of the derivative requires recursively expanding each of these data types as it is encountered.

The following pseudocode assumes that each f_j^i is stored as a linked list of edges and that a hash table or similar data structure is employed, so that any edge can be found in $O(1)$ time. To simplify the presentation, all the (many) tests for special cases such as null values, no previous or next edges, etc., have been eliminated. When the program terminates every f_j^i will consist of a set of paths each of which will be a sequence containing one, and only one, of the following types: edges, edge subgraphs, and edge pairs:

```
optimumSubproducts(graph G)
//count of paths edge e occurs on hash table. Counts: priority
    queue, Largest: sorted by edge path count
```

```
foreach(derivative graph Fij in G){
  foreach(edge eSub in Fij){
    if(eSub.isEdgeSubgraph){
      foreach(edge e, e.next in eSub){
        temp = new EdgePair(ei, e.next)
        Counts[temp].pathCount += 1
      }
    }
    else{
      temp = new EdgePair(ei, e.next)
      Counts[temp].pathCount += 1;
    }
  }
}

foreach(EdgePair e in Counts)Largest.insert(e)

while(Largest not empty){
  maxProduct = Largest.max
  foreach(Fij which has maxProduct){
    ei = Fij.find(maxProduct.edge1)
    eiNext = ei.next
    eiPrev = ei.previous
    eiNext2 = eiNext.next
    Fij.delete(ei)
    Fij.delete(eiNext)
    oldPair = new EdgePair(ei,eiNext)
    eiPrev.insertNext(oldPair)
    prevPair = new EdgePair(eiPrev,ei)
    nextPair = new EdgePair(eiNext,eiNext2)
    updateCounts(oldPair, prevPair,nextPair)
  }
}
}

updateCounts(oldPair, prevPair, nextPair){
  Counts.delete(oldPair)
  Largest.delete(oldPair)
  Counts[prevPair] -= 1
  Counts[nextPair] -= 1
  Largest.delete(prevPair)
  Largest.delete(nextPair)
  Largest.insert(prevPair)
  Largest.insert(nextPair)
}
```

7.3   Other Symbolic Forms

Automatic differentiation [16, 31] and symbolic differentiation have histor-
ically been viewed as completely different methods for computing derivatives. Automatic differentiation is generally considered to be strictly a
numerical technique, but by using operator overloading and two simple
recursive algorithms, both the forward and reverse forms of automatic differentiation can be used to create purely symbolic derivatives. In general,
D* will compute more efficient derivatives than either the forward or reverse
symbolic algorithms, but in special cases these alternative algorithms may
require less symbolic preprocessing time. For $f : \mathbb{R}^n \to \mathbb{R}^m$, the forward
symbolic algorithm may require less symbolic reprocessing when $m \gg n$,
and the reverse symbolic algorithm when $n \gg m$.

Symbolic forward automatic differentiation is implemented by the following recursive function:

```
/// Use this algorithm when the number of domain variables is less
      than the number of range functions.
/// example usage:
///
/// Function[] f = {v*c,Function.cos(c)};
///
/// Function[] DfDv = Function.forwardSymbolic(f, v);
/// Function[] DfDc = Function.forwardSymbolic(f, c);

public Function[] forwardSymbolic(Variable v) {
    Function[] deriv = new Function[range.Length];
    for (int i = 0; i < range.Length; i++) deriv[i] = range[i].
        forwardD(v);
    return deriv;
}

internal Function forwardD(Variable v) {
    Dictionary<Function, Function> dVal = new Dictionary<Function,
        Function>();
    Dictionary<Function, bool> visitedFunctions = new Dictionary<
        Function, bool>();
    return forwardD(visitedFunctions, v, dVal);
}

internal Function forwardD(Dictionary<Function, bool>
    visitedFunctions, Variable v, Dictionary<Function, Function>
    dVal) {
    bool visited;
```

```
if (this is Variable){
   if (ReferenceEquals(this, v)) { return 1.0; }
   else { return 0.0; }
}
if (this is Constant) return 0.0;
if (visitedFunctions.TryGetValue(this, out visited)) { return
   dVal[this]; }
visitedFunctions[this] = true;
Function sum = 0.0;
for (int i = 0; i < children.Length; i++){
   Function child = children[i];
   sum = sum + partial(i) * child.forwardD(visitedFunctions, v,
      dVal);
}
dVal[this] = sum;
return sum;
}
```

The function `partial(child)` computes the partial of the node function with respect to its child. For example, if the `sin()` function is the node, then `partial(child) = cos(child)`. Upon completion, entry i in the returned array contains $\frac{\partial f^i}{\partial v}$.

The symbolic reverse form is the following:

```
/// Use this algorithm when the number of range functions is less
///    than the number of domain variables
/// example usage:
///
/// Function f = v*c;
/// Function[] derivs = f.reverseSymbolic(new[]{v,c});
///
/// derivs[0] will contain Df/Dv, derivs[1] is Df/Dc.

public Function[] reverseSymbolic(Variable[] variables) {
   Dictionary<Variable, Function> deriv = new Dictionary<Variable,
      Function>();
   Dictionary<Function, Function> sum = new Dictionary<Function,
      Function>();
   Dictionary<Function, int> visited = new Dictionary<Function, int
      >();
   Dictionary<Function, int> numParents = new Dictionary<Function,
      int>();
   Function[] result = new Function[variables.Length];

   computeNumberOfParents(numParents, visited);
```

```
    visited.Clear();
    //reset visited for the next traversal of the graph
    foreach (Variable v in variables) { deriv[v] = null; }
    //initialize to just those variables want to take derivative w.r
        .t.
    this.reverseD(deriv, sum, numParents, visited, 1);
    for (int i = 0; i < variables.Length; i++) { result[i] = deriv[
        variables[i]]; }
    return result;
}


public void computeNumberOfParents(Dictionary<Function, int>
    numParents, Dictionary<Function, int> visited) {
    int numVisits = -1;
    if (visited.TryGetValue(this, out numVisits)) { numParents[this]
        += 1; }
    else{
        visited[this] = 1; numParents[this] = 1;
        if (children != null){//children array of Constant and
            Variable is null because these Function types have no
            children
            foreach (Function child in children) { child.
                computeNumberOfParents(numParents, visited); }
        }
    }
}


internal void reverseD(Dictionary<Variable, Function> deriv,
    Dictionary<Function, Function> sum, Dictionary<Function, int>
    numParents, Dictionary<Function, int> visited, Function
    cumDeriv) {
    int numVisits = -1;
    Function derivativeSoFar;

    if (visited.TryGetValue(this, out numVisits)) { visited[this] +=
        1; }
    else { visited[this] = 1; }
    if (sum.TryGetValue(this, out derivativeSoFar)) { sum[this] =
        sum[this] + cumDeriv; }
    else { sum[this] = cumDeriv; }
    if (visited[this] >= numParents[this]){//now recurse through to
        children since know this Function will never be visited
        again
```

```
if (children != null){//children array of Constant and
      Variable is null because these Function types have no
      children
    for (int i = 0; i < children.Length;i++ ) {
       Function child = children[i];
          child.reverseD(deriv, sum, numParents, visited, sum[
             this] * partial(i));
       }
    }
if (this is Variable){
    Function derivValue;
    //see if this is the variable we are taking a derivative
       with respect to.
    if (deriv.TryGetValue(this as Variable, out derivValue)) {
          deriv[this as Variable] = sum[this]; }
    }
  }
}
```

Upon completion, entry j in the returned array contains $\frac{\partial f}{\partial v_j}$.

To use the forward method for $f : \mathbb{R}^n \to \mathbb{R}^m$, apply the function forwardSymbolic to the n $\mathbb{R}^1 \to \mathbb{R}^m$ function subgraphs. To use the reverse method, apply the function reverseSymbolic to the m $\mathbb{R}^n \to \mathbb{R}^1$ function subgraphs.

The expression graph contained in the array returned by either the forwardSymbolic or reverseSymbolic algorithm is a purely symbolic representation of the derivative expression and can be used as an argument to any further desired functions in new expression graphs. Higher-order derivatives can trivially be computed by repeatedly applying either forwardSymbolic or reverseSymbolic.

7.4   Analysis of Forward and Reverse

Both the forward and reverse algorithms perform an implicit factorization of the derivative expression. This factorization makes the algorithms efficient for some functions and inefficient for others. Understanding this factorization is essential in determining which algorithm to apply to a given function.

Let us begin our analysis by writing out the derivative of the graph of Figure 7.18 in its expanded form as sums of all path products:[5]

---

[5]See section 7.1.

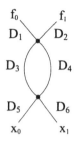

Figure 7.18. Derivative graph for some arbitrary function (see Plate XIX).

$$f_0^0 = D_1 D_3 D_5 + D_1 D_4 D_5,$$
$$f_1^0 = D_1 D_3 D_6 + D_1 D_4 D_6,$$
$$f_0^1 = D_2 D_3 D_5 + D_2 D_4 D_5,$$
$$f_0^1 = D_2 D_3 D_6 + D_2 D_4 D_6.$$

Now let us see the effect of running `forwardSymbolic` to compute $[f_0^0, f_0^1]$:

$$f_0^0 = D_1(D_3 D_5 + D_4 D_5),$$
$$f_0^1 = D_2(D_3 D_5 + D_4 D_5). \tag{7.6}$$

The `forwardSymbolic` algorithm factors out common *prefixes* of the sum-of-products derivative—the sum $D_3 D_5 + D_4 D_5$ is computed only once. If we run `forwardSymbolic` again to compute $[f_1^0, f_1^1]$, we get

$$f_1^0 = D_1(D_3 D_6 + D_4 D_6),$$
$$f_1^1 = D_2(D_3 D_6 + D_4 D_6). \tag{7.7}$$

Unfortunately, the sum $D_3 D_5 + D_4 D_5$ in Equation (7.6) is not the same as the sum $D_3 D_6 + D_4 D_6$ in Equation (7.7), so we end up doing some redundant work. To compute all the terms, $[f_0^0, f_1^0, f_0^1, f_1^1]$, in the derivative requires eight multiplications and two additions.

Now let us compute the same set of derivatives with `reverseSymbolic`, starting with $[f_0^0, f_1^0]$:

$$f_0^0 = (D_1 D_3 + D_1 D_4)D_5,$$
$$f_1^0 = (D_1 D_3 + D_1 D_4)D_6.$$

The `reverseSymbolic` algorithm factors out common *suffixes* of the sum-of-products derivative—the common term $D_1 D_3 + D_1 D_4$ is computed only once. If we run `reverseSymbolic` again to compute $[f_0^1, f_1^1]$, we get

$$f_0^1 = (D_2D_3 + D_2D_4)D_5,$$
$$f_1^1 = (D_2D_3 + D_2D_4)D_6. \tag{7.8}$$

As for the forward case, the common term $D_1D_3 + D_1D_4$ in Equation (7.8) is not the same as the common term $D_2D_3 + D_2D_4$ in (7.8), so we end up doing some redundant work. To compute all the terms, $[f_0^0, f_1^0, f_0^1, f_1^1]$, again requires eight multiplications and two additions.

By contrast, D* computes common factorable substrings occurring anywhere in the sum-of-products derivative. Here is the derivative that D* would compute for this function:

$$f_0^0 = (D_1(D_3 + D_4))D_5,$$
$$f_1^0 = (D_1(D_3 + D_4))D_6,$$
$$f_0^1 = (D_2(D_3 + D_4))D_5,$$
$$f_0^1 = (D_2(D_3 + D_4))D_6.$$

Each of the terms in parentheses is computed only once, so computing all the terms, $[f_0^0, f_1^0, f_0^1, f_1^1]$, takes only six multiplications and one addition. The savings in computation for D* versus either forwardSymbolic or reverseSymbolic can be much larger as the domain and range dimensions increase.

For $f : \mathbb{R}^1 \to \mathbb{R}^m$, the forward method is efficient, in the worst case doing only about twice as many multiplications as necessary. However, for $f : \mathbb{R}^n \to \mathbb{R}^1$, the implicit factorization of the forward method can result in an expression that takes n times more computation than necessary, in the worst case.

The reverse algorithm is efficient for $f : \mathbb{R}^n \to \mathbb{R}^1$, again doing no more than about twice as many multiplications as necessary, in the worst case. But for $f : \mathbb{R}^1 \to \mathbb{R}^m$, the reverse method may do m times more computation than necessary. For $f : \mathbb{R}^n \to \mathbb{R}^m$, the forward algorithm may do n times and the reverse m times as much work as necessary.

Unfortunately, for $f : \mathbb{R}^n \to \mathbb{R}^m$, it is hard to tell if forwardSymbolic or reverseSymbolic will be more efficient. You might think you could choose forwardSymbolic when $m > n$ and reverseSymbolic when $n \geq m$. Figure 7.19 shows examples where these simple tests fail. The simplest way is to run both algorithms and choose the most efficient result.

For $f : \mathbb{R}^n \to \mathbb{R}^m$, D* will generally find much more efficient derivatives than either the forward or reverse method. However, even for the $f : \mathbb{R}^n \to \mathbb{R}^1$ and $f : \mathbb{R}^1 \to \mathbb{R}^m$ cases, you are generally better off using D*, which automatically generates efficient derivatives in either case, and eliminates some redundant computations that neither of the other algorithms will eliminate. But the symbolic processing time of D* is greater than the

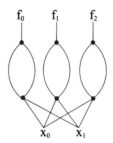

Forward: 4 multiplications, 3 additions.   Forward: 18 multiplications, 6 additions.
Reverse: 6 multiplications, 2 additions.   Reverse: 12 multiplications, 3 additions.

Figure 7.19. Failures of simple domain-range tests (see Plate XX).

symbolic processing time of the simple symbolic forward and reverse algorithms described here; for very large functions you might want to use these algorithms if the symbolic processing time of D* is too long.

8 Lagrangian Mechanics

In Chapter 5 you learned how to use Lagrangian dynamics to create complex mechanical systems and simulate their physical behavior. In this chapter you will learn the mathematical theory of Lagrangian dynamics.

Lagrangian mechanics is a reformulation of classical mechanics which is particularly useful for modeling systems with constrained motion; i.e., systems in which the individual rigid bodies are not free to move independently of each other. Essentially all useful mechanical systems have this property: industrial robots, the skeletal systems of animals, and automobile suspensions are just a few of many examples.

The great advantage of Lagrangian mechanics for constrained systems is that it is usually possible to formulate the equations of motion using just differential equations. By contrast, a Newtonian formulation will usually require differential equations *and* a set of nonlinear constraint equations which enforce the motion constraints.

For example, the Newtonian formulation for the simple point-mass pendulum shown in Figure 8.1 has two differential equations of motion,

$$m \begin{bmatrix} \ddot{x} \\ \ddot{y} \end{bmatrix} = \mathbf{f}_c + \begin{bmatrix} 0 \\ -mg \end{bmatrix},$$

and one nonlinear constraint equation, $\mathbf{x}^\mathrm{T}\mathbf{x} = 1$, which keeps the point mass the correct distance from the hinge point.

In this simple case it is easy to compute the constraint force, $\mathbf{f}_c$. However, the smallest numerical error in computing $\mathbf{f}_c$ will cause the point mass to be displaced from its correct position. This error will accumulate over time, eventually causing the position of the point mass to drift arbitrarily far. If we enforce the nonlinear constraint $\mathbf{x}^\mathrm{T}\mathbf{x} = 1$ while integrating the differential equation then the point mass will not drift; however, this is more complicated and computationally expensive than just integrating the differential equation and introduces numerical problems of its own.

Let us see how we would reformulate this problem using Lagrangian mechanics. There are three steps in writing the Lagrangian equations of motion:

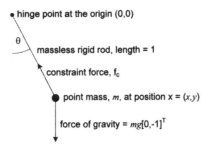

Figure 8.1. Point-mass pendulum with massless rigid rod.

1. Parameterize the kinematics of the mechanical system in terms of variables $q_1 \ldots q_n$ where n is the number of degrees of freedom of the system. The q_i are called the generalized coordinates of the system.

2. For each rigid body in the system write its differential equations of motion in world coordinates,[1] ignoring the constraint forces: $m_i \ddot{\mathbf{x}}_i = \mathbf{f}_{\text{ext}_i}$.

3. Project the differential equations of motion onto the constraint manifold, $\frac{\partial \mathbf{x}_i}{\partial q_j}$, defined by the kinematics of the mechanical system—this will result in a new set of differential equations in terms of the $q_1 \ldots q_n$ variables.[2]

Let us apply these steps to the simple dynamic system[3] of Figure 8.1.

1. Parameterize the kinematics:

$$\mathbf{x}(\theta(t)) = \begin{bmatrix} \sin(\theta(t)) \\ -\cos(\theta(t)) \end{bmatrix}.$$

2. Write the differential equations of motion in Cartesian coordinates:

$$m\ddot{\mathbf{x}} = mg \begin{bmatrix} 0 \\ -1 \end{bmatrix}. \tag{8.1}$$

---

[1] Actually in an inertial coordinate frame, i.e., one moving with constant linear velocity and not rotating with respect to the fixed stars—but this is a fine point we can ignore.

[2] Readers already familiar with Lagrangian mechanics will recognize this as the principle of virtual work.

[3] It is not this simple—we should compute the inertia matrix of the rigid body and account for the torque necessary to rotate it. Because the inertia matrix of a point mass is zero in the center of mass coordinate frame the torque will be zero, so we can ignore these rotational effects in this example.

3. Project the differential equations of motion onto the constraint surface. The constraint surface is

$$\frac{\partial \mathbf{x}(\theta(\mathbf{t}))}{\partial \theta} = \begin{bmatrix} \cos(\theta(t)) \\ \sin(\theta(t)) \end{bmatrix}.$$

Write the differential equation in terms of the parameterizing variable θ by using the chain rule to compute $\ddot{\mathbf{x}}$ in Equation (8.1):

$$\dot{\mathbf{x}} = \dot{\theta}(t) \begin{bmatrix} \cos(\theta(t)) \\ \sin(\theta(t)) \end{bmatrix},$$

$$\ddot{\mathbf{x}} = \ddot{\theta}(t) \begin{bmatrix} \cos(\theta(t)) \\ \sin(\theta(t)) \end{bmatrix} + \dot{\theta}^2(t) \begin{bmatrix} -\sin(\theta(t)) \\ \cos(\theta(t)) \end{bmatrix}.$$

Substitute the value for $\ddot{\mathbf{x}}$ into Equation (8.1) to get

$$m \left\{ \ddot{\theta}(t) \begin{bmatrix} \cos(\theta(t) \\ \sin(\theta(t)) \end{bmatrix} + \dot{\theta}^2(t) \begin{bmatrix} -\sin(\theta(t)) \\ \cos(\theta(t)) \end{bmatrix} \right\} = mg \begin{bmatrix} 0 \\ -1 \end{bmatrix}.$$

Now project onto the constraint surface:

$$m\ddot{\mathbf{x}}^T \frac{\partial \mathbf{x}}{\partial \theta} = mg \begin{bmatrix} 0 \\ -1 \end{bmatrix}^T \frac{\partial \mathbf{x}}{\partial \theta},$$

$$m \left\{ \ddot{\theta}(t) \begin{bmatrix} \cos(\theta(t)) \\ \sin(\theta(t)) \end{bmatrix} + \dot{\theta}^2(t) \begin{bmatrix} -\sin(\theta(t)) \\ \cos(\theta(t)) \end{bmatrix} \right\}^T$$

$$\times \begin{bmatrix} \cos(\theta(t)) \\ \sin(\theta(t)) \end{bmatrix} = mg \begin{bmatrix} 0 \\ -1 \end{bmatrix}^T \begin{bmatrix} \cos(\theta(t)) \\ \sin(\theta(t)) \end{bmatrix},$$

which gives

$$\left\{ \ddot{\theta}(t) \overbrace{\begin{bmatrix} \cos(\theta(t)) \\ \sin(\theta(t)) \end{bmatrix}^T \begin{bmatrix} \cos(\theta(t)) \\ \sin(\theta(t)) \end{bmatrix}}^{=1} \right.$$

$$\left. + \dot{\theta}^2(t) \overbrace{\begin{bmatrix} -\sin(\theta(t)) \\ \cos(\theta(t)) \end{bmatrix}^T \begin{bmatrix} \cos(\theta(t)) \\ \sin(\theta(t)) \end{bmatrix}}^{=0} \right\} = mg \begin{bmatrix} 0 \\ -1 \end{bmatrix}^T \begin{bmatrix} \cos(\theta(t)) \\ \sin(\theta(t)) \end{bmatrix},$$

which simplifies to

$$m\ddot{\theta}(t) = -mg\sin(\theta(t)),$$

$$\ddot{\theta}(t) = -g\sin(\theta(t)).$$

This is a great result; we went from two simultaneous differential equations and one nonlinear constraint equation to one scalar differential equation. However, you can see that even for this simple system, computing the required derivatives and simplifying them is a lot of work. The situation becomes much worse as the number of degrees of freedom increases—if we add one more point mass to make a double pendulum system the equations become surprisingly complex.

Before D* computing and simplifying these derivatives had to be done either by hand, with automatic differentiation, or with general-purpose symbolic math programs such as Mathematica or Maple. These methods become increasingly impractical for systems with more than a few degrees of freedom. This is why Lagrangian dynamics is rarely used for anything except textbook problems.

By contrast, with D* we can compute efficient derivatives for systems with many degrees of freedom,[4] making it possible to use Lagrangian dynamics on real world, rather than textbook, problems.

8.1   Kinematics of Mechanical Systems

Before we can begin describing the dynamics of our mechanical system we have to specify how the system moves; we have to parameterize the kinematics of the system. We will make the following assumptions:

- The system is tree structured, as shown in Figure 5.2. Each edge in the tree corresponds to a rigid-body transformation and each node corresponds to a rigid body, represented by a three-dimensional geometrical object. We will call the tree of transformations a transformation hierarchy.

- There is a set of n variables, $q_0 \ldots q_{n-1}$, called generalized coordinates, which completely specify the position of every rigid body in the system.

A rigid-body transformation, $\mathbf{A}$, is the product of two matrices, $\mathbf{A} = \mathbf{TR}$, where $\mathbf{T}$, a translation matrix, is

$$\mathbf{T} = \begin{bmatrix} 1 & 0 & 0 & t_x \\ 0 & 1 & 0 & t_y \\ 0 & 0 & 1 & t_z \\ 0 & 0 & 0 & 1 \end{bmatrix} = \begin{bmatrix} \mathbf{1}_{3x3} & \mathbf{t}_{3x1} \\ \mathbf{0}_{1x3} & 1 \end{bmatrix},$$

---

[4]The largest system we have attempted so far has 40 generalized degrees of freedom.

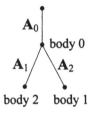

Figure 8.2. Transformation hierarchy.

and **R**, a rotation matrix, is

$$
\mathbf{R} = \begin{bmatrix} r_{11} & r_{12} & r_{13} & 0 \\ r_{21} & r_{22} & r_{23} & 0 \\ r_{31} & r_{32} & r_{33} & 0 \\ 0 & 0 & 0 & 1 \end{bmatrix} = \begin{bmatrix} \mathbf{R}_{3x3} & \mathbf{0}_{3x1} \\ \mathbf{0}_{1x3} & 1 \end{bmatrix}.
$$

The position of each rigid body in the mechanical system is the product of the transformation matrices on the path from the body node to the root. For example, in Figure 8.2, the transformation for body 0, $\mathbf{W}_0$, is $\mathbf{A}_0$. For body 1, the transformation $\mathbf{W}_1$ is $\mathbf{A}_0\mathbf{A}_2$. For body 2, the transformation $\mathbf{W}_2$ is $\mathbf{A}_0\mathbf{A}_1$.

Later in the text we will need to compute the inverse of a rigid-body transformation. The special structure of the **T** and **R** matrices makes computing the inverse very efficient. The translation matrix, **T**, is easily inverted:

$$
\mathbf{T}^{-1} = \begin{bmatrix} 1 & 0 & 0 & -t_x \\ 0 & 1 & 0 & -t_y \\ 0 & 0 & 1 & -t_z \\ 0 & 0 & 0 & 1 \end{bmatrix} = \begin{bmatrix} \mathbf{1}_{3x3} & -\mathbf{t}_{3x1} \\ \mathbf{0}_{1x3} & 1 \end{bmatrix}.
$$

Since the columns of a rotation matrix are orthogonal to each other and of unit length, the inverse of a rotation matrix is its transpose:

$$
\mathbf{R}^{\mathbf{T}}\mathbf{R} = \begin{bmatrix} r_{11} & r_{21} & r_{31} & 0 \\ r_{12} & r_{22} & r_{32} & 0 \\ r_{13} & r_{23} & r_{33} & 0 \\ 0 & 0 & 0 & 1 \end{bmatrix} \begin{bmatrix} r_{11} & r_{12} & r_{13} & 0 \\ r_{21} & r_{22} & r_{23} & 0 \\ r_{31} & r_{32} & r_{33} & 0 \\ 0 & 0 & 0 & 1 \end{bmatrix}
$$

$$
= \begin{bmatrix} 1 & 0 & 0 & 0 \\ 0 & 1 & 0 & 0 \\ 0 & 0 & 1 & 0 \\ 0 & 0 & 0 & 1 \end{bmatrix}.
$$

Given the inverses of the translation and rotation matrices, computing the inverse of a rigid-body transformation is straightforward:

$$
\begin{aligned}
\mathbf{A}^{-1} &= (\mathbf{TR})^{-1} \\
&= \mathbf{R}^{-1}\mathbf{T}^{-1} \\
&= \begin{bmatrix} \mathbf{R}_{3x3}^{\mathrm{T}} & \mathbf{0}_{3x1} \\ \mathbf{0}_{1x3} & 1 \end{bmatrix} \begin{bmatrix} \mathbf{1}_{3x3} & -\mathbf{t}_{3x1} \\ \mathbf{0}_{1x3} & 1 \end{bmatrix} \\
&= \begin{bmatrix} \mathbf{R}_{3x3}^{\mathrm{T}} & -\mathbf{R}_{3x3}^{\mathrm{T}}\mathbf{t}_{3x1} \\ \mathbf{0}_{1x3} & 1 \end{bmatrix}.
\end{aligned}
$$

8.2   Derivatives

Lagrangian mechanics is all about computing derivatives. In some sense that is all there is to it—if you can compute the derivatives then you have the differential equations which define the system dynamics.

In practice it is more difficult, because the derivatives do not naturally come out in the right form; the acceleration terms get jumbled together and need to be separated so we can integrate the equations numerically. We will worry about getting the derivative equations in the right form in the next section. In this section we will just concentrate on computing the derivatives.

First we will figure out how to compute the velocity of a point attached to a rigid body. Then we will derive the equations for angular velocity, the time derivative of the change in orientation of a rigid body.

8.2.1   Velocity of a Point

The entries in each transformation matrix, $\mathbf{A}_i$, are determined by some number of generalized coordinates

$$
\mathbf{A}_i\left(\mathbf{q}_i\left(t\right)\right) = \begin{bmatrix} \mathbf{R}(\mathbf{q}_i(t)) & \mathbf{t}(\mathbf{q}_i(t)) \\ \mathbf{0} & 1 \end{bmatrix},
$$

where $\mathbf{q}_i(t)$ is a vector of generalized coordinates

$$
\mathbf{q}_i(t) = [q_{i1}(t), q_{i2}(t), \ldots, q_{ik}(t)]^{\mathrm{T}}, \quad k \le 6.
$$

Because a rigid body has only six degrees of freedom, no more than six generalized coordinates can be used to specify any $\mathbf{A}_i$.

The transformation $\mathbf{W}_j$ for rigid-body j is

$$
\mathbf{W}_j(\mathbf{q}(t)) = \mathbf{A}_{p0}(\mathbf{q}_{p0}(t))\mathbf{A}_{p1}(\mathbf{q}_{p1}(t))\ldots\mathbf{A}_{pn}(\mathbf{q}_{pn}(t)),
$$

where $p_o, p_1, \ldots, p_n$ are edges along the path from the rigid-body j to the root of the tree.

Given a time invariant vector, $\mathbf{r}_j$, expressed in the jth coordinate system, we can compute its representation, $\mathbf{r}_j^w$, in the world coordinate frame by multiplying by $\mathbf{W}_j$:

$$\mathbf{r}_j^w\left(\mathbf{q}(t)\right) = \mathbf{W}_j(\mathbf{q}(t))\mathbf{r}_j.$$

From now on we will usually write quantities like $\mathbf{W}_j(\mathbf{q}(t))$ as $\mathbf{W}_j$ to reduce clutter in the equations. You will have to remember that these quantities depend on $\mathbf{q}(t)$. The time derivative of $\mathbf{r}_j^w$ is

$$\dot{\mathbf{r}}_j^w = (\mathbf{W}_j \mathbf{r}_j)$$
$$= \dot{\mathbf{W}}_j \mathbf{r}_j + \mathbf{W}_j \dot{\mathbf{r}}_j$$
$$= \dot{\mathbf{W}}_j \mathbf{r}_j$$
$$= \left[\begin{array}{cc} \dot{\mathbf{R}} & \dot{\mathbf{t}} \\ 0 & 0 \end{array} \right]_j \mathbf{r}_j.$$

8.2.2 Angular Velocity

Clearly, $\dot{\mathbf{R}}$, the time derivative of the rotational part of the transformation matrix, contains all the information about the rate of change of orientation of a rigid body but it is very inconvenient to write the equations of motion directly in terms of $\dot{\mathbf{R}}$. First, it has too many numbers: $\dot{\mathbf{R}}$ has nine entries, but only three are necessary to specify a rotation (or its derivative). Second, it is a matrix and we eventually want to be able to project the angular velocity onto the orientation constraint manifold—it is not obvious how to do this if our representation for angular velocity is a matrix. The solution to both of these problems is to represent angular velocity as a vector.

We will use a common matrix factorization trick to simplify $\dot{\mathbf{R}}$: multiplication by a rotation matrix.[5] Let us start with the identity $\mathbf{R}^\mathsf{T}\mathbf{R} = \mathbf{1}$ and differentiate it:

$$(\mathbf{R}^\mathsf{T}\mathbf{R}) = \mathbf{0},$$
$$\dot{\mathbf{R}}^\mathsf{T}\mathbf{R} + \mathbf{R}^\mathsf{T}\dot{\mathbf{R}} = \mathbf{0},$$
$$\mathbf{R}^\mathsf{T}\dot{\mathbf{R}} = -\dot{\mathbf{R}}^\mathsf{T}\mathbf{R}.$$

Making use of the fact that

$$\dot{\mathbf{R}}^\mathsf{T}\mathbf{R} = \left(\mathbf{R}^\mathsf{T}\dot{\mathbf{R}}\right)^\mathsf{T},$$

---

[5]This trick is used in the SVD factorization and the eigenvector diagonalization of a symmetric matrix, among many others.

we get the following result:

$$\mathbf{R}^T\dot{\mathbf{R}} = -\left(\mathbf{R}^T\dot{\mathbf{R}}\right)^T.$$

A matrix equal to minus its transpose is called an antisymmetric matrix. In this type of matrix the following must be true:

$$
\begin{bmatrix}
a_{11} & a_{12} & a_{13} \\
a_{21} & a_{22} & a_{23} \\
a_{31} & a_{32} & a_{33}
\end{bmatrix}
= -
\begin{bmatrix}
a_{11} & a_{21} & a_{31} \\
a_{12} & a_{22} & a_{32} \\
a_{13} & a_{23} & a_{33}
\end{bmatrix}
$$

$$
=
\begin{bmatrix}
0 & a_{12} & a_{13} \\
-a_{12} & 0 & a_{23} \\
-a_{13} & -a_{23} & 0
\end{bmatrix}.
$$

Because there are only three nonzero components in $\mathbf{R}^T\dot{\mathbf{R}}$, we do not need a matrix—we can map the elements in $\mathbf{R}^T\dot{\mathbf{R}}$ to $\omega = [\omega_x\omega_y\omega_z]^T$, the angular velocity vector, and use vector operations instead of matrix operations. If we use the mapping

$$\omega_x = -a_{23},$$
$$\omega_y = a_{13},$$
$$\omega_z = -a12,$$

then we get

$$
\begin{bmatrix}
0 & -\omega_z & \omega_y \\
\omega_z & 0 & -\omega_x \\
-\omega_y & \omega_x & 0
\end{bmatrix}
=
\begin{bmatrix}
0 & a_{12} & a_{13} \\
-a_{12} & 0 & a_{23} \\
-a_{13} & -a_{23} & 0
\end{bmatrix}.
$$

We did not choose this mapping arbitrarily; if you compute $\mathbf{R}^T\dot{\mathbf{R}}\mathbf{p}$,

$$
\begin{bmatrix}
0 & -\omega_z & \omega_y \\
\omega_z & 0 & -\omega_x \\
-\omega_y & \omega_x & 0
\end{bmatrix}
\begin{bmatrix}
p_x \\
p_y \\
p_z
\end{bmatrix}
=
\begin{bmatrix}
\omega_y p_z - \omega_z p_y \\
\omega_z p_x - \omega_x p_z \\
\omega_x p_y - \omega_y p_x
\end{bmatrix},
$$

you can see this is exactly equivalent to $\omega \times \mathbf{p}$:

$$
\begin{bmatrix}
\omega_x \\
\omega_y \\
\omega_x
\end{bmatrix}
\times
\begin{bmatrix}
p_x \\
p_y \\
p_z
\end{bmatrix}
=
\begin{bmatrix}
\omega_y p_z - \omega_z p_y \\
\omega_z p_x - \omega_x p_z \\
\omega_x p_y - \omega_y p_x
\end{bmatrix}.
$$

Instead of computing the matrix product $\mathbf{R}^T\dot{\mathbf{R}}\mathbf{p}$, we can compute the vector cross product $\omega \times \mathbf{p}$. Specifically, ω represents the angular velocity with respect to the moving frame itself, as the premultiplication of $\mathbf{R}^T$ to

$\dot{\mathbf{R}}$ implies. Converting between the vector and matrix representation will be indicated with a tilde ($\sim$):

$$\tilde{\omega} = \begin{bmatrix} 0 & -\omega_z & \omega_y \\ \omega_z & 0 & -\omega_x \\ -\omega_y & \omega_x & 0 \end{bmatrix},$$

$$\widetilde{\mathbf{R}^\mathsf{T}\dot{\mathbf{R}}} = \omega.$$

To sum up what we have learned,

$$\omega \times \mathbf{p} = \tilde{\omega}\mathbf{p}$$
$$= \mathbf{R}^\mathsf{T}\dot{\mathbf{R}}\mathbf{p}.$$

We will be using the following identity in future derivations: $\tilde{\omega}\mathbf{r} = -\tilde{\mathbf{r}}\omega$. It is easily verified by direct multiplication:

$$\tilde{\omega}\mathbf{r} = \begin{bmatrix} 0 & -\omega_z & \omega_y \\ \omega_z & 0 & -\omega_x \\ -\omega_y & \omega_x & 0 \end{bmatrix} \begin{bmatrix} r_x \\ r_y \\ r_z \end{bmatrix}$$

$$= \begin{bmatrix} \omega_y r_z - \omega_z r_y \\ \omega_z r_x - \omega_x r_z \\ \omega_x r_y - \omega_y r_x \end{bmatrix},$$

$$\tilde{\mathbf{r}}\omega = \begin{bmatrix} 0 & -r_z & r_y \\ r_z & 0 & -r_x \\ -r_y & r_x & 0 \end{bmatrix} \begin{bmatrix} \omega_x \\ \omega_y \\ \omega_z \end{bmatrix}$$

$$= \begin{bmatrix} \omega_z r_y - \omega_y r_z \\ \omega_x r_z - \omega_z r_x \\ \omega_y r_x - \omega_x r_y \end{bmatrix}$$

$$= -\tilde{\omega}\mathbf{r}.$$

8.2.3 Angular Momentum and Torque

Referring to Figure 8.3, the position $\mathbf{r}^w$ of a point of a rigid body with respect to the world frame is expressed in terms of its local position $\mathbf{p}$ as

$$\mathbf{r}^w = \mathbf{W}\mathbf{T}_{\mathrm{cm}}\mathbf{p}$$

$$= \begin{bmatrix} \mathbf{R} & \mathbf{t} \\ 0 & 1 \end{bmatrix} \begin{bmatrix} 1 & \mathbf{t}_{\mathrm{cm}} \\ 0 & 1 \end{bmatrix} \mathbf{p}$$

$$= \begin{bmatrix} \mathbf{R} & \mathbf{R}\mathbf{t}_{\mathrm{cm}} + \mathbf{t} \\ 0 & 1 \end{bmatrix} \mathbf{p}$$

$$= \begin{bmatrix} \mathbf{R} & \mathbf{r}_{\mathrm{cm}} \\ 0 & 1 \end{bmatrix} \mathbf{p}$$

$$= \mathbf{R}\mathbf{p} + \mathbf{r}_{\mathrm{cm}},$$

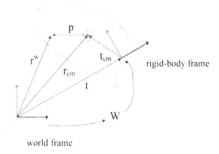

Figure 8.3. Angular momentum about the center of mass of the rigid body.

where the center of mass is denoted by $\mathbf{t}_{cm}$ and $\mathbf{r}_{cm}$ in the body frame and in the world frame, respectively. Then the angular momentum about its center of mass, represented in the world frame, is

$$
\begin{aligned}
\mathbf{H}_{cm} &= \int_V \mathbf{Rp} \times \dot{\mathbf{r}}^w \\
&= \int_V \mathbf{Rp} \times (\dot{\mathbf{r}_{cm} + \mathbf{Rp}}) \\
&= \int_V \mathbf{Rp} \times \dot{\mathbf{r}}_{cm} + \int_V \mathbf{Rp} \times \dot{\mathbf{R}}\mathbf{p} \\
&= \mathbf{R} \underbrace{\left(\int_V \mathbf{p} \right)}_{=0} \times \dot{\mathbf{r}}_{cm} + \int_V \mathbf{Rp} \times \dot{\mathbf{R}}\mathbf{p} \\
&= \int_V \mathbf{Rp} \times \dot{\mathbf{R}}\mathbf{p} \\
&= \int_V \widetilde{\mathbf{Rp}}\dot{\mathbf{R}}\mathbf{p}.
\end{aligned}
$$

We have to digress for a moment to figure out that $\widetilde{\mathbf{Rp}}$ term in the integral. The cross product is preserved under linear transformations; i.e., the transformation of the cross product of two vectors is equal to the cross product of each of the transformed vectors:

$$
\widetilde{\mathbf{As}}\mathbf{Av} = \mathbf{A}\left(\tilde{\mathbf{s}}\mathbf{v}\right),
$$
$$
\widetilde{\mathbf{As}}\mathbf{Av} - \mathbf{A}\left(\tilde{\mathbf{s}}\mathbf{v}\right) = 0,
$$
$$
\left(\widetilde{\mathbf{As}}\mathbf{A} - \mathbf{A}\tilde{\mathbf{s}}\right)\mathbf{v} = 0,
$$
$$
\widetilde{\mathbf{As}}\mathbf{A} - \mathbf{A}\tilde{\mathbf{s}} = 0,
$$

$$\widetilde{\mathbf{AsA}} = \mathbf{A\tilde{s}},$$

$$\widetilde{\mathbf{As}} = \mathbf{A\tilde{s}A}^{-1}.$$

Substituting $\widetilde{\mathbf{Rp}} = \mathbf{R\tilde{p}R}^{\mathrm{T}}$ into the equation for angular momentum, we get

$$\mathbf{H}_{\mathrm{cm}} = \int_V \widetilde{\mathbf{Rp}}\dot{\mathbf{R}}\mathbf{p}$$

$$= \int_V \mathbf{R\tilde{p}R}^{\mathrm{T}}\dot{\mathbf{R}}\mathbf{p}$$

$$= \int_V \mathbf{R\tilde{p}}\tilde{\omega}\mathbf{p}$$

$$= \int_V \mathbf{R\tilde{p}}\,(-\tilde{\mathbf{p}}\omega)$$

$$= \int_V \mathbf{R}\,(-\tilde{\mathbf{p}}\tilde{\mathbf{p}})\omega.$$

Because $\mathbf{R}$ and ω are independent of the variables of integration, we can move them both outside the integral:

$$\mathbf{H}_{\mathrm{cm}} = \mathbf{R}\left(\int_V -\tilde{\mathbf{p}}\tilde{\mathbf{p}}\right)\omega.$$

Let $\mathbf{I} = \int_V -\tilde{\mathbf{p}}\tilde{\mathbf{p}}$. $\mathbf{I}$ is called the inertia tensor. The integral is independent of the orientation and position of the rigid body with respect to the world frame, which is wonderful because it only needs to be evaluated once rather than every time the body moves.

Expanding out the matrix product $-\tilde{\mathbf{p}}\tilde{\mathbf{p}}$ term by term, we get

$$\mathbf{I} = \int_V (-\tilde{\mathbf{p}}\tilde{\mathbf{p}})$$

$$= \int_V \begin{bmatrix} 0 & z & -y \\ -z & 0 & x \\ y & -x & 0 \end{bmatrix} \begin{bmatrix} 0 & -z & y \\ z & 0 & -x \\ -y & x & 0 \end{bmatrix}$$

$$= \int_V \begin{bmatrix} y^2 + z^2 & -yx & -xz \\ -yx & x^2 + z^2 & -yz \\ -xz & -yz & x^2 + y^2 \end{bmatrix}$$

$$= \begin{bmatrix} \int_V y^2 + z^2 & \int_V -yx & \int_V -xz \\ \int_V -yx & \int_V x^2 + z^2 & \int_V -yz \\ \int_V -xz & \int_V -yz & \int_V x^2 + y^2 \end{bmatrix}. \tag{8.2}$$

Because **I** is symmetric it can be factored[6] into

$$\mathbf{I} = \mathbf{X}\Lambda\mathbf{X}^{\mathrm{T}}$$

$$= \begin{bmatrix} \mathbf{x}_1 & \mathbf{x}_2 & \mathbf{x}_3 \end{bmatrix} \begin{bmatrix} \lambda_1 & 0 & 0 \\ 0 & \lambda_2 & 0 \\ 0 & 0 & \lambda_3 \end{bmatrix} \begin{bmatrix} \mathbf{x}_1^{\mathrm{T}} \\ \mathbf{x}_2^{\mathrm{T}} \\ \mathbf{x}_3^{\mathrm{T}} \end{bmatrix},$$

where the $\mathbf{x}_i$ are the eigenvectors, and the λ_i the eigenvalues, of **I**. In this case only three numbers are needed to specify **I**. For simple shapes such as cylinders, rectangular prisms, etc., it is easy to choose a coordinate frame so that the inertia tensor integrals naturally result in a diagonal matrix.

Substituting $\mathbf{I} = \int_V -\tilde{\mathbf{p}}\tilde{\mathbf{p}}$ into the equation for angular momentum, we get

$$\mathbf{H}_{\mathrm{cm}} = \mathbf{R}\left(\int_V -\tilde{\mathbf{p}}\tilde{\mathbf{p}}\right)\omega$$

$$= \mathbf{R}\mathbf{I}\omega.$$

Torque is equal to the first derivative of the angular momentum:

$$\tau = \dot{\mathbf{H}}_{\mathrm{cm}}$$

$$= \frac{\mathrm{d}\left(\mathbf{R}\mathbf{I}\omega\right)}{\mathrm{d}t}.$$

8.3   Lagrangian Equations of Motion

If the inertia matrix is defined in the center of mass coordinate frame then we can separate the equations of motion into two parts: forces acting through the center of mass and torques defined relative to the center of mass [15]. Assuming we have a system of n rigid bodies with no kinematic constraints on their relative motion the Newtonian equation of motion look like this:

$$\sum_{i=1}^{n} m_i \ddot{\mathbf{r}}_{\mathrm{cm}_i}^{\mathrm{T}} = \sum_{i=1}^{n} \mathbf{F}_{\mathrm{ext}_i}^{\mathrm{T}}, \tag{8.3}$$

$$\sum_{i=1}^{n} \dot{\mathbf{H}}_{\mathrm{cm}_i}^{\mathrm{T}} = \sum_{i=1}^{n} \tau_{\mathrm{ext}_i}. \tag{8.4}$$

In the presence of kinematic constraints things become a little more complicated. We have two new types of forces: constraint forces and actuator forces.

---

[6]If your linear algebra is rusty, [36] is an excellent reference text.

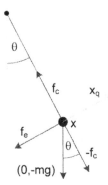

Figure 8.4. Constraint forces project to zero on the vector tangent to rigid-body motion.

Constraint forces hold the mechanical system together. Actuator forces arise from motors, pistons, etc. that are part of the mechanism; these are the forces we directly control to affect the motion of the mechanism. We will lump constraint and actuator forces into a single term, $\mathbf{F}_{\text{int}}$. We do not want to compute constraint forces if possible because this complicates things considerably. Fortunately, there is a simple way to reformulate the equations of motion so that all the constraint forces go to zero and can be ignored. To see how to do it, let us look more closely at the simple point-mass pendulum example shown in Figure 8.4. The point mass is constrained to move along the vector $\mathbf{x}_q = \frac{\partial x}{\partial q}$. The projection of the gravity force, $(0, -mg)$, on to $\mathbf{x}_q$ gives the only force, $\mathbf{f}_e = (0, -mg)^{\mathrm{T}} \mathbf{x}_q$, which has an effect on the motion of the point mass. The other forces, $-\mathbf{f}_c, \mathbf{f}_c$, exactly cancel, as they must if the point mass is to satisfy its kinematic constraints. Only forces which satisfy the kinematic constraints need be considered—all other forces can be ignored.

Let us modify Equation (8.3) to take into account kinematic constraints and internal forces. Constraints are accounted for by projecting all forces onto $\frac{\partial \mathbf{r}_{\text{cm}_i}}{\partial q_j}$. Constraint forces have zero projection on this vector, so they all vanish:[7]

$$\sum_{i=1}^{n} m_i \ddot{\mathbf{r}}_{\text{cm}_i}^{\mathrm{T}} \frac{\partial \mathbf{r}_{\text{cm}_i}}{\partial q_j} = \sum_{i=1}^{n} \left(\mathbf{F}_{\text{ext}_i}^{\mathrm{T}} + \mathbf{F}_{\text{int}_i}^{\mathrm{T}} \right) \frac{\partial \mathbf{r}_{\text{cm}_i}}{\partial q_j},$$

$$\sum_{i=1}^{n} \left(m_i \ddot{\mathbf{r}}_{\text{cm}_i}^{\mathrm{T}} - \mathbf{F}_{\text{ext}_i}^{\mathrm{T}} \right) \frac{\partial \mathbf{r}_{\text{cm}_i}}{\partial q_j} = \sum_{i=1}^{n} \mathbf{F}_{\text{int}_i}^{\mathrm{T}} \frac{\partial \mathbf{r}_{\text{cm}_i}}{\partial q_j},$$

[7]This is d'Alembert's principle of virtual work.

$$\sum_{i=1}^{n} (m_i \ddot{\mathbf{r}}_{\mathrm{cm}_i} - \mathbf{F}_{\mathrm{ext}_i})^{\mathrm{T}} \frac{\partial \mathbf{r}_{\mathrm{cm}_i}}{\partial q_j} = Q_{\mathbf{F}_j},$$

$$\sum_{i=1}^{n} \mathbf{a}_i^{\mathrm{T}} \frac{\partial \mathbf{r}_{\mathrm{cm}_i}}{\partial q_j} = Q_{\mathbf{F}_j}.$$

The quantity $Q_{\mathbf{F}_j}$ is called the generalized force associated with generalized coordinate q_j (due to forces—we will handle torques separately). What vector represents the tangent to the constraint manifold of the orientation of the rigid body? The differential change in orientation of rigid-body i due to generalized coordinate q_j is $\frac{\partial \mathbf{R}_i}{\partial q_j}$, but this partial derivative has nine terms and it is not a vector, so it is not clear how to project the torques onto it. We can use the same trick we used for computing angular velocity to compute a vector which represents the differential change in orientation due to q_j:

$$^b\omega_{q_j} = \left(\widetilde{\mathbf{R}_i^{\mathrm{T}} \frac{\partial \mathbf{R}_i}{\partial q_j}} \right).$$

Note that the above equation is expressed with respect to body frame. Since Equation (8.4) is expressed in the world coordinate, we want to transform its reference frame to the world frame:

$$\omega_{q_j} = \mathbf{R}_i \, ^b\omega_{q_j},$$

$$\widetilde{\omega_{q_j}} = \widetilde{\mathbf{R}_i \, ^b\omega_{q_j}},$$

$$= \mathbf{R}_i \, ^b\widetilde{\omega_{q_j}} \mathbf{R}_i^{\mathrm{T}},$$

$$= \mathbf{R}_i \left(\mathbf{R}_i^{\mathrm{T}} \frac{\partial \mathbf{R}_i}{\partial q_j} \right) \mathbf{R}_i^{\mathrm{T}},$$

$$= \frac{\partial \mathbf{R}_i}{\partial q_j} \mathbf{R}_i^{\mathrm{T}},$$

$$\omega_{q_j} = \widetilde{\frac{\partial \mathbf{R}_i}{\partial q_j} \mathbf{R}_i^{\mathrm{T}}}.$$

We project the torques onto this vector to eliminate constraint torques:

$$\sum_{i=1}^{n} \dot{\mathbf{H}}_{\mathrm{cm}_i}^{\mathrm{T}} \omega_{q_j} = \sum_{i=1}^{n} (\tau_{\mathrm{ext}_i} + \tau_{\mathrm{int}_i})^{\mathrm{T}} \omega_{q_j},$$

$$\sum_{i=1}^{n} \left(\dot{\mathbf{H}}_{\mathrm{cm}_i} - \tau_{\mathrm{ext}_i} \right)^{\mathrm{T}} \omega_{q_j} = \sum_{i=1}^{n} \tau_{\mathrm{int}_i}^{\mathrm{T}} \omega_{q_j},$$

$$\sum_{i=1}^{n} \mathbf{b}_i^{\mathrm{T}} \omega_{q_j} = Q_{\tau_j}.$$

The quantity Q_{T_j} is called the generalized force, due to torques, associated with generalized coordinate q_j. If we add the two generalized forces together, we get a single set of differential equations to represent the motion of the system:

$$Q_{\mathbf{F}_j} + Q_{T_j} = Q_j,$$

$$\sum_{i=1}^{n} \mathbf{a}_i^{\mathrm{T}} \frac{\partial \mathbf{r}_{\mathrm{cm}_i}}{\partial q_j} + \sum_{i=1}^{n} \mathbf{b}_i^{\mathrm{T}} \omega_{q_j} = Q_j,$$

$$\sum_{i=1}^{n} \left(\mathbf{a}_i^{\mathrm{T}} \frac{\partial \mathbf{r}_{\mathrm{cm}_i}}{\partial q_j} + \mathbf{b}_i^{\mathrm{T}} \omega_{q_j} \right) = Q_j.$$

This is compact and simple but not, it turns out, a computationally efficient form of the equations. Why the equations are inefficient and how they can be factored to make them more efficient is the subject of the next section.

8.3.1   Factoring the Equations of Motion

Let us look at the equations of motion more closely to understand how much computation we have to do in order to generate them. It is easier to understand what is going on if we consider the force and torque equations separately so let us start with the force equations:

$$\sum_{i=1}^{n} \mathbf{a}_i^{\mathrm{T}} \frac{\partial \mathbf{r}_{\mathrm{cm}_i}}{\partial q_j} = Q_{\mathbf{F}_j}.$$

Recalling that

$$\mathbf{r}_{\mathrm{cm}_i} = \mathbf{W}_i \mathbf{t}_{\mathrm{cm}_i},$$

we can make the substitution

$$\mathbf{a}_i^{\mathrm{T}} \frac{\partial \mathbf{r}_{\mathrm{cm}_i}}{\partial q_j} = \mathbf{a}_i^{\mathrm{T}} \frac{\partial \mathbf{W}_i \mathbf{t}_{\mathrm{cm}_i}}{\partial q_j}$$

$$= \mathbf{a}_i^{\mathrm{T}} \frac{\partial \mathbf{W}_i}{\partial q_j} \mathbf{t}_{\mathrm{cm}_i},$$

which gives us the set of equations for $Q_{\mathbf{F}_j}$

$$\sum_{i=1}^{i=n} \mathbf{a}_i^{\mathrm{T}} \frac{\partial \mathbf{W}_i}{\partial q_j} \mathbf{t}_{\mathrm{cm}_i} = Q_{\mathbf{F}_j}.$$

For a three-DOF system parameterized by generalized coordinates q_0, q_1, q_2 we get this system of equations:

$$\mathbf{a}_0^T \frac{\partial \mathbf{W}_0}{\partial q_0} \mathbf{t}_{\mathrm{cm}_0} + \mathbf{a}_1^T \frac{\partial \mathbf{W}_1}{\partial q_0} \mathbf{t}_{\mathrm{cm}_1} + \mathbf{a}_2^T \frac{\partial \mathbf{W}_2}{\partial q_0} \mathbf{t}_{\mathrm{cm}_2} = Q_{\mathbf{F}_0},$$

$$\mathbf{a}_0^T \frac{\partial \mathbf{W}_0}{\partial q_1} \mathbf{t}_{\mathrm{cm}_0} + \mathbf{a}_1^T \frac{\partial \mathbf{W}_1}{\partial q_1} \mathbf{t}_{\mathrm{cm}_1} + \mathbf{a}_2^T \frac{\partial \mathbf{W}_2}{\partial q_1} \mathbf{t}_{\mathrm{cm}_2} = Q_{\mathbf{F}_1},$$

$$\mathbf{a}_0^T \frac{\partial \mathbf{W}_0}{\partial q_2} \mathbf{t}_{\mathrm{cm}_0} + \mathbf{a}_1^T \frac{\partial \mathbf{W}_1}{\partial q_2} \mathbf{t}_{\mathrm{cm}_1} + \mathbf{a}_2^T \frac{\partial \mathbf{W}_2}{\partial q_2} \mathbf{t}_{\mathrm{cm}_2} = Q_{\mathbf{F}_2}.$$

We have hit a snag here: there are only three generalized coordinates, and three generalized forces, but we have to compute nine terms of the form

$$\mathbf{a}_i^T \frac{\partial \mathbf{W}_i}{\partial q_j} \mathbf{t}_{\mathrm{cm}_i}$$

to generate the equations of motion. That is n^2 terms for an n-coordinate system. Fortunately, there is a lot of redundancy in these equations; with a little algebra we can factor them so that computation grows as $O(n)$ rather than $O(n^2)$.

Let us start with two observations. First, because[8]

$$\frac{\partial \mathbf{A}_i}{\partial q_j} = 0, \quad i \neq j,$$

we can rewrite $\frac{\partial \mathbf{W}_i}{\partial q_j}$ as

$$\frac{\partial \mathbf{W}_i}{\partial q_j} = \mathbf{A}_1 \mathbf{A}_2 \ldots \mathbf{A}_{j-1} \frac{\partial \mathbf{A}_j}{\partial q_j} \mathbf{A}_{j+1} \ldots \mathbf{A}_i$$

$$= \mathbf{W}_{j-1} \frac{\partial \mathbf{A}_j}{\partial q_j} \mathbf{A}_{j+1} \ldots \mathbf{A}_i.$$

Second,

$$\frac{\partial \mathbf{W}_j}{\partial q_k} = 0 \text{ for } k \geq j,$$

where the expression $k \geq j$ means that generalized coordinate q_k is associated with a node in the transformation hierarchy that is further toward the leaves of the tree than transformation $\mathbf{W}_j$.

For example, in Figure 8.5,

$$\frac{\partial \mathbf{W}_0}{\partial q_1} = 0, \quad \frac{\partial \mathbf{W}_0}{\partial q_2} = 0,$$

---

[8]We are ignoring a technical detail that would unnecessarily complicate the equations at this point: the matrix $\mathbf{A}_j$ may be a function of up to six generalized coordinates q_k so the indices of the matrix $\mathbf{A}_j$ and the generalized coordinate may not be the same. This does not materially change the form of the equations or the factorization.

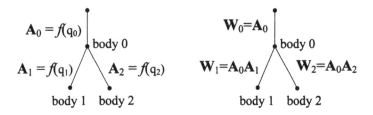

Figure 8.5. Ordering of nodes in transformation hierarchy.

because $\mathbf{W}_0$ is not a function of either q_1 or q_2, both of which affect only transformations further toward the leaves of the tree.

Applying these two observations to our equations of motion we get the slightly simpler set of expressions

$$\mathbf{a}_0^T \frac{\partial \mathbf{A}_0}{\partial q_0} \mathbf{t}_{cm_0} + \mathbf{a}_1^T \frac{\partial \mathbf{A}_0}{\partial q_0} \mathbf{A}_1 \mathbf{t}_{cm_1} + \mathbf{a}_2^T \frac{\partial \mathbf{A}_0}{\partial q_0} \mathbf{A}_1 \mathbf{A}_2 \mathbf{t}_{cm_2} = Q_{F_0},$$

$$\mathbf{a}_1^T \mathbf{W}_0 \frac{\partial \mathbf{A}_1}{\partial q_1} \mathbf{t}_{cm_1} + \mathbf{a}_2^T \mathbf{W}_0 \frac{\partial \mathbf{A}_1}{\partial q_1} \mathbf{A}_2 \mathbf{t}_{cm_2} = Q_{F_1},$$

$$\mathbf{a}_2^T \mathbf{W}_1 \frac{\partial \mathbf{A}_2}{\partial q_2} \mathbf{t}_{cm_2} = Q_{F_2}.$$

It still takes $O\left(n^2\right)$ time to generate these equations; but, we could factor out many common terms if we could move the $\mathbf{a}_i^T$ terms out from the left to the right-hand side.

The products

$$\mathbf{a}_i^T \mathbf{W}_{i-1} \frac{\partial \mathbf{A}_i}{\partial q_j} \mathbf{t}_{cm_i}$$

are of the form $\mathbf{x}^T \mathbf{y}$, where

$$\mathbf{x}^T = \mathbf{a}_i^T \text{ and } \mathbf{y} = \mathbf{W}_{i-1} \frac{\partial \mathbf{A}_i}{\partial q_j} \mathbf{t}_{cm_i}.$$

We can use the identity

$$tr\left(\mathbf{y}\mathbf{x}^T\right) = tr \begin{bmatrix} y_1 \\ y_2 \\ y_3 \end{bmatrix} \begin{bmatrix} x_1 & x_2 & x_3 \end{bmatrix}$$

$$= tr \begin{bmatrix} x_1 y_1 & & \\ & x_2 y_2 & \\ & & x_3 y_3 \end{bmatrix}$$

$$= \mathbf{x}^T \mathbf{y}$$

to rewrite these expressions so that the $\mathbf{a}_i^T$ term is on the right instead of the left:

$$\mathbf{a}_i^T \frac{\partial \mathbf{W}_i}{\partial q_j} \mathbf{t}_{cm_i} = tr\left(\frac{\partial \mathbf{W}_i}{\partial q_j} \mathbf{t}_{cm_i} \mathbf{a}_i^T\right)$$

$$= tr\left(\mathbf{W}_{j-1} \frac{\partial \mathbf{A}_j}{\partial q_j} \mathbf{A}_{j+1} \ldots \mathbf{A}_i \mathbf{t}_{cm_i} \mathbf{a}_i^T\right).$$

When we apply this to our three equations of motion the common terms are now in a form where they can be factored out:

$$tr\left(\frac{\partial \mathbf{A}_0}{\partial q_0} \mathbf{t}_{cm_0} \mathbf{a}_0^T + \frac{\partial \mathbf{A}_0}{\partial q_0} \mathbf{A}_1 \mathbf{t}_{cm_1} \mathbf{a}_1^T + \frac{\partial \mathbf{A}_0}{\partial q_0} \mathbf{A}_1 \mathbf{A}_2 \mathbf{t}_{cm_2} \mathbf{a}_2^T\right) = Q_{\mathbf{F}_0},$$

$$tr\left(\mathbf{W}_0 \frac{\partial \mathbf{A}_1}{\partial q_1} \mathbf{t}_{cm_1} \mathbf{a}_1^T + \mathbf{W}_0 \frac{\partial \mathbf{A}_1}{\partial q_1} \mathbf{A}_2 \mathbf{t}_{cm_2} \mathbf{a}_2^T\right) = Q_{\mathbf{F}_1},$$

$$tr\left(\mathbf{W}_1 \frac{\partial \mathbf{A}_2}{\partial q_2} \mathbf{t}_{cm_2} \mathbf{a}_2^T\right) = Q_{\mathbf{F}_2}.$$

If we factor out all common terms we end up with the following set of equations which, because of common subexpression elimination in D*, take $O(n)$ time to generate:

$$tr\left(\frac{\partial \mathbf{A}_0}{\partial q_0}\left(\mathbf{t}_{cm_0} \mathbf{a}_0^T + \mathbf{A}_1\left(\mathbf{t}_{cm_1} \mathbf{a}_1^T + \mathbf{A}_2 \mathbf{t}_{cm_2} \mathbf{a}_2^T\right)\right)\right) = Q_{\mathbf{F}_0},$$

$$tr\left(\mathbf{W}_0 \frac{\partial \mathbf{A}_1}{\partial q_1}\left(\mathbf{t}_{cm_1} \mathbf{a}_1^T + \mathbf{A}_2 \mathbf{t}_{cm_2} \mathbf{a}_2^T\right)\right) = Q_{\mathbf{F}_1},$$

$$tr\left(\mathbf{W}_1 \frac{\partial \mathbf{A}_2}{\partial q_2}\left(\mathbf{t}_{cm_2} \mathbf{a}_2^T\right)\right) = Q_{\mathbf{F}_2}.$$

Now let us look at the torque equations:

$$Q_{T_j} - \sum_{i=1}^{n} \omega_{q_j}^T \mathbf{b}_i$$

$$= \sum_{i=1}^{n} \widetilde{\frac{\partial \mathbf{R}_i}{\partial q_j} \mathbf{R}_i^T}^T \mathbf{b}_i.$$

We have a slightly different problem here than we had with the force equations. We want to move the $\frac{\partial \mathbf{R}_i}{\partial q_j}$ term to the left-hand side of the equation, because then the common terms will factor out just as they did for the force equations. But we cannot use the trick of taking the trace because $\frac{\partial \mathbf{R}_i}{\partial q_j}$ is inside a tilde conversion. Fortunately there is a simple identity that allows us to get the $\frac{\partial \mathbf{R}_i}{\partial q_j}$ term out from under the tilde conversion:

$$tr\left(\tilde{\mathbf{a}}\tilde{\mathbf{b}}\right) = tr\left\{\begin{bmatrix} 0 & -a_z & a_y \\ a_z & 0 & -a_x \\ -a_y & a_x & 0 \end{bmatrix}\begin{bmatrix} 0 & -b_z & b_y \\ b_z & 0 & -b_x \\ -b_y & b_x & 0 \end{bmatrix}\right\}$$

$$= tr\begin{bmatrix} -a_zb_z - a_yb_y & & \\ & -a_zb_z - a_xb_x & \\ & & -a_yb_y - a_xb_x \end{bmatrix}$$

$$= -2\left(a_xb_x + a_yb_y + a_zb_z\right)$$

$$= -2\mathbf{a}^T\mathbf{b},$$

$$-0.5tr\left(\tilde{\mathbf{a}}\tilde{\mathbf{b}}\right) = \mathbf{a}^T\mathbf{b}.$$

Now we can rewrite the $\omega_{q_j}^T\mathbf{b}_i$ terms,

$$\omega_{q_j}^T\mathbf{b}_i = -0.5tr\left(\tilde{\omega}_{q_j}\tilde{\mathbf{b}}_i\right)$$

$$= tr\left(-\frac{1}{2}\frac{\partial\mathbf{R}_i}{\partial q_j}\mathbf{R}_i^T\tilde{\mathbf{b}}_i\right),$$

which allows us to rewrite the torque equations with $\frac{\partial\mathbf{R}_i}{\partial q_j}$ on the left-hand side, where everything will factor nicely:

$$Q_{T_j} = \sum_{i=1}^{n}\omega_{q_j}^T\mathbf{b}_i$$

$$= \sum_{i=1}^{n}tr\left(-\frac{1}{2}\frac{\partial\mathbf{R}_i}{\partial q_j}\mathbf{R}_i^T\tilde{\mathbf{b}}_i\right)$$

$$= tr\left\{\sum_{i=1}^{n}\frac{\partial\mathbf{R}_i}{\partial q_j}\left(-\frac{1}{2}\mathbf{R}_i^T\tilde{\mathbf{b}}_i\right)\right\}.$$

There is just one more minor technical problem. The force equations used the full transformation $\mathbf{W}_i$ but the torque equations just use the rotation part of this matrix. If we define two new matrices, $\mathbf{U}_i$, $\mathbf{B}_i$,

$$\mathbf{U}_i = \begin{bmatrix} \mathbf{R}_i & 0 \\ 0 & 0 \end{bmatrix},$$

$$\mathbf{B}_i = \begin{bmatrix} \tilde{\mathbf{b}}_i & 0 \\ 0 & 0 \end{bmatrix},$$

then we can rewrite the torque equations using the full transformation

$$\mathbf{W}_i = \begin{bmatrix} \mathbf{R}_i & \mathbf{t}_i \\ \mathbf{0} & 0 \end{bmatrix},$$

$$\frac{\partial \mathbf{W}_i}{\partial q_j} \left(\mathbf{U}_i^{\mathrm{T}} \mathbf{B}_i \right) = \begin{bmatrix} \frac{\partial \mathbf{R}_i}{\partial q_j} & \frac{\partial \mathbf{t}_i}{\partial q_j} \\ \mathbf{0} & 0 \end{bmatrix} \left(\begin{bmatrix} \mathbf{R}_i & \mathbf{0} \\ \mathbf{0} & 0 \end{bmatrix} \begin{bmatrix} \tilde{\mathbf{b}}_i & \mathbf{0} \\ \mathbf{0} & 0 \end{bmatrix} \right)$$

$$= \frac{\partial \mathbf{R}_i}{\partial q_j} \left(\mathbf{R}_i^{\mathrm{T}} \tilde{\mathbf{b}}_i \right).$$

Using the same three-DOF system that we used for the force equations, we get the three torque equations

$$tr \left\{ \frac{\partial \mathbf{W}_0}{\partial q_0} \left(-\frac{1}{2} \mathbf{U}_0^{\mathrm{T}} \mathbf{B}_0 \right) + \frac{\partial \mathbf{W}_1}{\partial q_0} \left(-\frac{1}{2} \mathbf{U}_1^{\mathrm{T}} \mathbf{B}_1 \right) \right.$$
$$\left. + \frac{\partial \mathbf{W}_2}{\partial q_0} \left(-\frac{1}{2} \mathbf{U}_2^{\mathrm{T}} \mathbf{B}_2 \right) \right\} = Q_{\tau_0},$$

$$tr \left\{ \frac{\partial \mathbf{W}_0}{\partial q_1} \left(-\frac{1}{2} \mathbf{U}_0^{\mathrm{T}} \mathbf{B}_0 \right) + \frac{\partial \mathbf{W}_1}{\partial q_1} \left(-\frac{1}{2} \mathbf{U}_1^{\mathrm{T}} \mathbf{B}_1 \right) \right.$$
$$\left. + \frac{\partial \mathbf{W}_2}{\partial q_1} \left(-\frac{1}{2} \mathbf{U}_2^{\mathrm{T}} \mathbf{B}_2 \right) \right\} = Q_{\tau_1},$$

$$tr \left\{ \frac{\partial \mathbf{W}_0}{\partial q_2} \left(-\frac{1}{2} \mathbf{U}_0^{\mathrm{T}} \mathbf{B}_0 \right) + \frac{\partial \mathbf{W}_1}{\partial q_2} \left(-\frac{1}{2} \mathbf{U}_1^{\mathrm{T}} \mathbf{B}_1 \right) \right.$$
$$\left. + \frac{\partial \mathbf{W}_2}{\partial q_2} \left(-\frac{1}{2} \mathbf{U}_2^{\mathrm{T}} \mathbf{B}_2 \right) \right\} = Q_{\tau_2}.$$

Now we can apply the same observations that were used for the force equations

$$\frac{\partial \mathbf{W}_i}{\partial q_j} = \mathbf{W}_{j-1} \frac{\partial \mathbf{A}_j}{\partial q_j} \mathbf{A}_{j+1} \ldots \mathbf{A}_i,$$

$$\frac{\partial \mathbf{W}_j}{\partial q_k} = 0 \text{ for } k \geq j,$$

to get the equations first into an upper-triangular form,

$$tr \left\{ \frac{\partial \mathbf{A}_0}{\partial q_0} \left(-\frac{1}{2} \mathbf{U}_0^{\mathrm{T}} \mathbf{B}_0 \right) \right.$$
$$\left. + \frac{\partial \mathbf{A}_0}{\partial q_0} \mathbf{A}_1 \left(-\frac{1}{2} \mathbf{U}_1^{\mathrm{T}} \mathbf{B}_1 \right) + \frac{\partial \mathbf{A}_0}{\partial q_0} \mathbf{A}_1 \mathbf{A}_2 \left(-\frac{1}{2} \mathbf{U}_2^{\mathrm{T}} \mathbf{B}_2 \right) \right\} = Q_{\tau_0},$$

$$tr \left\{ \mathbf{W}_0 \frac{\partial \mathbf{A}_1}{\partial q_1} \left(-\frac{1}{2} \mathbf{U}_1^{\mathrm{T}} \mathbf{B}_1 \right) + \mathbf{W}_0 \frac{\partial \mathbf{A}_1}{\partial q_1} \mathbf{A}_2 \left(-\frac{1}{2} \mathbf{U}_2^{\mathrm{T}} \mathbf{B}_2 \right) \right\} = Q_{\tau_1},$$

$$tr \left\{ \mathbf{W}_1 \frac{\partial \mathbf{A}_2}{\partial q_2} \left(-\frac{1}{2} \mathbf{U}_2^{\mathrm{T}} \mathbf{B}_2 \right) \right\} = Q_{\tau_2},$$

and then to factor out common terms,

$$tr\left\{\frac{\partial \mathbf{A}_0}{\partial q_0}\left(\left(-\frac{1}{2}\mathbf{U}_0^T\mathbf{B}_0\right)\right.\right.$$
$$\left.\left.+\mathbf{A}_1\left(-\frac{1}{2}\mathbf{U}_1^T\mathbf{B}_1 + \mathbf{A}_2\left(-\frac{1}{2}\mathbf{U}_2^T\mathbf{B}_2\right)\right)\right)\right\} = Q_{\tau_0},$$

$$tr\left\{\mathbf{W}_0\frac{\partial \mathbf{A}_1}{\partial q_1}\left(-\frac{1}{2}\mathbf{U}_1^T\mathbf{B}_1 + \mathbf{A}_2\left(-\frac{1}{2}\mathbf{U}_2^T\mathbf{B}_2\right)\right)\right\} = Q_{\tau_1},$$

$$tr\left\{\mathbf{W}_1\frac{\partial \mathbf{A}_2}{\partial q_2}\left(-\frac{1}{2}\mathbf{U}_2^T\mathbf{B}_2\right)\right\} = Q_{\tau_2}.$$

Because they share common factors we can combine the generalized force and torque equations for each of the generalized forces, Q_0, Q_1, Q_2:

$$tr\left\{\frac{\partial \mathbf{A}_0}{\partial q_0}\left(\left(-\frac{1}{2}\mathbf{U}_0^T\mathbf{B}_0\right)\right.\right.$$
$$\left.\left.+\mathbf{A}_1\left(-\frac{1}{2}\mathbf{U}_1^T\mathbf{B}_1 + \mathbf{A}_2\left(-\frac{1}{2}\mathbf{U}_2^T\mathbf{B}_2\right)\right)\right)\right\} = Q_{\tau_0},$$

$$tr\left\{\frac{\partial \mathbf{A}_0}{\partial q_0}\left(\mathbf{t}_{cm_0}\mathbf{a}_0^T + \mathbf{A}_1\left(\mathbf{t}_{cm_1}\mathbf{a}_1^T + \mathbf{A}_2\mathbf{t}_{cm_2}\mathbf{a}_2^T\right)\right)\right\} = Q_{\mathbf{F}_0},$$

$$tr\left\{\frac{\partial \mathbf{A}_0}{\partial q_0}\left(\mathbf{t}_{cm_0}\mathbf{a}_0^T - \frac{1}{2}\mathbf{U}_0^T\mathbf{B}_0\right.\right.$$
$$\left.\left.+\mathbf{A}_1\left(\mathbf{t}_{cm_1}\mathbf{a}_1^T - \frac{1}{2}\mathbf{U}_1^T\mathbf{B}_1 + \mathbf{A}_2\left(\mathbf{t}_{cm_2}\mathbf{a}_2^T - \frac{1}{2}\mathbf{U}_2^T\mathbf{B}_2\right)\right)\right)\right\} = Q_{\tau_0} + Q_{\mathbf{F}_0}$$

$$= Q_0;$$

$$tr\left\{\mathbf{W}_0\frac{\partial \mathbf{A}_1}{\partial q_1}\left(-\frac{1}{2}\mathbf{U}_1^T\mathbf{B}_1 + \mathbf{A}_2\left(-\frac{1}{2}\mathbf{U}_2^T\mathbf{B}_2\right)\right)\right\} = Q_{\tau_1},$$

$$tr\left\{\mathbf{W}_0\frac{\partial \mathbf{A}_1}{\partial q_1}\left(\mathbf{t}_{cm_1}\mathbf{a}_1^T + \mathbf{A}_2\mathbf{t}_{cm_2}\mathbf{a}_2^T\right)\right\} = Q_{\mathbf{F}_1},$$

$$tr\left\{\mathbf{W}_0\frac{\partial \mathbf{A}_1}{\partial q_1}\left(\mathbf{t}_{cm_1}\mathbf{a}_1^T - \frac{1}{2}\mathbf{U}_1^T\mathbf{B}_1\right.\right.$$
$$\left.\left.+\mathbf{A}_2\left(\mathbf{t}_{cm_2}\mathbf{a}_2^T - \frac{1}{2}\mathbf{U}_2^T\mathbf{B}_2\right)\right)\right\} = Q_{\tau_1} + Q_{\mathbf{F}_1}$$

$$= Q_1;$$

$$tr\left\{\mathbf{W}_1\frac{\partial\mathbf{A}_2}{\partial q_2}\left(-\frac{1}{2}\mathbf{U}_2^T\mathbf{B}_2\right)\right\} = Q_{\tau_2},$$

$$tr\left(\mathbf{W}_1\frac{\partial\mathbf{A}_2}{\partial q_2}\left(\mathbf{t}_{\mathrm{cm}_2}\mathbf{a}_2^T\right)\right) = Q_{F_2},$$

$$tr\left\{\mathbf{W}_1\frac{\partial\mathbf{A}_2}{\partial q_2}\left(\mathbf{t}_{\mathrm{cm}_2}\mathbf{a}_2^T - \frac{1}{2}\mathbf{U}_2^T\mathbf{B}_2\right)\right\} = Q_{\tau_2} + Q_{F_2}$$

$$= Q_2.$$

When we put all the equations together we see the simple pattern

$$tr\left\{\frac{\partial\mathbf{A}_0}{\partial q_0}\left(\mathbf{t}_{\mathrm{cm}_0}\mathbf{a}_0^T - \frac{1}{2}\mathbf{U}_0^T\mathbf{B}_0\right.\right.$$

$$\left.\left.+\mathbf{A}_1\left(\mathbf{t}_{\mathrm{cm}_1}\mathbf{a}_1^T - \frac{1}{2}\mathbf{U}_1^T\mathbf{B}_1 + \mathbf{A}_2\left(\mathbf{t}_{\mathrm{cm}_2}\mathbf{a}_2^T - \frac{1}{2}\mathbf{U}_2^T\mathbf{B}_2\right)\right)\right)\right\} = Q_0,$$

$$tr\left\{\mathbf{W}_0\frac{\partial\mathbf{A}_1}{\partial q_1}\left(\mathbf{t}_{\mathrm{cm}_1}\mathbf{a}_1^T - \frac{1}{2}\mathbf{U}_1^T\mathbf{B}_1 + \mathbf{A}_2\left(\mathbf{t}_{\mathrm{cm}_2}\mathbf{a}_2^T - \frac{1}{2}\mathbf{U}_2^T\mathbf{B}_2\right)\right)\right\} = Q_1,$$

$$tr\left\{\mathbf{W}_1\frac{\partial\mathbf{A}_2}{\partial q_2}\left(\mathbf{t}_{\mathrm{cm}_2}\mathbf{a}_2^T - \frac{1}{2}\mathbf{U}_2^T\mathbf{B}_2\right)\right\} = Q_2,$$

from which the general formula follows directly:

$$tr\left\{\mathbf{W}_{j-1}\frac{\partial\mathbf{A}_j}{\partial q_j}\left(\mathbf{t}_{\mathrm{cm}_j}\mathbf{a}_j^T - \frac{1}{2}\mathbf{U}_j^T\mathbf{B}_j + \ldots\ldots\mathbf{A}_{n-1}\right.\right.$$

$$\left.\left.\left(\mathbf{t}_{\mathrm{cm}_{n-1}}\mathbf{a}_{n-1}^T - \frac{1}{2}\mathbf{U}_{n-1}^T\mathbf{B}_{n-1} + \mathbf{A}_n\left(\mathbf{t}_{\mathrm{cm}_n}\mathbf{a}_n^T - \frac{1}{2}\mathbf{U}_n^T\mathbf{B}_n\right)\right)\right)\right\} = Q_j.$$

$$(8.5)$$

8.4   Tree Structures

In Section 8.1 we said our mechanical systems could be tree structured, but Equation (8.5) is for a linear chain of links, not a tree. In this section we will generalize the equations to handle tree structured systems.

That was a lot of work to get this one equation but as you will see in the next section this is everything we need to do dynamics simulations.

8.5   Dynamics Applications

There are several ways to use the equations of motion. If you know the motion you want then you can use the equations of motion to find the generalized forces to apply in order to get that motion. This is the *inverse* *dynamics* problem. If you know only the forces applied to your system and you want to compute the motion of the system over time, using an ODE numerical integration program, then you have to solve the *forward dynamics* problem. If you know neither, but instead have an objective function to minimized and a set of constraints to be satisfied then you have to solve the optimal control problem.[9] The next three sections describe each of these problems and show how D* can be used to solve them.

8.5.1 Inverse Dynamics

If you know the motion you want then you can use the equations of motion to find the generalized forces to apply in order to get that motion. This is the *inverse dynamics* problem. For example, in industrial robotics applications it frequently happens that you know the motion required of a robot arm, say to pick an object off a conveyor belt and move it to a box, but you have no idea what joint torques would be required to accomplish this movement. Since the only way you can move the robot arm is by specifying the torques to be generated by the motors at each joint you must somehow compute the torques.

More than 60 research papers[10] have been published on the topic of solving the inverse dynamics problem for robot manipulators. From the timeline in Figure 8.6 you can see that more than a decade elapsed before the first $O(n)$ solution was found and two decades passed before the most efficient $O(n)$ solutions were developed [12].D* makes the computation of inverse dynamics very simple.

Given the motion specification, $\mathbf{q}(t)$, you can use the equations of motion

$$tr\left\{ \mathbf{W}_{j-1} \frac{\partial \mathbf{A}_j}{\partial q_j} \left(\mathbf{t}_{\mathrm{cm}_j} \mathbf{a}_j^{\mathrm{T}} - \frac{1}{2}\mathbf{U}_j^{\mathrm{T}}\mathbf{B}_j + \ldots \mathbf{A}_{n-1} \right. \right.$$
$$\left. \left. \left(\mathbf{t}_{\mathrm{cm}_{n-1}} \mathbf{a}_{n-1}^{\mathrm{T}} - \frac{1}{2}\mathbf{U}_{n-1}^{\mathrm{T}}\mathbf{B}_{n-1} + \mathbf{A}_n \left(\mathbf{t}_{\mathrm{cm}_n} \mathbf{a}_n^{\mathrm{T}} - \frac{1}{2}\mathbf{U}_n^{\mathrm{T}}\mathbf{B}_n \right) \right) \right) \right\} = Q_j,$$

$$\mathbf{U}_i = \left[\begin{array}{cc} \mathbf{R}_i & 0 \\ 0 & 0 \end{array} \right], \qquad \mathbf{B}_i = \left[\begin{array}{cc} \tilde{\mathbf{b}}_i & 0 \\ 0 & 0 \end{array} \right],$$

$$\mathbf{a}_i = m_i \ddot{\mathbf{r}}_{\mathrm{cm}_i} - \mathbf{F}_{\mathrm{ext}_i},$$
$$\mathbf{b}_i = \dot{\mathbf{H}}_{\mathrm{cm}_i} - \tau_{\mathrm{ext}_i},$$
$$\mathbf{H}_{\mathrm{cm}_i} = \mathbf{R}_i \mathbf{I}_i \omega_i,$$

---

[9]Known as space-time optimization in the computer graphics literature.
[10]See Chapter 5 of [3] for an extensive bibliography.

History of inverse dynamics algorithms

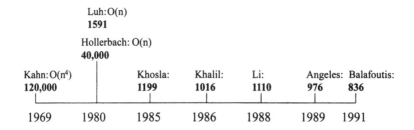

Roughly 60 papers published on this topic

Bold numbers = number of multiplications/additions

Figure 8.6. Solving the inverse dynamics problem was surprisingly difficult. The first $O(n^4)$ algorithm was published in 1969 but it took an additional 22 years for efficient $O(n)$ algorithms to appear.

to compute the joint torques that will make the arm move the way you want it to. Q_j is a function of $\mathbf{q}(t)$, $\dot{\mathbf{q}}(t)$, and $\ddot{\mathbf{q}}(t)$, all of which you can compute from your motion specification. Computing the joint torques will take time linear in the number of generalized coordinates of the system. For now, do not worry about the details of setting up the equations—we will do several detailed examples in Chapter 5.

It is interesting to compare D^* to one of the best published linear recursive inverse dynamics algorithms [3]. The comparison is complicated by the fact that no single number will suffice for describing the relative performance of D^*. This is because the Balafoutis algorithm computation is independent of the number of zero and one elements of the inertia matrices, $\mathbf{I}_i$, and the vectors $\mathbf{r}_i$ to the center of mass of link i but the D^* derivative, because of symbolic simplification, *will* depend on these values. There are an extremely large number of possible ways to insert zero and one elements in the $\mathbf{I}_i, \mathbf{r}_i$, each leading to a different computational cost. We have tried to bracket the range of these costs by choosing values for $\mathbf{I}_i, \mathbf{r}_i$ that we believe are close to the best and worst cases for D^*.

For example, in Table 8.1 we see the D^* derivative has only 1.5% more computation[11] than the Balafoutis algorithm when all joint axes are parallel and the inertia matrices have all nonzero elements. But if the inertia matrices are diagonal the D^* derivative is approximately 30% faster. Sim-

---

[11]If we assume multiplication and addition take the same number of clock cycles.

Operation	$\pm$	$\times$	sin	cos
Balafoutis	386	450	6	6
D* parallel axes (**I**, **r** full)	416	433	6	6
Ratio	*.93*	*1.04*	*1*	*1*
D* parallel axes (**I** diagonal, **r** sparse)	305	350	6	6
Ratio	*1.3*	*1.3*	*1*	*1*
D* perp. axes (**I**, **r** full)	587	546	6	6
Ratio	*.66*	*.82*	*1*	*1*
D* perp. axes (**I** diagonal, **r** sparse)	449	457	6	6
Ratio	*.86*	*.98*	*1*	*1*

Table 8.1. Balafoutis recursive inverse dynamics vs. D*, $n = 6$: For all joint axes parallel, all $\mathbf{I}_i$ diagonal, and each $\mathbf{r}_i$ having only one nonzero element, D* is approximately 30% faster than the $O(n)$ Balafoutis algorithm (see text), which is among the most efficient manually derived recursive inverse dynamics algorithms. For all axes perpendicular, each $\mathbf{I}_i, \mathbf{r}_i$ all nonzero, D* is 74% as fast. These two extremes are probably close to the best and worst cases, respectively, for D*.

ilarly, for all axes perpendicular and $\mathbf{I}_i$ all nonzero, D* is 74% as fast, but for all $\mathbf{I}_i$ diagonal, D* is 92% as fast.

This is a surprisingly good result because evaluating the dynamics equations in the most straightforward way has computational complexity $O(n^4)$, where n is the number of links in the manipulator. For a six-DOF manipulator this formulation requires roughly 120,000 multiplications/additions [3]. D* has eliminated virtually all of the redundant computation in spite of the fact that the D* program uses 4×4 homogeneous transformations, an inefficient, but simple, way to represent rotation. By contrast, the best manually derived inverse dynamics algorithms use more complex specialized representations for transformation matrices.[12]

8.5.2   Forward Dynamics

If you know only the forces applied to your system and you want to compute the motion of the system over time, using an ODE numerical integration program, then you have to solve the *forward dynamics* problem. The ODE software needs the equations to be manipulated into the form

$$\ddot{q}_0 = f_0(\mathbf{q}, \dot{\mathbf{q}}) + a_0 Q_0,$$

$$\vdots$$

$$\ddot{q}_n = f_n(\mathbf{q}, \dot{\mathbf{q}}) + a_n Q_n,$$

---

[12]The Balafoutis algorithm, for example, uses a Cartesian tensor representation for which the author provides 80 pages of background mathematics.

```
nd: node to find coefficient of
lc: true if left child graph of this contains nd
rc: true if right child graph of this contains nd

coeff(function nd)
  if this is leaf return this
  else
      foreach (node c in this.children) c.coeff(nd)
      if(this.type not one of {+,-,*,/}) ERROR


      if (this.is '*' && lc && rc) ERROR
      if (this.is '/' && rc) ERROR


      if (!(this.is '+' || this.is '-')) return this
  else if (lc && !right) return this.leftchild
  else if (rc && !lc) return this.rightchild
      else return this
```

Listing 8.1. Coefficient algorithm.

but our equations have the form

$$f_1(\mathbf{q}, \dot{\mathbf{q}}, \ddot{\mathbf{q}}) = Q_0,$$

$$\vdots$$

$$f_n(\mathbf{q}, \dot{\mathbf{q}}, \ddot{\mathbf{q}}) = Q_n,$$

where $f_i(\mathbf{q}, \dot{\mathbf{q}}, \ddot{\mathbf{q}})$ is a complicated mess. Fortunately, D* has two functions, coefficent and substitute, which make it trivial to reorganize these equations into a form that can be easily solved. Listing 8.1 shows the algorithm for the coefficient function.

Assume we have a D* function, fi, which computes $f_i(\mathbf{q}, \dot{\mathbf{q}}, \ddot{\mathbf{q}})$, and a D* variable, qiddt, which corresponds to $\ddot{q}_i$. Then fi.coefficient(qiddt) returns the symbolic expression which represents the coefficient of $\ddot{q}_i$. If we call this function for every $\ddot{q}_i$ in each f_i, we end up with a set of equations that look like this:

$$c_{00}\ddot{q}_0 + c_{01}\ddot{q}_1 \dots c_{0n}\ddot{q}_n + g_0(\mathbf{q}, \dot{\mathbf{q}}) = Q_0,$$

$$\vdots$$

$$c_{n0}\ddot{q}_0 + c_{n1}\ddot{q}_1 \dots c_{nn}\ddot{q}_n + g_n(\mathbf{q}, \dot{\mathbf{q}}) = Q_n,$$

The $g_i(\mathbf{q}, \dot{\mathbf{q}})$ are easily computed by calling
fi.substitute(new[]{q0ddt,...qnddt}, new[]{0,...,0})

This will substitute zero for all the $\ddot{q}_i$; the only thing left will be the symbolic expression for $g_i(\mathbf{q}, \dot{\mathbf{q}})$.

Finally, we have a set of simultaneous linear equations in the $\ddot{q}_i$,

$$c_{00}\ddot{q}_0 + c_{01}\ddot{q}_1 \ldots c_{0n}\ddot{q}_n = Q_0 - g_0(\mathbf{q}, \dot{\mathbf{q}})$$

$$\vdots$$

$$c_{n0}\ddot{q}_0 + c_{n1}\ddot{q}_1 \ldots c_{nn}\ddot{q}_n = Q_n - g_n(\mathbf{q}, \dot{\mathbf{q}})$$

which we can rewrite as

$$\mathbf{C}\ddot{\mathbf{q}} = \mathbf{d},$$

where

$$\mathbf{d}[i] = Q_i - g_i(\mathbf{q}, \dot{\mathbf{q}}).$$

You can solve the equation $\mathbf{C}\ddot{\mathbf{q}} = \mathbf{d}$ using any numerical matrix solver to get $\ddot{\mathbf{q}} = \mathbf{f}(\mathbf{q}, \dot{\mathbf{q}})$.

8.5.3 Optimal Control

Optimal control is a sophisticated technique for automatically generating animations of complex articulated figures. For a representative, but by no means complete, sampling of these types of algorithms see [11,26,27,37,38]. The animation problem is cast as an optimization problem with objective function

$$F = \int_0^{t_f} f(q_0(t), q_1(t), \ldots, q_n(t)) \tag{8.6}$$

to be minimized, where the q_i are the generalized coordinates of the system, and the set of constraints

$$c(q_0(t), q_1(t), \ldots, q_n(t)) = 0$$

to be satisfied. The $q_i(t)$ are defined in terms of basis functions, which have enough degrees of freedom to contain the desired motion but allow for tractable numerical solutions. Piecewise polynomial splines and multiresolution splines, among others, have been used with considerable success.

To avoid unnecessary complexity in the example we will assume that our physical system is an n-DOF manipulator with rotary joints, that each q_i is defined by the single cubic polynomial

$$q_i(t) = a_{i,0}t^3 + a_{i,1}t^2 + a_{i,2}t + a_{i,3},$$

and that we wish to minimize the sum of the joint torques:

$$f(t) = \sum_i \tau_i^2(t).$$

The integral of Equation (8.6) is typically evaluated with numerical quadrature

$$\tilde{F} = \sum_i w_i f(t_i) \approx \int_0^{t_f} f(q_0(t), q_1(t), \dots, q_n(t)).$$

Gradient-based optimization is frequently used to compute a local minimum of $\tilde{F}$: this requires computing the derivative of f with respect to the free parameters of the basis functions

$$D(f) = \left(\frac{\partial f}{\partial a_{0,0}}, \frac{\partial f}{\partial a_{0,1}}, \frac{\partial f}{\partial a_{0,2}}, \frac{\partial f}{\partial a_{0,3}}, \dots, \frac{\partial f}{\partial a_{n,0}}, \frac{\partial f}{\partial a_{n,1}}, \frac{\partial f}{\partial a_{n,2}}, \frac{\partial f}{\partial a_{n,3}} \right).$$

Computing the gradient of the space-time objective function is straightforward using D*. Assuming that the array tau[] contains the torques, τ_i, computed using the inverse dynamics equations, and that indVars is an array containing the variables we wish to differentiate with respect to, we can compute the gradient with the following code:

```
F f = 0;

for(int i=0;i<tau.rangeDim;i++) {f += tau[i]*tau[i]}
F Df = gradient(f,indVars);
```

where the gradient function is

```
F gradient(F f, F[] indVars)
    int n = indVars.GetLength(0);
    F[] derivs = new F[n];
    for (int i = 0; i < n; i++) {derivs[i] = D(f,0,indVars[i]);}
    return evalDeriv(derivs);
```

Derivative evaluations per second for the compiled D* derivative is changing almost perfectly linearly as a function of n. D* appears to be taking time cubic in the number of links to compute the symbolic derivative. As mentioned in Section 7.2.1, this is because we run the dominator algorithm on the entire graph after every subgraph factorization. The algorithm is fast enough to be used for space-time optimization of relatively complex articulated figures such as human beings. Table 8.2 shows the performance of D* for space-time optimization.

It is not possible to precisely compare D* to the best manually derived recursive formulas because no operation counts are given in [24], and important details are left to the reader to fill in. For example, the authors state, "It should be noted that many of the computations embedded in the forward and backward recursions above need only be evaluated once, thereby

number of links, n	D*	D* symbolic time (secs.)
6	332,225	7
12	172,830	53
18	109,589	199
40	41,000	3660

Table 8.2. Space-time optimization: Number of derivative evaluations per second. The last column in the table shows the amount of time D* took to compute the symbolic derivative.

reducing the computational burden," [24, p. 662] without giving details as to precisely which computations are redundant; as a result it would be difficult, if not impossible, to precisely reproduce their implementation.

However, we can compare the D* derivative to the best results that might be achieved. The lower bound for the gradient is certainly no less than the amount of computation required for the space-time objective function, f. For $n = 6$, f has 501 additions/subtractions, 537 multiplications, 6 cosine operations, and 6 sine operations. The D* derivative of f has 1226 additions/subtractions, 1419 multiplications, 6 cosine operations, and 6 sine operations, which is less than 2.8 times the operations of f. Clearly the D* derivative is close to the lower bound.

8.6 Conclusion

The Lagrangian formulation always maintains kinematic constraints, and thus it is possible to take very large time steps when precise modeling of the true dynamics is unnecessary. In computer games and animation for film or television it is rarely necessary to model dynamics to high precision, since human viewers do not notice small dynamic errors. By comparison, kinematic constraint errors are much more noticeable, since they result in parts of the mechanism failing to connect properly.

Figure 8.7 shows two frames from a dynamic simulation of a bead constrained to move along a wire: (a) shows a step along the tangent to the constraint manifold, as would be done when using nonlinear constraint equations, and (b) shows the step taken by our symbolic Lagriangian formulation. The tangent step moves the bead far off the constraint manifold; convergence of a nonlinear constraint solver to the correct point on the constraint manifold is highly unlikely. To guarantee convergence a much smaller time step would be necessary to correctly maintain the kinematic constraints.

We do not deal with simulating contact and collision in this book since it is a separate problem that is resolved after computing the dynamics of a

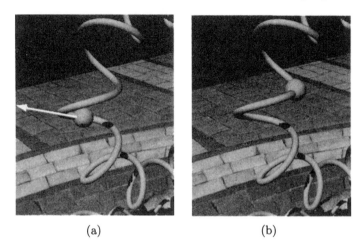

(a)   (b)

Figure 8.7. (a) Yellow arrow shows differential equation step, ignoring constraints. (b) Actual step with constraints (see Plate XXI).

system. Any collision and contact handling techniques for minimal coordinate approaches can be used with the new algorithm. For example, [23] can be used for simulating collision response, enforcing unilateral and bilateral constraints as well as joint limits, and computing contact or friction forces when the system is in contact with environment.

Handling topology change can be an issue with Lagrangian mechanics. If we can predefine a set of subsystems that a system can break into, then we can compute the motion equations of the subsystems offline and switch between the equations in real time. However, to simulate completely general topological changes, such as breaking a system into arbitrary combinations of its constituent rigid bodies, a maximal coordinate approach is probably a better choice.

The great strength of the algorithm introduced in this chapter is that complex joints can be easily specified and robustly and rapidly simulated. For example, a common weakness of human figure animations is that the knee joint is modeled as a hinge when it is more accurately modeled as a four-bar linkage. This gives natural human knees a significantly larger range of motion than artificial knee joints, which are simple hinges. Similarly, the human scapula is a complex joint which can be modeled as a surface-surface joint type. Incorporating these complex joints in a human body simulation would be straightforward with our algorithm but considerably more problematic using existing algorithms. In addition, the robustness, efficiency, and simplicity of the algorithm make it an attractive choice for real-time applications, such as computer simulations or games, where numerical simulation failure is not an option.

9 CSG on Procedural Geometry

In Chapter 4 we showed how you could represent parametric surfaces as D*
programs. The objects you can make this way are very compact and resolution independent, but it becomes increasingly difficult to write an explicit
parametric representation of the surface as objects become more complicated. In particular it is very difficult to figure out how to parameterize
surfaces with holes which penetrate into the interior of the object.

Constructive solid geometry, or CSG, is a powerful way of extending the
modeling techniques of Chapter 4. You create CSG models by adding and
subtracting solid shapes. For example, you could cut a hole in an object
by subtracting a cylindrical shape.

CSG models [34] have many desirable characteristics for real-time rendering. They are powerful enough to model many types of objects, es-
pecially manufactured things which frequently have simple procedural de-
scriptions. The abstract definition of a CSG model is extremely compact
and resolution independent because surfaces are represented as piecewise
continuous functions.

Compactness is particularly important because of a long term trend in
computer hardware: GPU processor performance has been increasing at a
rate of roughly 71% per year while memory bandwidth has been increasing
at only 25% per year [29]. Fetching data from memory is steadily becoming
more expensive relative to computation. A more compact representation
can be faster to render than a larger one, even if more computation is
required to process the compact representation. Memory-constrained plat-
forms, such as game consoles, directly benefit from the reduction in object
size since more complex virtual worlds can be stored in the same amount
of RAM. In addition, the effective IO bandwidth of slow peripherals, such
as DVD drives or Internet connections, is increased when a more compact
representation is used.

CSG models have not previously been used for real-time graphics because no algorithms existed which could both maintain their compact representation and render them efficiently at runtime. The key difficulty in
doing this was finding a compact, exact representation of the curves of intersection that arise from CSG operations. This chapter describes a new

Figure 9.1. Real-time screen capture of a generative model of a speaker. Memory footprint of the object is approximately 8.9 KBytes. Rendering speed for this and the other objects illustrated in the paper is approximately 20 million triangles/second on an NVidia GeForce 6800. All the objects in this chapter are CSG operations on executable procedures representing surfaces of revolution, extrusions, offset surfaces, etc. None of the objects are represented as polynomial surface patches (see Plate XXII).

algorithm for finding a piecewise parametric representation for the implicit curve of intersection between two general parametric surfaces involved in a CSG operation. This parametric representation is compact and exact to the limits of precision of floating point arithmetic. Arbitrary points on the intersection curve can be efficiently evaluated at runtime which allows triangulation density to be adapted dynamically.

The CSG models are represented as D* programs. We have implemented a code generation back end that transforms the high level D* programs to HLSL code which is executed directly on the GPU. Figure 9.1 shows an example of a model rendered with the new algorithm.

9.1 Previous Work

The algorithms described in this chapter are largely complementary to previous work on real-time CSG rendering. The work of [1, 6, 30] computed discrete 3D approximations of the CSG operation. The CSG operations were approximated in screen space in [19, 35]. In particular, the ingenious algorithm of [19] effectively utilizes the GPU to evaluate the CSG operation in parallel across multiple pixels without requiring excessive runtime processing. This algorithm requires minimal preprocessing and has runtime complexity $O(Nk)$ where N is the number of primitives and k is the average depth complexity. In the worst case when $k = N$ complexity is $O(N^2)$.

When the CSG operation is constantly being changed, for example when previewing CSG operations in a modeling tool, this algorithm is very efficient. However, if the CSG operation is fixed and one desires to display the CSG surface as quickly as possible, then the screen space algorithms are less than ideal, since the rendering speed is a complex function of the orientation of the object and its projection to screen space. This makes rendering speed somewhat unpredictable. In addition, many writes and reads to screen memory may be required and, as mentioned previously, memory access is becoming ever more expensive.

In contrast to the screen space methods, we compute an exact boundary surface representation of CSG objects and dynamically trim the domains at runtime, using the implicit curves of intersection, to determine the precise subset of each of the surface domains to render. Our algorithm requires significantly more preprocessing than the screen space methods but has much less runtime overhead and makes far fewer reads and writes to screen memory. Our algorithm does not suffer from discrete approximation errors. In addition, rendering time is not dependent on the number of primitives or on average depth complexity. For applications where predictable performance and high speed are important, with computer games being the preeminent example, the new representation has many advantages.

The work of [18] differs from our work in that their system only allows NURBS patches. The NURBS patches are then approximated by Bezier patches, which are rendered on the GPU. CSG intersection curves are not rendered exactly so cracks may appear in the surface. These are patched over with a thin strip of polygons so that they are not visible.

By contrast, our system allows a very general class of surface functions, which includes polynomial surfaces as a subset. Intersection curves are computed exactly so no cracks ever appear in the rendered surface.

9.2   Overview of the Algorithm

Figure 9.2 shows the steps involved in transforming a geometric object first into a D* program, and then, at runtime, into triangles the GPU can render. The object is interactively created on a conventional 3D modeling package, and the sequence of operations used to create it is translated into D* programs, which are dynamically compiled and used in the first stage of the algorithm to compute the exact representation of the CSG intersection curves. This takes from a few seconds up to five or ten minutes, so this process is done offline after the object is modeled.

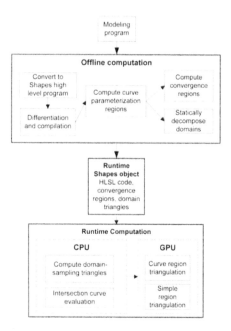

Figure 9.2. Flow diagram of procedural model processing.

Next the domains of the parametric surfaces are decomposed into a small number of triangular domain regions called static domain triangles. These domain regions have the property that they can be easily subdivided and sampled at whatever resolution is necessary at runtime.

The compiled D* code, the intersection curve descriptors, and the static domain triangles are bundled together to make a runtime D* object that contains everything necessary to triangulate the surface at runtime.

The last phase of processing occurs at runtime. First, the intersection curves are used to dynamically trim the domain of the parametric function into regions. The particular CSG operation used to create the object determines which regions will be triangulated and rendered. Then the regions to be rendered are subdivided into domain-sampling triangles.

The domain-sampling triangles are passed to the GPU, along with the compiled D* program representing the surface. The D* program is evaluated on the GPU at a large number of points in each sampling triangle using geometry instancing and vertex shaders. The resulting n-dimensional surface points become vertices in a triangle mesh. A typical vertex might be $[x, y, z, n_x, n_y, n_z, u, v]^T$, but one could have additional elements for color, reflection parameters, etc. D* places no limitations on the dimension or contents of this vector.

9.3   Finding Exact Curves of Intersection

In our system, surfaces are general parametric functions of two variables. Polynomial surfaces are a subset of the surfaces that can be represented in D^* (but none of the objects illustrated in the paper are modeled as polynomial surfaces). In a typical CSG operation, two surfaces defined by

$$f_1(u_0, u_1) = [f_{1x}(u_0, u_1), f_{1y}(u_0, u_1), f_{1z}(u_0, u_1)]^T,$$
$$f_2(u_2, u_3) = [f_{2x}(u_2, u_3), f_{2y}(u_2, u_3), f_{2z}(u_2, u_3)]^T$$

are intersected. The functions $f_i : R^2 \to R^3$ are assumed to be non-self-intersecting, with a Lipschitz first derivative everywhere except perhaps at a set of points that can be found with minimal computation, as, for example, if two curve segments were joined with a known first derivative discontinuity. This is essentially equivalent to requiring the functions to be piecewise C^2.

Each CSG operation gives rise to a set of closed four-dimensional intersection curves in the variables u_0, u_1, u_2, u_3 defined by the implicit function $f : R^4 \to R^3$:

$$f(u_0, u_1, u_2, u_3) = f_1(u_0, u_1) - f_2(u_2, u_3) = [0, 0, 0]^T.$$

The exact representation of the intersection curves is computed in two steps. First we use the implicit function theorem to partition the intersection curve into regions, each of which can be parameterized by at least one variable in each domain. In a region parameterized by variable u_i, the implicit function theorem guarantees that there exists a function $g(u_i) : R^1 \to R^3$ that defines the remaining three variables in terms of u_i:

$$g(u_i) = [g_{u_j}(u_i), g_{u_k}(u_i), g_{u_l}(u_i)]^T \quad j \neq k \neq l \neq i.$$

More generally we will write

$$g(u_{\text{ind}}) = u_{\text{dep}},$$

where u_{dep} is a 3-vector of functions that define the dependent variables in terms of the scalar parameterizing variable u_{ind}. The implicit function theorem asserts that such a function exists but does not offer any suggestions about how it may be computed.

The second step of the algorithm finds an explicit, computable representation of this implicit function that is valid over the region parameterized by variable u_i. This step is the fundamentally new part of our algorithm and is described in Section 9.3.1.

The parameterization regions are computed using an algorithm quite similar to the one in [34], although our slightly stronger parameterization requirements simplify our real-time triangulation algorithm. We include this detailed description here because it forms the foundation for the next section and because [34] is out of print and so may be difficult to find. For those readers familiar with the parameterization algorithm, we advise skipping to Section 9.3.1.

First the four-dimensional domain is subdivided into a set of boxes that completely enclose the intersection curve. Inside each box the curve can be parameterized by at least one variable in each domain; i.e., the curve must be parameterizable by at least two variables. This slightly stronger parameterizability requirement is necessary for the real-time triangulation algorithm. We then fuse boxes of common parameterization into larger parameterization regions (Figure 9.3). These parameterization regions are used in the next phase of our algorithm (Section 9.3.1), where we find a computable representation of the implicit function.

We define f, the intersection curve function, over the four-dimensional interval box

$$\overline{\mathbf{u}} = [\overline{u}_0, \overline{u}_1, \overline{u}_2, \overline{u}_3]^{\mathrm{T}},$$

where $\overline{\mathbf{u}}$ is initialized to the entire domain of the surface. The notation $\overline{x}$ indicates an interval over the variable x, where $\overline{x}$ is the upper and $\underline{x}$ the lower bound (see [20] for a good recent introduction to interval analysis). The initial vector interval $\overline{\mathbf{u}}$ is then recursively subdivided until all boxes $\underline{\overline{\mathbf{p}}}_b$ are found that satisfy

$$0 \in f(\overline{\mathbf{p}}_b), \tag{9.1}$$

as well as

$$\begin{aligned} \{0 \notin \mathrm{Det}(\mathbf{D}_{-u_1} f(\overline{\mathbf{p}}_b)) \quad \text{or} \quad 0 \notin \mathrm{Det}(\mathbf{D}_{-u_0} f(\overline{\mathbf{p}}_b))\} \\ \text{and} \quad \{0 \notin \mathrm{Det}(\mathbf{D}_{-u_2} f(\overline{\mathbf{p}}_b)) \quad \text{or} \quad 0 \notin \mathrm{Det}(\mathbf{D}_{-u_3} f(\overline{\mathbf{p}}_b))\} \end{aligned}, \tag{9.2}$$

where the dependent derivative, $\mathbf{D}_{-u_i} f$, is $\mathbf{D}f$ minus the column containing derivatives with respect to variable u_i. For example, $\mathbf{D}_{-u_2} f$ is

$$\mathbf{D}_{-u_2} f = \begin{bmatrix} \frac{\partial f_x}{\partial u_0} & \frac{\partial f_x}{\partial u_1} & \frac{\partial f_x}{\partial u_3} \\ \frac{\partial f_y}{\partial u_0} & \frac{\partial f_y}{\partial u_1} & \frac{\partial f_y}{\partial u_3} \\ \frac{\partial f_z}{\partial u_0} & \frac{\partial f_z}{\partial u_1} & \frac{\partial f_z}{\partial u_3} \end{bmatrix}.$$

The conditions of Equation (9.2) guarantee parameterizability. By the implicit function theorem, if $0 \notin \mathbf{D}_{-u_i}(f(\overline{\mathbf{p}}_b))$, then there exists a function $\mathbf{g}(u_i) = \mathbf{u}_{\mathrm{dep}}$; i.e., we can parameterize the curve by variable u_i everywhere in $\overline{\mathbf{p}}_b$. Since we require that at least one of the $\mathbf{D}_{-u_i}$ be nonsingular in each domain, we are guaranteed that we can parameterize every part of the curve by at least one of the domain variables.

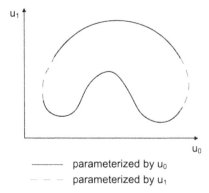

Figure 9.3. An intersection curve in one domain is partitioned into regions parameterizable by at least one of the variables.

In general, the conditions of the implicit function theorem will not be satisfied at points where the two surfaces are tangent or at points where the parameterization itself is singular as, for example, occurs at the north and south poles of the simple parametric definition of a sphere. Tangent surfaces give rise to a host of numerical robustness issues, and one can model many interesting surfaces without allowing them. As a consequence, CSG operations on tangent surfaces will not be considered further in this paper, although extending our work to handle this case is an interesting research problem. Similarly, our system does not currently allow CSG operations that result in implicit curves of intersection passing through singular parameterization points.

Condition (9.1) eliminates those boxes that cannot contain the intersection curve: if $f \neq 0$ everywhere in the box, then clearly the curve cannot be in the box so it is discarded and not subdivided further. Because the range bounds on f are not tight, it is possible that the box does not contain the curve even though condition (9.1) is met. We eliminate these false boxes by computing the intersection of the curve with each box face using interval Newton root finding. If there are no face intersections, then the box does not contain the curve and it is discarded. A few additional steps are performed to minimize box size, but they are not relevant to our discussion. The details can be found in [34].

The boxes that have satisfied Equations (9.1) and (9.2) and the face intersection test are linked together into connected components by matching face intersection points. The result is a linked list of four-dimensional boxes that completely contain the curve. Sequential boxes of common parameterization are fused to form a single parameterization region, which is defined by an interval in the parameterizing variable $\overline{u}_i$ (Figure 9.3).

9.3.1 Proving Convergence of Newton's Iteration

While techniques for computing parameterizability have been known for some time, up to now there has not been an efficient way to use this information to evaluate points on the curve rapidly enough to be useful for real-time rendering. Our new algorithm uses Newton's iteration to solve the implicit curve equation at runtime. Convergence of the Newton iteration is assured by finding regions of guaranteed convergence over intervals of the parameterizing variable, and storing these regions as part of the D* runtime object.

Assume we have a parameterization region $\underline{\bar{u}}_i$ and that we wish to solve for a point on the curve corresponding to the parametric value $c \in \underline{\bar{u}}_i$. The parametric function $\mathbf{g}(\underline{\bar{u}}_i)$ gives the unique 3-vector $\mathbf{u}_{\text{dep}}$ that satisfies

$$f(\mathbf{c}) = 0,$$

where the notation

$$\mathbf{c} = [c, \mathbf{u}_{\text{dep}}]$$

denotes a 4-vector consisting of the independent scalar parameterizing variable, in this case equal to c, and the 3-vector of dependent variables $\mathbf{u}_{\text{dep}}$. For example, if the parameterizing variable is u_1 and $\mathbf{u}_{\text{dep}} = [4, 5, 6]$, then

$$\mathbf{c} = [c, \mathbf{u}_{\text{dep}}] = [4, c, 5, 6].$$

The parametric function $\mathbf{g}(\underline{\bar{u}}_i)$ is constructed by partitioning $\underline{\bar{u}}_i$ into intervals of guaranteed convergence $\underline{\bar{u}}_{\text{con}_k}$, each of which has an associated dependent variable starting point $\mathbf{u}_{\text{dep}_k}$. To compute a curve point $[c, \mathbf{u}_{\text{dep}}]$, the appropriate convergence region

$$\{\underline{\bar{u}}_{\text{con}_k} | c \in \underline{\bar{u}}_{\text{con}_k}\}$$

is found. Then $[c, \mathbf{u}_{\text{dep}_k}]$ is used as the starting point for the Newton iteration

$$\mathbf{u}_{\text{dep}_{j+1}} = \mathbf{u}_{\text{dep}_j} - \mathbf{h}_j, \tag{9.3}$$

where $\mathbf{h}_j$ is

$$\mathbf{h}_j = \left[\mathbf{D}_{-u_i} f([c, \mathbf{u}_{\text{dep}_j}])\right]^{-1} f([c, \mathbf{u}_{\text{dep}_j}]).$$

On average three to four iterations are enough to get seven–eight digits of accuracy. This iteration is evaluated at runtime to compute points on the intersection curve.

To compute the regions of guaranteed convergence, $\underline{\bar{u}}_{\text{con}_k}$, one can use an interval extension of Kantorovich's theorem (see Appendix C), which gives sufficient conditions to guarantee convergence of Newton's iteration. The interval extension is essentially equivalent to Hubbard's balls of convergence [21], used in his constructive proof of the implicit function theorem. The result of the interval extension is a function $\overline{K}$,

$$\overline{\mathbf{u}} = [\overline{u}_i, \overline{\mathbf{u}}_{\text{dep}}],$$

$$\overline{K}(\overline{\mathbf{u}}) = \|f(\overline{\mathbf{u}})\| \| [\mathbf{D}_{-u_i} f(\overline{\mathbf{u}})]^{-1} \|^2 \overline{M},$$

which depends on f, its derivative, and the Lipschitz first derivative bound $\overline{M}$. If $\overline{K}(\overline{\mathbf{u}}) < .5$, then for any $u_{\text{ind}} \in \overline{u}_i, u_{\text{dep}0} \in \overline{\mathbf{u}}_{\text{dep}}$ Newton's iteration starting from $u_{\text{dep}0}$ will converge quadratically to the solution of $f([u_{\text{ind}}, \mathbf{u}_{\text{dep}}]) = 0$.

One could attempt to use the interval extension of Kantorovich's theorem directly to find regions of guaranteed convergence. Unfortunately, Kantorovich's theorem provides only sufficient conditions for convergence and in general yields quite pessimistic estimates of the size of convergence regions. For the surfaces we have modeled in our system, thousands of these convergence regions would be required to completely cover a single curve of intersection. The convergence regions are required to compute curve points at runtime, so minimizing their number reduces the memory footprint of the procedural object. Thousands of regions would take up far too much space to be practical.

While a naive application of Kantorovich's theorem is not practical, it does form the basis for our new algorithm, which computes regions of convergence that are orders of magnitude larger than those predicted by the interval form of Kantorovich's theorem.

9.3.2 Finding Large Regions of Convergence

Assume that we want to prove convergence from starting interval

$$\overline{\mathbf{u}}_0 = [\overline{u}_i, \mathbf{u}_{\text{dep}_0}],$$

but that $\overline{K}([\overline{u}_i, \mathbf{u}_{\text{dep}_0}]) > .5$. Compute a new interval box $\overline{\mathbf{u}}_1$ that is the image of $\overline{\mathbf{u}}_0$ under the Newton transformation

$$\overline{\mathbf{h}}_0 = \left[\mathbf{D}_{-ui} f([c, \overline{\mathbf{u}}_{\text{dep}_0}]) \right]^{-1} f([c, \overline{\mathbf{u}}_{\text{dep}_0}]),$$

$$\overline{\mathbf{u}}_{\text{dep}_1} = \mathbf{u}_{\text{dep}_0} + \overline{\mathbf{h}}_0,$$

$$\overline{\mathbf{u}}_1 = [\overline{u}_i, \overline{\mathbf{u}}_{\text{dep}_1}].$$

If $\overline{K}(\overline{\mathbf{u}}_1) \geq .5$, continue computing points $\overline{\mathbf{u}}_j$ until at some step k, $\overline{K}(\overline{\mathbf{u}}_k) < .5$. By the interval extension of Kantorovich's theorem, we know that Newton's iteration starting from any point in $\overline{\mathbf{u}}_k$ will converge. Since all of the points in $\underline{\overline{u}}_{k-1}$ map into $\underline{\overline{u}}_k$, then all points in $\underline{\overline{u}}_{k-1}$ must converge. By continuing this argument backwards through the $\underline{\overline{u}}_i$, we arrive at the conclusion that every point in $\underline{\overline{u}}_0$ will converge.

If after some maximum number of steps, m, none of the $\underline{\overline{u}}_j$ satisfy the condition

$$\overline{K}(\underline{\overline{u}}_k) < .5 \quad k = 0..m,$$

then $\underline{\overline{u}}_i$ is split in half and new starting points are computed at the midpoint of each half using standard interval Newton root finding. The test is then performed recursively on each half:

```
findConvergenceRegions(interval up, list cR){
    us = curveDependentValues(up.mid)
    if(convergence(up,us)){
        append (up(interval),us) to cR
    }
    else{
        lowHalf = (up.low,up.mid)
        highHalf = (up.mid,up.high)
        //attempt to prove convergence on new intervals
        //with new starting points
        findConvergenceRegions (lowHalf, cR)
        findConvergenceRegions (highHalf, cR)
    }
}


boolean convergence(interval up, vector us){
    up1 = up
    while(K(up1,us)<alpha*K(up,us)){
        hi = inverse(Dup(f(up,us)))*f(up,us)
        up1 = up - hi
        if(K(up1) < .5 && inParamBox(up1)) return true
    }
    low = (up.low,up.mid)
    high = (up.mid,up.high)
    //attempt to prove convergence on new intervals
    //using the same starting point
    return convergence(low,us) && convergence(high,us)
}
```

The Lipschitz first derivative and parameterizability conditions in Equation (9.2) guarantee that eventually we will find convergence regions of nonzero size. Since $\|\mathbf{D}^{-1}f\|$ and M are both bounded in the parameterizability boxes that completely enclose the curve but $\|f([\underline{\overline{u}}_i, \mathbf{u}_{\mathrm{dep}_k}])\|$ becomes arbitrarily small as we decrease the width of $\overline{\underline{u}}_i$, then

$$\overline{K}([\overline{\underline{u}}_i, \mathbf{u}_{\mathrm{dep}_k}]) \to 0 \quad \text{as} \quad \mathrm{width}(\overline{\underline{u}}_i) \to 0.$$

Uniqueness of the point of convergence is guaranteed by the parameterizability condition associated with each parametric region. Assume the convergence region $\overline{\underline{u}}_0$ is part of parametric region $\overline{\underline{u}}_p$ and that $\overline{\underline{u}}_k$ is the image of $\overline{\underline{u}}_0$ after k Newton steps. For width$(\overline{\underline{u}}_i)$ small enough, there will be such a $\overline{\underline{u}}_k$. If

$$\overline{K}(\overline{\underline{u}}_k) < .5 \quad \text{and} \quad \overline{\underline{u}}_k \subseteq \underline{\overline{p}}_b,$$

where $\underline{\overline{p}}_b$ is a parameterizability box containing some part of the curve parameterized by $\overline{\underline{u}}_p$, then for every $u_c \in \overline{\underline{u}}_0$, Newton's iteration converges to some $\mathbf{u}_{\mathrm{dep}} \in \underline{\overline{p}}_b$. Since the curve is parameterizable everywhere in $\underline{\overline{p}}_b$, $\mathbf{u}_{\mathrm{dep}}$ is the unique point such that

$$f([u_c, \mathbf{u}_{\mathrm{dep}}]) = 0.$$

Overestimation of bounds due to interval analysis, combined with the widening caused by outward rounding, increase the size of the $\overline{\underline{u}}_j$ at each iteration, which tends to increase $\overline{K}(\overline{\underline{u}}_j)$ when the boxes become very wide. But the $\overline{\underline{u}}_j$ are also typically getting closer to the solution curve at each

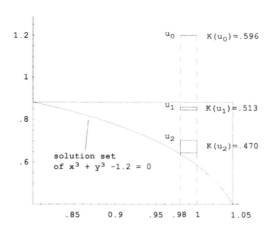

Figure 9.4. Proving convergence of Newton's iteration for every point in $[\{.98, 1\}, 1.2]$ to the solution of $x^3 + y^3 - 1.2 = 0$. Here x is the parameterizing variable and y is the dependent variable; $\overline{K}\overline{\underline{u}}_0 > .5$ so Kantorovich's theorem is not satisfied. In the next step, $\overline{\underline{u}}_0$ is transformed by a Newton step into $\overline{\underline{u}}_1$.

iteration, which reduces $\|f(\underline{\mathbf{u}}_j)\|$ and frequently $\overline{K}(\underline{\mathbf{u}}_j)$ as well. It is this effect that makes convergence() so effective at proving convergence over large regions.

A simplified two-dimensional example illustrates both phenomena described above (Figure 9.4). Function convergence() is applied to the function $x^3 + y^3 - 1.2 = 0$ parameterized by x in the range $\{.98, 1\}$ with dependent variable starting point $y = 1.2$. Initially, at $\underline{\mathbf{u}}_0 = [\{.98, 1\}, 1.2)]$, $\overline{K}(\underline{\mathbf{u}}_0)$ is .596, because $\underline{\mathbf{u}}_0$ is far away from the solution curve. Each succeeding $\underline{\mathbf{u}}_j$ comes closer to the curve, but the width of the dependent variable interval becomes much larger as well: $\underline{\mathbf{u}}_1 = [\{.98, 1\}, \{.846, .86\}], \underline{\mathbf{u}}_2 = [\{.98, 1\}, \{.643, .703\}]$. The reduction in $\|f(\underline{\mathbf{u}}_j)\|$ dominates for the first few iterations, so that by the second iteration $\overline{K}(\underline{\mathbf{u}}_2) = .470 < .5$, and convergence from $\underline{\mathbf{u}}_0$ is proven.

9.4   Orienting the Curve of Intersection

To perform a CSG operation, we triangulate only those regions of the domain that satisfy the predicate of the CSG operation. We use the exact curve of intersection to make this process simple and robust.

For simplicity let the two objects in a CSG operations be $A = f_A(u_0, u_1)$ and $B = f_B(u_2, u_3)$ intersecting in a single 4D curve, $curve_{4D}$. Choose a random 4D point $\overline{\mathbf{c}}$ on the curve. This 4D point projects to two 2D points c_A, c_B, one in each domain. Call the 2D projection of $curve_{4D}$ into the domain of B $curve_B$.

The notation becomes very messy if we leave the parameterization of the curve at $\overline{\mathbf{c}}$ indeterminate. Therefore, without loss of generality, assume that the curve is parameterizable by variable u_2 at $\overline{\mathbf{c}}$.

To orient the curve, project the 3D surface normal into the 2D domain, and then compute the 2D tangent of the curve. Begin by computing the outward pointing surface normal of A, $\overline{\mathbf{n}}_A$, at point c_A and then project $\overline{\mathbf{n}}_A$ onto the basis vectors $\mathbf{D}_{u_2}f_B, \mathbf{D}_{u_3}f_B$ that define the tangent plane of B at c_B by solving the least squares equation

$$[\mathbf{D}_{u_2}f_B(\overline{\mathbf{c}}) \mid \mathbf{D}_{u_3}f_B(\overline{\mathbf{c}})][\overline{\mathbf{n}}_{A_{\mathrm{proj}}}]^{\mathrm{T}} = \overline{\mathbf{n}}_A,$$

where

$$\mathbf{D}_{u_i}f_B = \left[\frac{\partial f_{B_x}}{\partial u_i}, \frac{\partial f_{B_y}}{\partial u_i}, \frac{\partial f_{B_z}}{\partial u_i}\right]^{\mathrm{T}}. \tag{9.4}$$

Compute the implicit derivative at point $\overline{c}$ with respect to u_2 (see Appendix D),

$$\mathbf{D}_{u_2}\overline{g}(\overline{u_2}) = \left[\frac{\partial u_0}{\partial u_2}, \frac{\partial u_1}{\partial u_2}, \frac{\partial u_3}{\partial u_2}\right]^{\mathrm{T}}$$
$$= -\left[\mathbf{D}_{-u_2}f(\overline{c})\right]^{-1}\mathbf{D}_{u_2}f(\overline{c}).$$

The partial terms in Equations (9.4) and (9.4) are intervals, but we have avoided using the interval notation

$$\frac{\overline{\partial f_{u_j}}}{\partial u_i}$$

for these terms because it is too cluttered.

The 2D tangent of $curve_B$ at $\overline{c}$ is

$$\overline{\mathbf{t}}_B = \left[1, \frac{\partial u_3}{\partial u_2}\right].$$

The orientation of the curve is

$$\overline{o} = \overline{\mathbf{t}}_B[0] \times \overline{\mathbf{n}}_{A_{\mathrm{proj}}}[1] - \overline{\mathbf{n}}_{A_{\mathrm{proj}}}[0] \times \overline{\mathbf{t}}_B[1].$$

If $\underline{o} > 0$, then points in domain B that map to 3D points inside of A will be to the left of the curve. If $\overline{o} < 0$, then points in domain B that map to 3D points outside of A will be to the left of the curve. The CSG operation along with the orientation of the curve give all the information needed to determine which parts of the domain to triangulate.

The orientation point, $\overline{c}$, is computed with standard interval Newton root finding. It is typically a very narrow interval with $\overline{c}$ and $\underline{c}$ differing only in the last few decimal places. As a consequence, $\overline{o}$ is also very narrow and allows orientation to be unambiguously determined except in those very rare cases when $0 \in \overline{o}$. In general this will only occur when on points of the curve where the two surfaces are nearly tangent at $\overline{c}$ or when one or more of the parameterizations is nearly singular there. These regions of the curve can be detected in earlier stages of processing and avoided.

9.5 Triangulation

There are two different types of computation performed at runtime: evaluating 4D intersection curve points using Equation (9.3) and evaluating surface points and normals. Curve points are evaluated on the CPU because it is difficult to make this computation run efficiently on the GPU. All surface points and normals are computed on the GPU.

For the objects we have constructed to date, we can evaluate approximately 200,000 4D curve points per second. For some applications this is fast enough to get real-time update rates. With many objects visible on the screen, this rate is not quite fast enough. In this case the curve can be sampled densely and the curve points cached. This is done just once when an object first changes from a dormant state to an active state, meaning from an invisible to a visible or potentially-visible-soon state. For all succeeding frames, curve points are read from the cache rather than computed. Most objects will require only a few hundred curve points to render intersection curves accurately, so activation time will be a few milliseconds. When the object goes back to a dormant state, the cache space is reclaimed and used for another object.

CSG operations are effected by triangulating only that part of the domain which corresponds to visible parts of the CSG surface. The first phase of triangulation is performed offline. The parts of the domain to be triangulated are subdivided into a small number of triangular domain regions of two types. Curve visibility triangles, v_i, are bounded along one side by an intersection curve and along the other two edges by line segments. Simple triangles, s_i, are bounded on all three sides by line segments.

The second phase of triangulation is performed at runtime just before the object is to be rendered. The static domain triangles are subdivided into smaller domain-sampling triangles if necessary, and these triangles are passed to the GPU for evaluation. The GPU uses the compiled HLSL D* code representing the surface and geometry instancing, a feature available in cards that support the DirectX Vertex Shader 3.0 model, to evaluate the surface. After the surface is rendered, the domain-sampling triangles are discarded.

9.5.1 Offline Processing

Curve visibility triangles, v_i, are computed for each parametric segment of every intersection curve. There are two visibility triangles for each segment (Figure 9.5). Each triangle shares two 2D vertices, c_0, c_1, on the curve. Two additional 2D points, p_1, p_2, not on the curve are the apices of the two triangles. The part of the curve between c_0 and c_1 is defined by an interval over a single parameterizing variable, $\bar{u}_p$. Each apex p_i has the property that every point of the curve segment associated with the visibility triangle is visible from either p_i.

Visibility regions are easily computed by using implicit differentiation (see Appendix D) over the interval $\bar{u}_p$ to compute the extreme values of the 2D tangent. The intersection of the min and max tangent lines gives the two visibility points p_1, p_2. By the mean value theorem, if $u_c \in \bar{u}_p$, the curve must lie entirely within the shaded region bounded by the max and

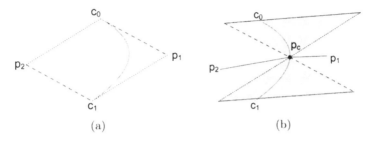

Figure 9.5. (a) Intersections of the min and max values of the 2D tangent over the curve segment give visibility points p_1 and p_2. (b) Every point on the curve must lie in the shaded cone bounded by the tangent lines. All points of the curve segment are visible from p_1 and p_2.

min slope lines centered at p_c. A line segment from p_i to p_c clearly will lie outside this region except exactly at the endpoints of $\bar{u}_p$, so there will be a single intersection with the curve for any $u_c \in \bar{u}_p$.

Edges are added between the endpoints of each parametric segment, and the domain is triangulated with constrained Delaunay triangulation. Visibility triangles are then subdivided until they do not intersect any other visibility triangle edges.

9.5.2 Runtime Processing

Runtime triangulation uses vertex shaders and geometry instancing to move most of the work of surface evaluation onto the GPU. Geometry instancing is a kind of primitive looping construct that has as input two vertex streams. The instance vertex stream contains vertices of a triangle mesh called the instance mesh. The per-instance vertex stream has one vertex per instance to be displayed. Conceptually, the looping works like this:

```
foreach(vertex v in the per-instance vertex stream)
  foreach(vertex iv in the instance vertex stream)
    run the vertex shader with inputs v,iv
```

Instance mesh vertices contain the barycentric coordinates of sample points defined on a canonical base triangle. There are three different types of instance meshes (low-sampling-level versions of these are shown in Figure 9.6). The NNN type is used for all noncurve triangles. It has N vertices along each edge and roughly $.5N^2$ interior vertices. The $NN1$ type is used for curve visibility triangles bounded along one side by an intersection curve. It has N vertices along two edges and 2 vertices along the curve edge. The $NN2N$ type is for triangles generated during the subdivision of

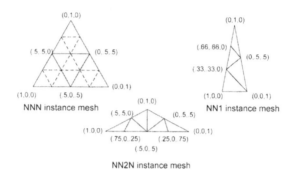

Figure 9.6. Barycentric coordinates stored in the instance mesh.

curve visibility triangles. This type lies inside the curve visibility triangle but is not bounded on any side by an intersection curve. It has roughly N vertices along the two short edges and $2N$ vertices along the long edge.

At each frame time, we perform the following steps on the CPU: 4D points along the CSG intersection curve are computed using (9.3), or cached points are read from the cache. These points are used to subdivide the curve visibility triangles. Because the intersection curve points are shared between the intersecting surfaces, the triangles along the curve boundary will be completely consistent (Figure 9.7). The subdivided curve triangles and all noncurve static domain triangles are dynamically subdivided into domain-sampling triangles (Figure 9.8). Edge length is computed in the parametric space of the domain and subdivision continues until it is below some user defined minimum value. The three 2D vertices of each resulting sampling triangle make up one vertex in the per-instance stream. The sampling triangle vertices are copied into the per-instance vertex stream and this, along with the instance meshes, is sent to the GPU for evaluation of surface points. After each object is rendered, the per-instance vertex buffer used to store the domain-sampling triangle data is discarded.

This snippet of HLSL code shows how a point in the domain of the surface function is computed on the GPU from the per-instance vertex data (variables p0,p1,p2) and the instance mesh barycentric coordinates (variable bary):

```
struct VSIN{float3 bary, float2 p0, float2 p1, float2 p2};
main( VSIN In ){
  float2 pos = In.bary.x*In.p0
             + In.bary.y*In.p1
             + In.bary.z*In.p2;
}
```

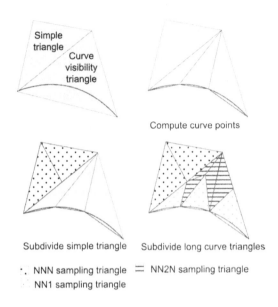

Subdivide simple triangle   Subdivide long curve triangles

∴ NNN sampling triangle   ≡ NN2N sampling triangle
  NN1 sampling triangle

Figure 9.7. Runtime subdivision of static domain curve and simple triangles. Red edges are not subdivided further on the CPU. Edges are subdivided based on parametric length. The subdivision length for curve edges is $1/N$ the length for all other edges because 2D domain coordinates of all curve samples are computed on the CPU. Curve edges are proportionally much shorter than they appear here. The scale has been changed to make the curve triangle subdivision process easier to see.

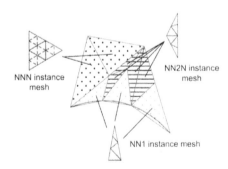

Figure 9.8. Instance meshes that will be evaluated on the GPU for each type of sampling triangle. Simple domain-sampling triangles use an NNN instance mesh. Domain-sampling triangles bounded by a curve edge use an $NN1$ instance mesh. Thin triangles not bounded by a curve edge are sometimes generated in the curve triangle subdivision, in order to ensure consistency of sampling along shared edges. They use an $NN2N$ instance mesh.

This 2D domain point is then used by the HLSL surface function to evaluate the surface position and normal.

For any one object, all three instance meshes of types NNN, $NN1$, $NN2N$ that are used to render the object have the same value of N, the number of sample points along an edge. We do this for efficiency and simplicity. If N could vary on a per-sampling-triangle basis, then in order to ensure consistent sampling along shared edges, we would have to create instance meshes with all possible combinations of edge sampling numbers. Even worse, we would have to set up the vertex streams and issue a DirectX drawPrimitive call for each different resolution instance mesh used to render the object. Both of these operations have high overhead and their use should be minimized in order to achieve high frame rates.

9.6   Results

All of the timings in the results section were measured on a Pentium Xeon 2.6 GHz processor with an NVidia 6800 Ultra graphics card. Objects exist in two states: dormant and active. A dormant object contains only static object data. An active object has both the static data plus cached intersection curve points, if any. As mentioned in Section 9.5, our current implementation computes approximately 200,000 intersection curve points per second. This rate is high enough for interactive rendering of a few objects, but when the number of objects increases, it is better to cache the 4D intersection curve points at the instant the object first becomes active, i.e., potentially visible soon. When the object becomes dormant again, the cache is cleared. This is the method we have used to measure all our rendering speeds.

All of the objects shown in the illustrations render at approximately 20 million triangles/second. Each triangle is texture mapped and environment mapped with a DirectX 9.0 pixel shader that is approximately 40 lines of HLSL code.

Each object is made up of procedural surfaces and CSG operation between the surfaces. The size of an object is determined by the number of lines of code required to represent each surface, and the number of convergence regions and static domain triangles.

There are two types of code: the HLSL surface and normal function, and the C# derivative function. Both of these pieces of code share whatever 2D spline control points were used to make the extrusions or surfaces of revolution, so we count this only once. The derivative code is shared between the two surfaces involved in a CSG operation, so we will also count it only once. The code for all the surfaces is nearly the same size: roughly 36 lines of HLSL code and 80 lines of C# code.

name	HLSL	C#	data	total	t_{pr}	t_{conv}
speaker	720	2K	6.2K	8.9K	3s	76s
wheel 0	432	960	6.9K	8.2K	57s	104s
wheel 1	432	960	10K	11.4K	63s	148s
wheel 2	432	960	5.6K	7K	121s	270s
tire	288	960	10.7K	11.9K	8s	683s

Table 9.1. Computed memory size, in bytes, of procedural objects and offline processing time, in seconds, to compute parameterization regions, t_{pr}, and to prove convergence, t_{conv}. The data column includes space required for the convergence regions, the static domain triangles, and the two-dimensional splines used in surfaces of revolution or extrusion. See Figures 9.10 through 9.16.

Both the HLSL and C# code consist almost entirely of statements of the form "$a = b$ op c", where op is one of the arithmetic operators $(+, -, *, /)$, so there should be a nearly one-to-one mapping from lines of code to number of assembly instructions. Since HLSL compiles to proprietary object code in the graphics card driver and C# compiles to an intermediate language which is jit'ed at load time, we cannot measure the true size of the object code. We will assume each assembly instruction is 6 bytes long on average and that each source line translates to a single assembly instruction.

Table 9.1 shows the storage requirements and offline processing time for each of the objects in the illustrations. Compare the sizes to the memory required to store a polygon mesh. If we assume each vertex in a polygon mesh has components $x, y, z, n_x, n_y, n_z, u, v$, then each vertex requires 32 bytes. Assuming there are roughly twice as many triangles as vertices and that the triangle connectivity information takes 6 bytes (three 2-byte indices), each triangle in the mesh requires roughly 22 bytes. The memory required for Wheel 2, 7 KBytes, is equivalent to that required for 320 triangles. The system does a good job of minimizing the number of parametrization regions in each intersection curve. Figure 9.9 shows a typical domain triangulation and parameterization. Both intersection curves have four parameterization regions, which is the minimum theoretically possible in this case. Figures 9.10 through 9.16 show the range of geometric features that can be created.

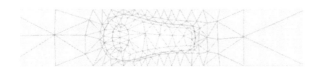

Figure 9.9. Domain parameterization regions and triangulation for a typical procedural model.

Figure 9.10. Wheel 0: 8.2KBytes (see Plate XXIII).

Figure 9.11. Wheel 1: 11.4 KBytes (see Plate XXIV).

Figure 9.12. Closeup of Figure 9.11 (see Plate XXV).

Figure 9.13. Wheel 2: 7 KBytes (see Plate XXVI).

Figure 9.14. Rear view of the wheel in Figure 9.13 (see Plate XXVII).

Figure 9.15. Closeup of bolt cutouts in Figure 9.13 (see Plate XXVIII).

Figure 9.16. The tire treads are geometric detail resulting from CSG operations, not a bump or normal map. Tire by itself: 11.9 KBytes (see Plate XXIX).

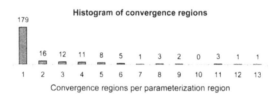

Parameterization regions per intersection curve

Figure 9.17. Histogram of the number of parameterization regions per intersection curve. For closed curves that do not cross domain boundaries, at least four regions will be required.

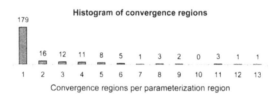

Convergence regions per parameterization region

Figure 9.18. Histogram of the number of convergence regions per parameterization region. Ideally all parameterization regions would have just one convergence region.

Figures 9.17 and 9.18 show histograms of the number of parameterization regions per intersection curve and the number of convergence regions per parameterization region, respectively. These histograms represent the combined statistics of all the objects shown in the illustrations. Most intersection curves have five parameterization regions or fewer. Most parameterization regions have only a single convergence region, which is the best possible result, with a relatively small number having more.

9.7 Conclusion

Our new representation for generative CSG models is compact, resolution independent, and renders quickly on modern GPUs. Future DirectX10 style geometry shaders will make it possible to execute virtually all the computations on the GPU, which will significantly increase speed.

The proof of large regions of convergence for Newton's iteration, which applies to a very broad class of functions, is quite general and should have applications outside of real-time graphics rendering.

List of Symbols

$\mathbf{W}_i$ | Transformation from the ith coordinate frame to the global coordinate frame.

$\mathbf{A}_i$ | Transformation from the ith coordinate frame to its parent coordinate frame.

$\tilde{\omega}_i = \mathbf{R}_i^{\mathrm{T}}\dot{\mathbf{R}}_i$ | Angular velocity for the ith coordinate frame expressed in the ith coordinate frame, where $\mathbf{R}_i$ is the rotation part of $\mathbf{W}_i$.

$\mathbf{t}_{\mathrm{cm}_i}$ | The position of the center of mass of the ith rigid body with respect to the ith coordinate frame.

$\mathbf{r}_{\mathrm{cm}_i}$ | The position of the center of mass of the ith rigid body with respect to the global coordinate frame.

$\mathbf{q}_i, \dot{\mathbf{q}}_i, \ddot{\mathbf{q}}_i$ | The generalized coordinates of the ith coordinate frame and their time derivatives.

Q_i | Generalized force for the ith generalized coordinate.

$\mathbf{F}_{\mathrm{ext}_i}$ | External forces applied to the ith rigid body expressed in the global coordinate frame.

τ_{ext_i} | External torque applied to the ith rigid body expressed in the global coordinate frame.

$\mathbf{H}_{\mathrm{cm}_i}$ | Angular momentum of the ith rigid body about its center of mass, expressed in the global coordinate frame.

m_i | Mass of the ith rigid body.

$\mathbf{I}_i$ | The inertia tensor of the ith rigid body with respect to a coordinate frame that is located at the center of mass and is parallel to the ith coordinate frame.

$\mathbf{b}_i^{\mathrm{T}}$ | The torque due to the change in the angular momentum and external torque applied to the ith rigid body:

$$\mathbf{b}_i^{\mathrm{T}} = \left(\dot{\mathbf{H}}_{\mathrm{cm}_i} - \tau_{\mathrm{ext}_i}\right)^{\mathrm{T}}.$$

Expressed in the global coordinate frame.

$\mathbf{a}_i^{\mathrm{T}}$ The sum of the force due to acceleration of the ith mass and
the external force applied on that body:

$$\mathbf{a}_i^{\mathrm{T}} = (m_i \ddot{\mathbf{r}}_{\mathrm{cm}_i} - \mathbf{F}_{\mathrm{ext}_i})^{\mathrm{T}}.$$

Expressed in the global coordinate frame.

$\mathbf{U}_i$ The ith rotation matrix embedded in a 4×4 matrix:

$$\mathbf{U}_i = \begin{bmatrix} \mathbf{R}_i & 0 \\ 0 & 0 \end{bmatrix}.$$

$\mathbf{B}_i$

$$\mathbf{B}_i = \begin{bmatrix} \tilde{\mathbf{b}}_i & 0 \\ 0 & 0 \end{bmatrix}.$$

Properties of a Unitary Mapping

Assume we have a two-dimensional vector $\mathbf{c} : \|\mathbf{c}\| = 1$ and a 3×2 matrix $\mathbf{P}$ that maps $\mathbf{c}$ from $\mathbb{R}^2$ to $\mathbb{R}^3$:

$$\mathbf{P} = \begin{bmatrix} p_{11} & p_{12} \\ p_{21} & p_{22} \\ p_{31} & p_{32} \end{bmatrix} = \begin{bmatrix} \mathbf{p}_1 & \mathbf{p}_2 \end{bmatrix}.$$

What properties must hold on the elements of $\mathbf{P}$ so that $\|\mathbf{Pc}\| = 1$? By inspection we can see that each column vector of $\mathbf{P}$ must have length 1:

$$\left\| \begin{bmatrix} \mathbf{p}_1 & \mathbf{p}_2 \end{bmatrix} \begin{bmatrix} 1 \\ 0 \end{bmatrix} \right\| = 1 = \|\mathbf{p}_1\|,$$

$$\left\| \begin{bmatrix} \mathbf{p}_1 & \mathbf{p}_2 \end{bmatrix} \begin{bmatrix} 0 \\ 1 \end{bmatrix} \right\| = 1 = \|\mathbf{p}_2\|.$$

Also, for an arbitrary two-dimensional vector with both elements nonzero, $\left\| [a, b]^\mathrm{T} \right\| = 1$, $a, b \neq 0$:

$$1 = \left\| \begin{bmatrix} \mathbf{p}_1 & \mathbf{p}_2 \end{bmatrix} \begin{bmatrix} a \\ b \end{bmatrix} \right\|,$$

$$1 = (a\mathbf{p}_1 + b\mathbf{p}_2)^\mathrm{T} (a\mathbf{p}_1 + b\mathbf{p}_2),$$

$$1 = a^2 \mathbf{p}_1^\mathrm{T} \mathbf{p}_1 + 2ab\mathbf{p}_1^\mathrm{T} \mathbf{p}_2 + b^2 \mathbf{p}_2^\mathrm{T} \mathbf{p}_2,$$

$$1 = a^2 + b^2 + 2ab\mathbf{p}_1^\mathrm{T} \mathbf{p}_2,$$

$$1 = 1 + 2ab\mathbf{p}_1^\mathrm{T} \mathbf{p}_2,$$

$$0 = \mathbf{p}_1^\mathrm{T} \mathbf{p}_2.$$

To yield a unitary mapping, the columns of the matrix $\mathbf{P}$ must have unit magnitude and must be orthogonal to each other.

Kantorovich's Theorem

$$\mathbf{D}f$$ Derivative of f with respect to all variables in the vector $\mathbf{u}$.

$$\mathbf{D}_{u_i}f$$ Derivative of f with respect to the single variable u_i.

$$\mathbf{D}_{-u_i}f$$ $\mathbf{D}f$ with the column $\mathbf{D}_{u_i}f$ removed.

$$\overline{\underline{u}}$$ Interval in u with upper bound $\overline{u}$ and lower bound $\underline{u}$.

For the point version of Kantorovich's theorem see [21]. The interval extension is a matter of substituting intervals for points and suitably extending the intervals over which the Lipschitz constant $\overline{M}$ must exist and the function f must have nonzero determinant.

Given a function

$$f([\overline{\underline{u}}_p, \overline{\underline{u}}_{\mathrm{dep}_0}])$$

assumed to be continuously differentiable over a region as large as is necessary, a parameterizing variable $\overline{\underline{u}}_p$ that is the ith argument of f, and dependent variable starting point $\overline{\underline{u}}_{\mathrm{dep}_0}$, compute the Newton displacement, $\overline{\mathbf{h}}_0$,

$$\overline{\mathbf{h}}_0 = \left[\mathbf{D}_{-ui} f([\overline{\underline{u}}_p, \overline{\underline{u}}_{\mathrm{dep}_0}]) \right]^{-1} f([\overline{\underline{u}}_p, \overline{\underline{u}}_{\mathrm{dep}_0}]),$$

and the image, $\overline{\underline{u}}_{\mathrm{dep}_1}$, of $\overline{\underline{u}}_{\mathrm{dep}_0}$ after a single Newton step,

$$\overline{\underline{u}}_{\mathrm{dep}_1} = \overline{\underline{u}}_{\mathrm{dep}_0} + \overline{\mathbf{h}}_0.$$

Form the interval box

$$\overline{\underline{\mathbf{P}}}_0 = \left[\overline{\underline{u}}_p, \left[\overline{\underline{u}}_{\mathrm{dep}_1} + [\overline{\underline{r}}, \overline{\underline{r}}, \overline{\underline{r}}] \right] \right],$$

where $\overline{\underline{r}}$ is

$$\overline{\underline{r}} = \{ -|\overline{\mathbf{h}}_0|, |\overline{\mathbf{h}}_0| \}.$$

Suppose that $0 \notin \mathbf{D}_{-u_i}(f(\overline{\mathbf{P}}_0))$ and the Lipschitz constant $\overline{M}$,

$$\|\mathbf{D}_{-u_i}(\mathbf{x}) - \mathbf{D}_{-u_i}(\mathbf{y})\| \leq \overline{M}\|\mathbf{x} - \mathbf{y}\|,$$

exists for any $\mathbf{x}, \mathbf{y} \in \overline{\mathbf{P}}_0$; if

$$\overline{K}([\underline{\overline{u}}_p, \underline{\overline{\mathbf{u}}}_{\mathrm{dep}_0}]) = \|f([\underline{\overline{u}}_p, \underline{\overline{\mathbf{u}}}_{\mathrm{dep}_0}])\|\|\left[\mathbf{D}_{-u_i}f([\underline{\overline{u}}_p, \underline{\overline{\mathbf{u}}}_{\mathrm{dep}_0}])\right]^{-1}\|^2\overline{M} < .5,$$

then for any $u_p \in \underline{\overline{u}}_p, \mathbf{u}_{\mathrm{dep}0} \in \underline{\overline{\mathbf{u}}}_{\mathrm{dep}_0}$, Newton's iteration starting from $\mathbf{u}_{\mathrm{dep}0}$ will converge quadratically to the solution of $f([u_p, \mathbf{u}_{dep}]) = 0$.

Implicit Differentiation

See [21] for a derivation that applies to functions of any codimension. This derivation is valid only for functions with codimension 1, since this is the class of functions the CSG intersection curves belong to.

A point $\mathbf{u}$ on the curve can be written as $[u_i, g(u_i)]$, where

$$\mathbf{g}(u_i) = [g_{u_j}(u_i), g_{u_k}(u_i), g_{u_l}(u_i)]^T \quad j \neq k \neq l \neq i$$

is the parameterizing function for this part of the curve. For any $\mathbf{u}$ on the curve, $f(\mathbf{u}) = 0$ and consequently $\mathbf{D}_{u_i} f(\mathbf{u}) = 0$ as well. By the chain rule,

$$\mathbf{D}_{u_i} f([u_i, g(u_i)]) = \mathbf{D}f(\mathbf{u})\mathbf{D}_{u_i}[u_i, g(u_i)] = 0, \qquad (\text{D.1})$$

where

$$\mathbf{D}_{u_i}[u_i, g(u_i)] = \left[\frac{\partial u_0}{\partial u_i}, \frac{\partial u_1}{\partial u_i}, \frac{\partial u_2}{\partial u_i}, \frac{\partial u_3}{\partial u_i} \right]^T.$$

The ith element in $\mathbf{D}_{u_i}[u_i, g(u_i)]$ will be 1. Reorder the variables so that u_i is the last element in $\mathbf{u}$. Then

$$\mathbf{D}_{u_i}[u_i, g(u_i)] = [\mathbf{D}_{u_i} g(u_i), 1]^T,$$

and the columns of $\mathbf{D}f(\mathbf{u})$ will also be reordered so that $\mathbf{D}_{u_i} f(\mathbf{u})$ is the last column,

$$\mathbf{D}f(\mathbf{u}) = \left[\mathbf{D}_{u_j} f(\mathbf{u}) \mid \mathbf{D}_{u_k} f(\mathbf{u}) \mid \mathbf{D}_{u_l} f(\mathbf{u}) \mid \mathbf{D}_{u_i} f(\mathbf{u}) \right] \qquad (\text{D.2})$$

The first three columns of (D.2) are just $\mathbf{D}_{-u_i} f(\mathbf{u})$, so (D.1) becomes

$$[\mathbf{D}_{-u_i} f(\mathbf{u}) \mid \mathbf{D}_{u_i} f(\mathbf{u})] \, [\mathbf{D}_{u_i}[g(u_i)], 1]^T = 0,$$
$$\mathbf{D}_{-u_i} f(\mathbf{u})\mathbf{D}_{u_i}[g(u_i)] + \mathbf{D}_{u_i} f(\mathbf{u}) = 0,$$
$$\mathbf{D}_{u_i}[g(u_i)] = -\mathbf{D}_{-u_i}^{-1} f \mathbf{D}_{u_i} f(\mathbf{u}).$$

Code Listings

E.1 Geometry Programs

```
public delegate Function R1ToR2(Function t); //This should be an R1
    -> R2 function.

/// input: an arbitrary R1->R2 function, a planar parametric curve
/// output: an R2->R3 function, a 3D parametric surface formed by
    sweeping the planar curve about the y axis

public static Function makeSurfaceOfRevolution(
  Variable theta,
  Variable t,
  R1ToR2 xyFunction,
  bool normalizedNormal) {

  Function result;
  const int xIndex = 0, yIndex = 1;
  Function cosTheta = Function.cos(theta), sinTheta = Function.sin(
      theta);
  Function f = xyFunction(t);
  Function Dx = Function.D(f,0,t), Dy = Function.D(f,1,t);
  Function.orderDerivatives(Dx,Dy);
  Function denominator = Function.sqrt(Function.square(Dx) +
      Function.square(Dy));
  Function denomReciprocal = 1 / denominator;

  if (normalizedNormal) {
    result = new Function(
      Function.cos(theta) * f[xIndex],
      f[yIndex],
      Function.sin(theta) * f[xIndex],
      cosTheta * Dy * denomReciprocal,
      -Dx * denomReciprocal,
```

```
      sinTheta * Dy * denomReciprocal);
    }
  else {
    result = new Function(
      Function.cos(theta) * f[xIndex],
      f[yIndex],
      Function.sin(theta) * f[xIndex],
      cosTheta * Dy,
      - Dx,
      sinTheta * Dy);
    }
  return result;
}


public static parametricPartial(F surface, Var parameter)
  //now take partials with respect to parameter
  List<Derivative> derivs = new List<Derivative>();

  for(int i=0;i<surface.rangeDimension;i++)
    {derivs.Add(D(surface,i,parameter);}
  return new F(derivs);
}


public static Function cross(Function a,Function b) {
  return new Function(a[1]*b[2] - a[2]*b[1], a[2]*b[0] - a[0]*b[2],
      a[0]*b[1] - a[1]*b[0]);
}
```

E.2   Dynamics Programs

```
private RigidBodySystem torusLinkSystem(GraphicsDevice device,
    Texture2D texture, int numJoints)
{
    Function.newContext();
    Variable t = new Variable("t");
    double m = 1.0;
    Function[,] r0 = { { 0}, {0}, { 0 }, { 1 } }; //point so need 1
        in 4th position
    double largeRad = 1, smallRad = .2;
    //Function[,] I0 = inertiaMatrixCylinder(m, rad, h);
    Function[,] I0 = inertiaMatrixTorus(m, largeRad, smallRad);
```

```
Geometries.Torus tor = new Geometries.Torus(largeRad, smallRad);
Function[,] flip ={ { 0, -1, 0, 0 }, { 1, 0, 0, 0 }, { 0, 0, 1,
    0 }, { 0, 0, 0, 1 } };

RigidBody ji = null, jiPlus1 = null;
List<RigidBody> allJoints = new List<RigidBody>();
for (int i = numJoints -1; i >= 0 ; i--)
{
    Function[,] A0;

    UnspecifiedFunction qi_0 = UnspecifiedFunction.functionOf("q"
        + i + "_0", t), qi_1 = UnspecifiedFunction.functionOf("q
        " + i + "_1", t);
    Function[,] RBi0 = tor.SurfaceTangentFrame(qi_0, qi_1);
    UnspecifiedFunction qi_2 = UnspecifiedFunction.functionOf("q"
        + i + "_2", t), qi_3 = UnspecifiedFunction.functionOf("q
        " + i + "_3", t);
    Function[,] RBi1 = tor.SurfaceTangentFrame(qi_2, qi_3);

    if (i == 0) {
        A0 = VM.mult(VM.translate(0, 2*numJoints, 0),VM.
            rigidBodyInverse(RBi0));
        ji = new RigidBody(A0, new Function[] { qi_0,qi_1 },
            frictionForce(t, qi_0, qi_1), r0, I0, 1, i.ToString(),
            t);
    }
    else {
        A0 = VM.mult(RBi0, VM.mult(flip, VM.rigidBodyInverse(RBi1)
            ));
        //A0 = VM.mult(RBi0, VM.rigidBodyInverse(RBi1));
        ji = new RigidBody(A0, new Function[] { qi_0, qi_1, qi_2,
            qi_3 }, frictionForce(t, qi_0, qi_1, qi_2, qi_3), r0,
            I0, 1, i.ToString(), t);
    }

    ji.CreateGeometry(device, tor, texture);
    ji.force = new Function[,] { { 0 }, { -10 * m }, { 0 }, { 0 }
        }; //vector not point
    ji.torque = new Function[,] { { 0 }, { 0 }, { 0 }, { 0 } };
    allJoints.Add(ji);
    if (jiPlus1 != null) { ji.c(jiPlus1); }
    jiPlus1 = ji;
}
allJoints.Reverse();
```

```
    Graph<JointNode> g = new Graph<JointNode>(ji, allJoints.ToArray
        ());
    RigidBodySystem temp = new RigidBodySystem(g, t, device);
    temp.initialize();
    return temp;
}
```

E.3   Miscellaneous

```
F SHDerivatives(int maxL, double x, double y, double z){
  List harmonics = new List();
  for (int l = 0; l <= maxL; l++)
    for (int m = -1; m <= 1; m++)
      harmonics.Add(Y(l,m,x,y,z));

  F[] dY = new F[harmonics.Count * 3];
  for (int i = 0; i < dY.GetLength(0) / 3; i++){
    dY[i * 3] = D((F)harmonics[i],0,x);
    dY[i * 3 + 1] = D((F)harmonics[i],0,y);
    dY[i * 3 + 2] = D((F)harmonics[i],0,z);
  }
  return evalDeriv(dY);
}


F P(int l, int m, Var z){
  if(l==0 && m==0)return 1.0;
  if(l==m)return (1-2*m)*P(m-1,m-1,z);
  if(l==m+1)return (2*m + 1)*z*P(m,m,z);
  return(((2*l -1)/(l-m))*z*P(l-1,m,z) - ((l+m-1)/(l-m))*P(l-2,m,z)
      );
}


F S(int m, Var x, Var y){
  if(m==0)return 0;
  else return x*C(m-1,x,y) - y*S(m-1,x,y);
}


F C(int m, Var x, Var y){
  if(m==0)return 1;
  else return x*S(m-1,x,y) + y*C(m-1,x,y);
}

F N(int l, int m){
```

```
  int absM = Math.Abs(m);
  if(m==0)return Math.Sqrt((2*l+1)/(4*Math.PI));
  else return Math.Sqrt((2*l+1)/(2*Math.PI)*(factorial(l-absM)/
      factorial(l+absM)));
}


F Y(int l, int m, Var x, Var y, Var z){
  int absM = Math.Abs(m);
  if(m<0)return N(l,absM)*P(l,absM,z)*S(absM,x,y);
  else return N(l,absM)*P(l,absM,z)*C(absM,x,y);
}
```

```
F StructureFromMotionDerivs(Var f, a, s, px, py, ptx ,pty ,ptz , wx
    , wy, wz, tx, ty, tz){
  F[,] affine = f,s,px , 0,f * a,py , 0,0,1 ;
  F pt = new F(ptx,pty,ptz);
  F t = new F(tx,ty,tz);
  F q = quaternion(wx,wy,wz);
  F r = quaternionRotation(q,pt);
  F[] T = VM.plus(r,t);
  F K = new F(VM.mult(affine,new F[] T[0],T[1],T[2] )); F proj =
    new F(K[0] / K[2],K[1] / K[2]);
  F error = new F(proj[0] - zx,proj[1] - zy);
  F[,] derivs;derivs = D(new F[]error[0],error[1], new Var[] f,a,s,
    px,py,ptx,pty,ptz,wx,wy,wz,tx,ty,tz );
  return evalDeriv(derivs);
}


F quaternion(Var wx,Var wy,Var wz){
  return new F(F.sqrt(1 - (wx * wx - wy * wy - wz * wz) / 4),wx /
    2,wy / 2,wz / 2);
}


F quaternionRotation(F q,F p){
  F x = q[0],y = q[1],z = q[2],w = q[3],px = p[0],py = p[1],pz = p
    [2];
  F[,] R = 1-2*(y*y) - 2*(z*z), 2*(x*y) - 2*(w*z), 2*(z*x) + 2*(w*y
    ), 2*(x*y) + 2*(w*z), 1- 2*(x*x) - 2*(z*z), 2*(y*z) - 2*(w*x)
    , 2*(z*x) - 2*(w*y), 2*(y*z) + 2*(w*x), 1 - 2*(x*x) - 2*(y*y)
    ;
  F[] temp = VM.mult(R,new F[] px,py,pz );
  F s = new F(temp);
  return s;
}
```

Bibliography

[1] Bart Adams and Philip Dutre. "Interactive Boolean Operations on Surfel-Bounded Solids." *Proc. SIGGRAPH '03, Transactions on Graphics* 22:3 (2003), 651–656.

[2] Aseem Agarwala, Maneesh Agrawala, Michael Cohen, David Salesin, and Rick Szeliski. "Photographing Long Scenes with Multi-Viewpoint Panoramas." *Proc. SIGGRAPH '06, Transactions on Graphics* 25:3 (2006), 853–862.

[3] Constantinos A. Balafoutis and Rajnikant V. Patel. *Dynamic Analysis of Robot Manipulators: A Cartesian Tensor Approach.* Boston: Kluwer Academic Publishers, 1991.

[4] F. L. Bauer. "Computational Graphs and Rounding Error." *SIAM J. Numer. Anal.* 11:1 (1974), 87–96.

[5] J. Baumgarte. "Stabilization of Constraints and Integrals of Motion in Dynamical Systems." *Computer Methods in Applied Mechanics and Engineering* 1 (1972), 1–16.

[6] Henning Biermann, Daniel Kristjansson, and Denis Zorin. "Approximate Boolean Operations on Free-Form Solids." In *Proceedings of SIGGRAPH '01: Computer Graphics Proceedings, Annual Conference Series,* edited by E. Fiume, pp. 185–194, New York: ACM SIGGRAPH, 2001.

[7] Christian H. Bischof, Alan Carle, Peyvand Khademi, and Andrew Mauer. "ADIFOR 2.0: Automatic Differentiation of Fortran 77 Programs." *IEEE Computational Science & Engineering* 3:3 (1996), 18–32.

[8] Christian H. Bischof, Lucas Roh, and Andrew Mauer. "ADIC—An Extensible Automatic Differentiation Tool for ANSI-C." *Software–Practice and Experience* 27:12 (1997), 1427–1456. Available at http://www-fp.mcs.anl.gov/division/software.

[9] K. Cooper, T. Harvey, and K. Kennedy. "A Simple, Fast Dominance Algorithm." *Software Practice and Experience.* Available at citeseer.ist.psu.edu/cooper01simple.html.

[10] P. Debevec, C. Taylor, and J. Malik. "Modeling and Rendering Architecture from Photographs: A Hybrid Geometry- and Image-Based Approach." In *Proceedings of SIGGRAPH '96, Computer Graphics Proceedings, Annual Conference Series*, edited by Holly Rushmeier, pp. 21–30, Reading, MA: Addison Wesley, 1996.

[11] A. C. Fang and N. S. Pollard. "Efficient Synthesis of Physically Valid Human Motion." *Proc. SIGGRAPH '03, Transactions on Graphics* 22:3 (2003), 417–426.

[12] Roy Featherstone and David Orin. "Robot Dynamics: Equations and Algorithms." In *Proceedings of the IEEE International Conference on Robotics and Automation*, pp. 826–834, Los Alamitos, CA: IEEE Press, 2000.

[13] Roy Featherstone. *Robot Dynamics Algorithms*. Boston: Kluwer Adademic Publishers, 1987.

[14] Roy Featherstone. *Rigid Body Dynamics Algorithms*. New York: Springer, 2008.

[15] Herbert Goldstein, Charles P. Poole, and John L. Safco. *Classical Mechanics*, San Francisco: Addison Wesley, 2002.

[16] Andreas Griewank. *Evaluating Derivatives: Principles and Techniques of Algorithmic Differentiation*. Lecture Notes in Computer Science 120, Philadelphia, PA: SIAM, 2000.

[17] Andreas Griewank. "A Mathematical View of Automatic Differentiation." *Acta Numerica*, 12 (2003), 321–398.

[18] Michael Guthe, Akos Balazs, and Reinhard Klein. "GPU-based Trimming and Tessellation of NURBS and T-Spline Surfaces." *Proc. SIGGRAPH '05, Transactions on Graphics* 24:3 (2005), 1016–1023.

[19] John Hable and Jarek Rossignac. "Blister:GPU-Based Rendering of Boolean Combinations of Free-Form Triangulated Shapes." *Proc. SIGGRAPH '05, Transactions on Graphics* 24:3 (2005), 1024–1031.

[20] Eldon Hansen and G. William Walster. *Global Optimization Using Interval Analysis*. New York: Marcel Dekker, 2004.

[21] John H. Hubbard and Barbara Burke Hubbard. *Vector Calculus, Linear Algebra, and Differential Forms: A Unified Approach*. Upper Saddle River, NJ: Prentice Hall, 2002.

[22] David Kincaid and Ward Cheney. *Numerical Analysis, Second Edition*. Pacific Grove, CA: Brooks/Cole Publishing Company, 1996.

[23] E. Kokkevis and D. Metaxas. "Efficient Dynamic Constraints for Animating Articulated Figures." *Multibody System Dynamics* 2:2 (1998) 89–114.

[24] Sung-Hee Lee, Junggon Kim, F.C. Park, Munsang Kim, and James E. Bobrow. "Newton-Type Algorithms for Dynamics-Based Robot Movement Optimization." *IEEE Trans. Robotics* 21:4 (2005), 657–667.

[25] M. Levoy and P. Hanrahan. "Light Field Rendering." In *Proceedings of SIGGRAPH '96, Computer Graphics Proceedings, Annual Conference Series*, edited by Holly Rushmeier, pp. 31–42, Reading, MA: Addison Wesley, 1996.

[26] Z. Liu, S. J. Gortler, and M. F. Cohen. "Hierarchical Spacetime Control." In *Proceedings of SIGGRAPH '94, Computer Graphics Proceedings, Annual Conference Series*, edited by Andrew Glassner, pp. 35–42, New York: ACM Press, 1994.

[27] C. Karen Liu, Aaron Hertzmann, and Zoran Popovic. "Learning Physics-Based Motion Style with Inverse Optimization." *Proc. SIGGRAPH '05, Transactions on Graphics* 24:3 (2005), 1071–1081.

[28] Richard M. Murray, Zexiang Li, and S.Shankar Sastry. *A Mathematical Introduction to Robotic Manipulation*. Boca Raton, FL: CRC Press, 1994.

[29] John Owens. "Streaming Architectures and Technology Trends." In *GPU Gems 2*, edited by Matt Pharr, Chapter 29. Reading, MA: Addison Wesley, 2005.

[30] Mark Pauly, Richard Kaiser, Leif Kobbelt, and Markus Gross. "Shape Modeling with Point Sampled Geometry." *Proc. SIGGRAPH '03, Transactions on Graphics* 22:3 (2003), 641–650.

[31] Louis B. Rall. *Automatic Differentiation: Techniques and Applications*. Berlin: Springer Verlag, 1981.

[32] Peter-Pike Sloan, Ben Luna, and John Snyder. "Local, Deformable Precomputed Radiance Transfer." *Proc. SIGGRAPH '05, Transactions on Graphics* 24:3 (2005), 1216–1224.

[33] Noah Snavely, Steven M. Seitz, and Richard Szeliski. "Photo Tourism: Exploring Photo Collections in 3D." *Proc. SIGGRAPH '06, Transactions on Graphics*, 25:3 (2006), 835–846.

[34] John Snyder. *Generative Modeling for Computer Graphics and CAD*. Boston: Academic Press, 1992.

[35] N. Stewart, G. Leach, and S. John. "Improved CSG Rendering Using Overlap Graph Subtraction Sequences." *International Conference on Computer Graphics and Interactive Techniques in Australasia and South East Asia—GRAPHITE 2003*, pp. 47–53. Available at citeseer.ist.psu.edu/stewart03improved.html.

[36] Gilbert Strang. *Linear Algebra, Third Edition*. San Diego: Harcourt Brace Jovanovich, 1988.

[37] M. van de Panne, J. Lazlo, and E. L. Fiume. "Interactive Control for Physically-Based Animation." In *Proceedings of SIGGRAPH 2000, Computer Graphics Proceedings, Annual Conference Series*, edited by Kurt Akeley, pp. 201–208, Reading, MA: Addison-Wesley, 2000.

[38] A. Witkin and M. Kass. "Spacetime Constraints." *SIGGRAPH '88, Computer Graphics* 22 (1988), 159–168.

Index

angular momentum, 126
angular velocity, 122
antisymmetric matrix, 122
automatic differentiation
    forward, 34
    reverse, 34
    symbolic, 108

Baumgarte stabilization, 79
Bspline, 25

center of mass, 56
Chebyshev polynomials, 22
closed loops, 76
coefficent, 140
common subexpression elimination, 32
computed torque control, 83
constraint
    forces, 127
    holonomic, 79
    nonholonomic, 79
    orientation, 69
    Pfaffian, 79
    rolling, 79
    stabilization, 79
cubic B-splines, 25
curvature of a surface, 43

D'Alembert's principle, 76
dependent coordinate, 66

derivative graph, 95
differential-algebraic equations, 76
dominance, 97
dynamics
    classes
        MultiBodySystem, 82
    functions
        coefficient, 140
        inverseDynamics, 82
        inverseKinematics, 81
        Jacobian, 81
        substitute, 140
D* language
    ceiling, 24
    compile, 29
    compileFromFile, 32
    compileToFile, 32
    D, 19
    derivative, 27
    eval, 30
    FArray, 24
    floor, 24
    IntegerValue, 25
    max, 24
    Memoize, 24
    min, 24
    orderVariablesInDomain, 31
    printCompilerSource, 29
    printOperatorCounts, 22

Reference, 25
UnspecifiedFunction, 30

equations of motion, 52
Euler-Lagrange equations, 20

factor subgraphs, 99
forward dynamics, 137, 139
forward Euler method, 54

generalized coordinate, 51, 118
generalized force, 53, 128
geometry
    classes
        DDiff, 37
        DGeom, 37
        DMat, 37
        DOp, 37
    functions
        cross product, 38
        normalize, 39
        parametric partial, 38
        principal curvatures, 46
        revSurf, 21
        surface normal, 38
        surfaceAndNormal, 39
    operators
        extrude, 40
gimbal lock, 57

holonomic constraint, 79

independent coordinate, 66
inertia tensor, 125
inverse dynamics, 137
    computed torque control, 83
    recursive linear algorithms, 139
    robot arm, 82
inverse kinematics, 80

Jacobian
    constraint, 77
    inverse kinematics, 81

Lagrange multiplier method, 76
Lagrangian dynamics, 51, 115

memoization, 24
moment of inertia, 56

nonholonomic constraint, 79

offset function, 42
optimal control, 141
orientation constraints, 69

Pfaffian constraint, 79
postdominance, 97
principal curvatures, 45
profile product surface, 3
proportional-derivative control, 64

recursive functions, 22
Richardson's extrapolation, 34
rigid-body transformation, 118
rigid-body transformation inverse, 120
rolling constraint, 79
rotational joints, 57

spherical harmonics, 86
splines, 24
substitute, 140
surface
    cross-section, 3
    curvature, 43
    normal, 38
    of revolution, 3, 21
    parametric tangents, 38
    principal curvature, 45
    profile product, 3
    wire product, 3
SymGeom, 3
SymMech, 7

transformation hierarchy, 118
translational constraints, 67
translational joints, 58

unspecified function, 20

VM, 59

wire product surface, 3